Strong...
Shaken

A Biblical Examination of
Religious Cults and World Faiths

DAVID LEGGE

AMBASSADOR INTERNATIONAL
Greenville, South Carolina • Belfast, Northern Ireland

STRONGHOLDS SHAKEN

ISBN 978-1-84030-192-2

Ambassador Publications
a division of
Ambassador Productions Ltd.
Providence House
Ardenlee Street,
Belfast,
BT6 8QJ
Northern Ireland
www.ambassador-productions.com

Emerald House
427 Wade Hampton Blvd.
Greenville
SC 29609, USA
www.emeraldhouse.com

For though we walk in the flesh, we do not war after the flesh:
(For the weapons of our warfare are not carnal, but mighty through God to the pulling down of strongholds;)
Casting down imaginations, and every high thing that exalteth itself against the knowledge of God, and bringing into captivity every thought to the obedience of Christ;

The Apostle Paul, 2 Corinthians 11:3-5

For still our ancient foe
Doth seek to work his woe;
His craft and power are great,
And armed with cruel hate –
On earth is not his equal.

Did we in our own strength confide,
Our striving would be losing;
Were not the right Man on our side,
The Man of God's own choosing.
Doth ask who that may be?
Christ Jesus, it is He!
Lord Sabaoth His Name,
From age to age the same;
And He must win the battle.

Martin Luther

Here I stand. I can do no other. Martin Luther

In loving memory of my Grandfathers who are now with Christ: David Nicol who died 24 March 2005 and Harold Legge who died 7 November 2006.

This book is dedicated to Andrew Watkins: originator and webmaster of www.preachtheword.com 'Remembering without ceasing your work of faith, and labour of love, and patience of hope in our Lord Jesus Christ, in the sight of God and our Father;' 1 Thessalonians 1:3.

Thanks to my wife, Barbara, and children, Lydia and Noah, for their understanding and help throughout the writing of this book.

Thanks also to the Iron Hall Assembly for their encouragement, prayers and practical support.

Special thanks to all those who have helped in the publication of this book.

List of Contents

Introduction

How many times have we heard the expression, 'All roads lead to God'? This sentiment captures a widely endorsed, relativistic worldview, which assumes that what really counts is that a believer is sincere and devoted to his or her faith, for ultimately we are worshipping the same deity. In this book, we will examine whether or not this modern view is a reasonable and rational assertion.

Many seekers in our world, having been exposed to the plethora of religious variety and choice, are confused and, like Pontius Pilate, they are asking, 'What is truth?' (John 18:38). Perhaps they are not satisfied with the shallow explanation that all religions and gods are ultimately one and the same; perhaps they see the blatant conflict among so many faiths and they ask, 'Who is right?' This book turns to the Old and New Testament to show what the truth is; and where it is, and is not, to be found.

From the outset, however, let me make it clear that whilst this book is a biblical critique of various religious cults and world faiths, I would seek to defend and maintain the right of all people everywhere, at home and abroad, regardless of culture and race, to worship according to their conscience in freedom and peace.

Indeed, as Christians, we ought to welcome, love and care for people of other faiths in our midst. The Bible teaches that 'the truth' is a message for all peoples, regardless of race or culture. Therefore, it should not be construed by any who read this book that we have personal animosity towards the adherents of another faith.

An atheist once said to me, 'There is enough religion in the world to cause men to hate each other but not enough to make them love one another.' I agree with this statement; man-made religion has been the scourge of humanity.

As Christians we love and pray for all men; in this spirit we must make it clear that this publication is not intended to offend or ostracise anyone. Rather, it is an attempt to introduce all men and women to the One who is 'the truth', 'the way' and 'the life' (John 14:6): the Lord Jesus Christ.

This is not an attempt to present a particular faith as an alternative religion for mankind, but rather, an attempt to introduce people to a Person who is the answer to all humanity's questions: the Lord Jesus Christ.

The content of these chapters was originally delivered as sermons preached in the Iron Hall, Belfast, Northern Ireland from September 2004 to May 2005. Since sermons, by nature, have time and content parameters, the written explications of these sermons are far from a complete study of each religious group but rather each sermon seeks to highlight specific inconsistencies of each group as judged by comparison with biblical teachings.

The following belief systems are biblically examined within this book in this order: Jehovah's Witnesses, Christian Science and Scientology, Mormonism, Unitarianism, Spiritism, the Church of Christ, Christadelphianism, Buddhism, the Baha'i Faith, Islam, Roman Catholicism, the Cooneyites, Hinduism, Oneness Pentecostalism and Freemasonry.

Most readers will already accept that there are differences among religions in the world, the most obvious being different concepts of God and how He can be approached and known. In this book, we have identified particular ways of thinking as cults that come under the umbrella of 'Christendom'. In other words, in some way they recognise the Christ of history and the Bible as being important. As we shall see from a biblical perspective, some of these cult-like characteristics are also evident in religions outside Christendom.

It may be helpful to define the following in more detail at this juncture: the characteristics of a cult, the people who join a cult and the characteristics of a cult member.

The Characteristics Of A Cult

1. THEOLOGICAL	2. STRUCTURAL	3. BEHAVIOURAL
New Revelation Exclusivity Loss of Salvation	Authoritarian Leadership Financial Emphasis	Isolationism Deprivation Indoctrination Sense of Persecution

How can you distinguish a cult from the true Christian Church? Matt Slick, founder of the Christian Apologetics and Research Ministry: abbreviated 'CARM' - www.carm.org, has given some helpful guidelines in order to differentiate between a cult and a Christian Church in the biblical sense. I have elaborated on his research in order to emphasise the distinctive characteristics of a cult and to group these characteristics in terms of theological, structural and behavioural orientations.

It should be stressed that not all religious groups will demonstrate all these characteristics. Some of the religous groups examined in this book will exhibit many of these characteristic traits and others may only display a few.

Often the first characteristic of a cult is that it claims a **new revelation: char 1,** from God; a new teaching, that hitherto has not been known to man. Whether it is through a prophet or particular organisation, a cult purports to shed a new light on the gospel of Jesus Christ: a new prophetic revelation that God has given exclusively to this particular organisation. For example, we shall see that the 'new light' of the Jehovah's Witness movement is supposedly revealed in the *New World Translation* and also by their prophet Charles Taze Russell. According to the Mormons, 'new light' has been revealed through Joseph Smith and the *Book of Mormon*, and many other of their 'inspired' writings.

Cults demonstrate in their 'new' teaching a defective view of the Bible, a dishonouring view of the Lord Jesus Christ, a denial of justification by faith, and a dangerous stress on trivial matters. Indeed, most of the 'new revelations', upon a close examination of Church history, can be identified as a duplication of old heresy faced by the Church in the past. Perhaps this is why cults so readily discount the record of Church history.

A second characteristic of a cult, one that flows out from the first claim of a new revelation, is a claim of **exclusivity: char 1**. Cult members believe that they constitute the only true Church, and that they have the only true teaching on this new way to God. As far as cults are concerned, all other Churches are apostates and damned. Cults claim that other Churches have lost *the true gospel* at some stage, but they, as God's new chosen channel, have rediscovered it and are now the sole contemporary bastions of its truth. An implication of this claim is that cult members despise much of the two thousand years of Christian history and in doing so regard this history as deficient Christianity.

A third characteristic of a cult is an out-flowing of the second characteristic of exclusivity. Cults teach that to leave their exclusive fellowship will result in the **loss of salvation: char 1**, and so this teaching creates another emotional dependency. Furthermore, this impression of exclusivity is deepened through practices such as meditation, and the repetition of phrases and mantras. Cults often have their own language, common clichés and 'in' phrases. By using this language followers are able to identify whether a person is in the group or not. There is a sense of belonging that comes with the exclusive jargon and phraseology adopted.

A fourth characteristic of a cult is a strong **authoritarian leadership: char 2**. It may be the individual who has established the cult or a group of individuals who collectively lead the group but all of the cults examined here seem to have a leadership base that exerts strict control over its followers. What the leaders say is final, and their word is received almost as the Word of God with the leaders themselves as prophets of God.

A fifth characteristic of a cult is often an overt **financial emphasis: char 2**. Compulsory tithing is required within many cults. Furthermore, some cults even acquire their follower's personal assets and inheritances after death.

A sixth characteristic of a cult is **isolationism: char 3**. Cults may attempt to reduce or even sever their followers from the world in general, their Church background, or their family relationships. This goal of a cult is to lessen a follower's dependence on outside influences in order to make them more dependent on the cult thereby gaining more control over multiple aspects of a person's life. This control can be attempted physically, by isolating a person from their family, friends and other religious influences. Mental Control can be exerted through using mind control techniques; commonly referred to as 'brainwashing'. Emotional dependency is another aspect where cults may seek to gain control. Here the aim is to encourage followers into a deeper dependence on group members rather than on family and friends.

In addition, cults can assert financial control as leaders influence how personal money of followers is spent. This can create in followers a sense of obligation to the group.

A seventh characteristic of a cult is that control may be exercised over followers through **deprivation: char 3**. Sleep deprivation is sometimes imposed by encouraging excessive time to be taken up with praying, reading and studying the

Bible. Food deprivation is another tactic used by cults that also weakens the body. Ultimately any kind of deprivation has the goal of weakening the will in order to exert more control over the individual. Cult members are therefore susceptible to suggestions made by the cults' strong leadership.

An eighth characteristic of a cult is **indoctrination: char 3**. There is often a prohibition of alternative views and beliefs. Followers are actively discouraged from studying broadly and searching widely. Critiques of their beliefs are deliberately misrepresented in order to dissuade their disciples from ever considering an alternative viewpoint.

A ninth characteristic of a cult is that cult members sense that they are **under constant persecution: char 3**. It is true that some cult followers have at times experienced persecution, however, at times their perception of persecution is as a result of their exclusivity. Believing that they alone have the truth, cult followers conclude that anyone who is not in their group must be against the truth, and consequently against them. Cult leaders instruct their members that any challenge to their beliefs is persecution and this in turn adds to this perception of persecution. Cult followers in general therefore, avoid argumentation, questioning or reasoning.

The critical reader will not miss the fact that some of these cult characteristics could also, somewhat ironically, be ascribed to my own faith and Church. In response to such a charge I would invite those readers who take such a view to read on with an open mind and to re-examine the Scriptures and come to your own conclusion.

People Likely to Join a Cult

Having briefly assessed how a cult may be recognised, let us consider what manner of person may join a cult or, indeed, the characteristics of people on whom a cult may prey.

First, it is observed that cults often identify potential converts as those in society who may be **vulnerable** in some way. Such individuals may be emotionally vulnerable;

possibly having experienced a recent bereavement in their life. Perhaps they lack family members or friends. The spiritually vulnerable may also be susceptible to a cult. Often these people are searching for the truth, seeking a religious community to join and in doing so to feel a sense of belonging and meaning. Such people may also be financially vulnerable, struggling with debt or budgeting their income and so when someone comes along and claims that their organisation will take full control of their finances: this is welcomed.

The vulnerable person then becomes dependent upon the cult member and the cult member gains a measure of control. Cults exploit vulnerability.

A second feature of the nature of people that seek to join a cult is that they are often **supernaturally curious**. This is, more than just searching for the truth; these individuals are intrigued by supernatural activity and the realities of eternity, such as heaven, hell, angels and the end of the world.

A third characteristic of a potential cult member is that they are often **intellectually confused.** By this I mean these individuals have looked, in depth, into religions and beliefs in the world and are confused by the variety and divergence of opinion. They ask, 'What is true?'

The Characteristics Of Cult Members

What is the profile of a cult member, a person who is 'under the influence' of a cult? This section will help in identifying cult members who approach you for recruitment, or perhaps in recognising a cult influence in the life of a friend or family member.

Generally speaking there is a **change of character** in a person who joins a cult.

First, there is often a **loss of a sense of humour** among cult members thereby losing the ability to laugh at themselves or at other people, particularly those from among their own group.

Second, there can be a manifestation of **childlike behaviour**. Specifically this is witnessed in an increased dependence on other people. A member may constantly seek the approval of their leaders, of their prophets and elders; as a child would behave toward a parent.

Third, an outcome of this childlike behaviour is a degree of **indecisiveness**. Members, seeking God's will, are known to constantly consult their leaders over the most insignificant decisions.

Fourth, there is often **tunnel vision** with cult members. This characteristic is observed particularly among Mormons and Jehovah's Witnesses. However strong the evidence is to disprove their claims, however complete the exposé of their doctrine, cult followers cannot or will not see it!

I spoke recently to some Mormon elders regarding the historical facts proving the moral duplicity of Joseph Smith and Brigham Young, yet it made no difference to them. In fact they admitted to me that they are not depending on historical fact but a certain 'inner light', subjective experience, that cannot be verified.

Having outlined in introduction the characteristics of a cult and of those who become influenced by cults, this book seeks to 'test the spirits' according to the indisputable evidence of the Bible, God's Word. This book will set out this evidence in an unmistakable fashion to shake spiritual strongholds that hold many **religious** followers in bondage.

I challenge you to weigh the evidence for yourself as you study God's Word through these pages.

May you encounter the One who is 'the way, the truth and the life' – Jesus Christ the Lord.

David Legge

Chapter 1
The Jehovah's Witnesses

Mention 'Jehovah's Witnesses' to people and there is a varied response.

For some people, an image will spring to mind of two well-dressed individuals knocking on doors at inconvenient times: talking about the end of the world. Other people may recall reading in the newspaper, or, may have even seen portrayed on film, the controversial stories of parents who refuse blood transfusions for their children because of their devout religious views.[1] There are those people who do not know the origins of the Jehovah's Witnesses Movement, or what their followers actually believe. However, to most people who meet them the zeal and devotion of Jehovah's Witnesses are obvious.

What perhaps is not realised is the true extent of their fervour. *The Watchtower* magazine claims that the average Jehovah's Witness spends ten hours per month in door-to-door evangelism. This is in addition to attending five hours of meetings during one week.

Is it any wonder that the organisation is said to be growing at a rate of 4000 converts per week?

The *2005 Report of Jehovah's Witnesses Worldwide* claims that the global membership of the Watchtower Movement is 6.6 million. These members are active witnesses in 98 congregations throughout 235 countries.

It is claimed the Jehovah's Witnesses erect five 'Kingdom Halls' a week worldwide and publish *The Watchtower* magazine twice per month in 120 languages. Each issue, on average, has over 16 million copies printed and 600,000 of those copies are for distribution in the United Kingdom alone.

Clearly, the Jehovah's Witnesses is not a small and insignificant religious fringe group. It is a movement making great strides in our modern age!

To what extent do the Jehovah's Witnesses meet the **theological**, **structural** and **behavioural** characteristics of a cult as defined in our introduction?

The Witness Of Their History

Charles Taze Russell was the founder and first President of the Watchtower Movement: hence the group was known by many as 'The Russellites'.

Charles Taze Russell was born in Pittsburgh in Pennsylvania in 1852, and was brought up as a Congregationalist and a Presbyterian. It was not long, however, until he became sceptical regarding some of the views of those Christian denominations. Eventually he came to oppose organised religion of any kind. In doing so, he rejected outright many of the teachings that traditional historical orthodox Christians hold as sacred and fundamental.

Here we see the classic **theological** characteristics of a cult: claiming to have **new revelation** from God and **exclusivity** of truth.

Having rejected mainstream Christianity, Charles Taze Russell began in 1870 to organise small Bible classes in Pittsburgh. These met regularly to study, in their own way, God's Word. A magazine from this group was published in 1879 entitled *Zion's Watchtower and Herald of Christ's Presence*. It was later renamed *The Watchtower - announcing Jehovah's Kingdom*. We know the publication today as *The Watchtower* magazine.

The Jehovah's Witnesses, as a movement, was eventually incorporated in Pennsylvania in 1884 under the name 'Zion's Watchtower Tract Society'. In 1886 Charles Taze Russell was involved in publishing the first volume of the *Millennial Dawn*, which is now known by Jehovah's Witnesses, as a series of books entitled *Studies in Scripture*.

All this information may at first seem irrelevant. However, when the Jehovah's Witness Movement is studied in any depth it becomes obvious that *Studies in Scripture* by Charles Taze Russell is more important to the Jehovah's Witnesses than the Word of God. It is of even more value than their translation of the Bible.

The influence of the writings of Jehovah's Witness leaders and an unquestioning adherence to their teaching display a **structural** characteristic common to a cult, namely, **authoritarian leadership.**

When Charles Taze Russell died in 1916, this **authoritarian leadership** was exercised through a Missouri lawyer called Judge Joseph Franklin Rutherford. The Movement was known then as *The Dawn Bible Students' Association*.

Judge Joseph Franklin Rutherford claimed that in 1931 an angel appeared to him and revealed that the Movement's name should be changed from 'The Dawn Bible Students Association' to 'The Jehovah's Witness Movement'. This name was taken from Isaiah 43:10-12,

> Ye are my **witnesses**, saith the **LORD** *(Yahweh or Jehovah)*[2], and my
> servant whom I have chosen: that ye may know and believe me, and

understand that I am he: before me there was no God formed, neither shall there be after me. I, even I, am the **LORD** *(Yahweh or Jehovah)*[3]; and beside me there is no saviour. I have declared, and have saved, and I have shewed, when there was no strange god among you: therefore ye are my **witnesses**, saith the **LORD** (*Yahweh* or *Jehovah*)[4], that I am God.

It was Judge Joseph Franklin Rutherford who established the headquarters in Brooklyn, New York; and it was he who claimed for himself absolute authority over the whole of the Watchtower Movement. This was a new concept for the Jehovah's Witnesses.

Judge Joseph Franklin Rutherford's word became law: he occupied a position of dictatorship.

In 1942, Nathan Knorr took over the presidency and he probably did more to build up the Watchtower Movement than any other leader. Under his leadership the membership soared from 115,000 people to, over 2 million members. It was during Nathan Knorr's reign in 1961 that the *New World Translation* of the Bible was produced.

In 1977 Nathan Knorr's associate, Frederick William Franz succeeded him as president. Frederick Franz had been the spokesperson on the committee for the *New World Translation*. More recent presidents of the organisation have been Milton Henschel in 1992 and Don Adams in the year 2000.

Theologically, the Jehovah's Witness Movement embodies the characteristic of a cult in claiming **new revelation**. Central to this is the over emphasis on the teachings of their own prophets at the expense of the teachings of Holy Scripture. The **theological** characteristic of **exclusivity** and the **behavioural** characteristic of **indoctrination** are evidenced also in the fact that the Movement encourages extensive and intense study of their own publications whilst discouraging their members examining the beliefs and writings of other faiths.

In the January 15th 1993 issue of *The Watchtower* magazine the readers were instructed, 'to avoid independent thinking.' This, perhaps, is one reason why Jehovah's Witnesses devote a purported 85% of their personal study time to Watchtower publications. The balance of their personal study time is then dedicated to a study of their own prophets and their own particular version of the Bible: the *New World Translation*.

Thus, it is immediately clear where Jehovah's Witnesses' emphasis lies; not in the Holy Scriptures, nor even in their own interpretation of the Bible, but, in the teaching of their own prophets.

Are Jehovah's Witnesses, as they claim, 'Jehovah's Witnesses' upon the earth, or are they what the New Testament describes as 'false witnesses'?

What are the claims this group makes and what witness do they actually present?

The Witness Of Their Prophecies

Watchtower literature claims that the Jehovah's Witness Movement is the one true Church; Christ's authentic representatives on the earth today proclaiming God's message. This is another example of displaying the **theological** characteristics of claiming **new revelation** and **exclusivity**. Jehovah's Witnesses assert that they, alone, are the true proclaimers of God's Kingdom and that they, exclusively, possess the correct interpretation of the Scriptures.

If these claims are true it is reasonable to expect that any prophecies the Jehovah's Witnesses have made, based on their teachings and new revelations, would come true.

The truth is that every prophecy, without exception, that the Watchtower Movement has made, has not come to pass.

Jehovah's Witnesses may accuse me of taking their statements out of context. They may also try to argue that those who spoke these predictions did not claim to be the prophets of God. Furthermore they may attempt to reason in their own terms that, 'the light is getting brighter for us now, and we know more today than we did then: we're understanding Bible prophecy better now than ever.'

The reality is that Movement *does* claim to be the only prophet of God today in the world. *The Watchtower* magazine 1st April 1972 asks the question,

> So does Jehovah have a prophet to help them, to warn them of the dangers and to declare things to come? These questions can be answered in the affirmative. Who is this prophet? This prophet was not one man, but was a body of men and women. It was the small group of footstep followers of Jesus Christ known at the time as 'International Bible Students', today they are known as 'Jehovah's Christian Witnesses'.

God's Word in Deuteronomy 18:22 warns concerning prophets whose prophecies do not come to pass,

> When a prophet speaks in the name of the LORD, if the thing follow not, nor come to pass, that is the thing which the LORD hath not spoken, but the prophet hath spoken it presumptuously: thou shalt not be afraid of him.

The Lord says such prophecies are not from Him and we should not listen to the false prophets that make them.

Charles Taze Russell made two predictions of the Second Coming of Jesus Christ. The first forecast that Doomsday would occur in 1874 ushering in the coming of the Lord Jesus. A later prophecy predicted that in the year 1914 Christ, after Armageddon, would reign from the skies. Both prophecies failed despite *Studies in Scripture; volume 4*, p.621 stating,

> Our Lord, the appointed King, is now present since October 1874.

Jehovah's Witnesses maintain this return was an invisible return, because no one saw Christ return in 1914. To these followers though, He is reigning from the heavens as King of kings and Lord of lords over His Kingdom.

Jehovah's Witnesses believe that these **new revelations** are true prophecies.

Judge Joseph Franklin Rutherford was the second Jehovah's Witness to make false prophecies. He predicted that in 1925 Christ would usher in Paradise upon the earth. This prophecy failed.

To perpetuate the myth the Movement built a house in California called 'Beth-Sarim' that they claimed was the house to which the princes of God would come at the Second Coming. This was seen as visible proof that the Jehovah's Witnesses really believed that the Lord Jesus was going to bring in Paradise in 1925.

Significantly it was Judge Joseph Franklin Rutherford, and not princes of God such as Abraham, Isaac and Jacob, who ended up inhabiting 'Beth-Sarim'!

When Paradise did not materialise in 1925 and Hitler rose to prominence in Europe, Judge Joseph Franklin Rutherford taught that Jehovah's Witnesses should not enter into the war. The reasoning behind this was his insistence that no side would win as World War II was going to usher in Armageddon upon the world.

Armageddon did not come, and Judge Joseph Franklin Rutherford was proven, like Charles Taze Russell, to be a false prophet.

Nathan Knorr, influenced by his predecessor Judge Joseph Franklin Rutherford, was the president responsible for the prediction that the Lord Jesus Christ would return in 1975. This prophecy was announced in the magazine *Awake*.

Many sincere and dedicated Jehovah's Witnesses sacrificially sold all their possessions, giving their money to the poor and to the Movement, as they waited for the coming of the Christ. Many of them made life-changing decisions on the ground of Nathan Knorr's prediction. Dave Riccoboni, and his wife were former headquarter members in the Watchtower Movement in 1974. Dave recalls,

> 1974 was a very difficult time for me, I was freaking out. I had to make a decision, a critical decision, because my wife had to undergo surgery and the doctor said she needed a blood transfusion. I had to make the decision, and the brothers were encouraging me to make the right decision to please Jehovah, because after all Armageddon was only a year away, so even if she died she'd be resurrected right away.

Mrs Riccoboni testifies also,

> You can just imagine the fear, I had so much fear, and it was so frightening. I was near death, I was in hospital, and the brothers and sisters told me to take my stand for Jehovah - don't accept a blood transfusion. If I accepted the blood transfusion I would die at Armageddon, if I didn't and I died I'd be resurrected - the Great Tribulation was coming, it was 1974 and 1975 was at our doorstep. By staying loyal to Jehovah I would be resurrected, so that was the hope I was given.[5]

Mrs Riccoboni survived this incident and eventually both she and her husband left the Jehovah's Witness Movement because of their false teachings.

At this time the **authoritarian leadership** of the Jehovah's Witnesses was so strong that some members of the Movement decided not to have any children believing that Armageddon was imminent. Others decided they would not answer the call of conscription to serve in the U.S. Army, and consequently they were sent to prison. Many forfeited their freedom, family, savings, even potentially their lives, because of the false claims of these false teachers.

Recent Jehovah's Witness publications; 1999, indicated the Movement's belief that the Lord was going to come back to earth in the year 2000.

All of these prophecies are said to originate from 'new light'. Jehovah's Witnesses claim that this is how God reveals new truth to His people.

Realistically all false prophets need new light, because as time passes, and their prophecies fail, new prophecies are needed to perpetuate their beliefs.

Time is the enemy of the false prophet.

The Lord Jesus warned in Matthew 24:24,

> There shall arise false Christs, and false prophets, and shall shew great signs and wonders; insomuch that, if it were possible, they shall deceive the very elect.

The prophet Isaiah in Isaiah 8:20 writes,

> To the law and to the testimony: if they speak not according to this word, it is because there is no light in them.

The Witness Of Their Bible

In 1993 a Watchtower publication: *The Proclaimers of God's Kingdom* referred to the *New World Translation* as a,

> . . . literal translation that faithfully presents what is in the original writing.

The Proclaimers of God's Kingdom book then claims that the entire translation committee were Spirit-anointed Christians.

This statement is problematic.

First and foremost the *New World Translation* is not a literal translation of the original

Scriptures. Fred Franz, who later became the fourth president of the Movement, was the chairman and spokesman of the translation committee and he was mainly responsible for the whole work. Astoundingly he had not one Hebrew or Greek qualification to his name. How could he translate the Scriptures from the original languages?

Furthermore, when the Watchtower Movement was asked who these Spirit-anointed Christians were and who it was who translated the work, they would not tell!

The translation's authenticity and credibility must be questioned.

The *New World Translation* is not a translation; rather it is an invention of men intended to reflect the peculiar doctrines of this Movement. Leading Bible scholar Bruce M. Metzger was asked his opinion of the *New World Translation* and he stated that rather than a version of the Bible, the *New World Translation* is,

> . . . a perversion of the Bible.

Bruce M. Metzger went on to remark that the New Testament of the *New World Translation* contains the word 'Jehovah' 237 times, when in fact the word 'Jehovah' is not found in one Greek manuscript extant. He goes on to comment,

> I don't think this is responsible scholarship.

Indeed every opportunity the translators got they denigrated the Lord Jesus Christ in His person from being the Eternal Son of God, co-equal with the Father, to be a mere creature.[6]

The Witness Of Their Theology

How could the Movement get so many dates wrong regarding the Second Coming of Christ, if their theology is correct?

The reason is simple: their theology is not based on the leading of the Holy Spirit through the Scriptures. The theology of Jehovah's Witnesses owes much to pyramidology, which in effect is a form of occultism.

Pyramidology is the belief that in the Great Pyramid of Giza, Egypt, there is a witness of God to the times and the seasons of all the generations of humanity. Charles Taze Russell believed that the Pyramid of Giza was God's 'stone witness' corroborating the biblical time periods that is needed in order to work out when the Lord Jesus will return.

It was by this method that Charles Taze Russell obtained his prophecy that Christ would return in 1914.

Significantly, beside Charles Taze Russell's grave is a monument dedicated to him: in the shape of a pyramid. A pyramid was used because pyramidology was the source of his theology.

Charles Taze Russell, however, was not the only president of the Watchtower Movement with occultic associations. Judge Joseph Franklin Rutherford claimed to contact the deceased Charles Taze Russell. The result of this contact, Judge Joseph Franklin Rutherford maintained, was Charles Taze Russell telling him how to take the Movement forward.

As noted previously, Judge Joseph Franklin Rutherford claimed that an angel told him to change the Movement's name to 'Jehovah's Witnesses'. However, Judge Joseph Franklin Rutherford also made the staggering statement that the Jehovah's Witness Movement was not led by the Holy Spirit, 'but by a collection of spirits.'

Such a blatant admission of occultic influence must indicate that the origins of the Jehovah's Witness Movement are dangerously suspect.

As the founder of the Watchtower Movement, Charles Taze Russell's personal life, also casts doubt on the claims of the group.

Matthew 7:15-17 records that the Lord Jesus warned,

> Beware of false prophets, which come to you in sheep's clothing, but inwardly they are ravening wolves. Ye shall know them by their fruits. Do men gather grapes of thorns, or figs of thistles? Even so every good tree bringeth forth good fruit; but a corrupt tree bringeth forth evil fruit.

At various points in Charles Taze Russell's life he was involved in both legal and marital conflicts.

Historical records show that in 1913 the courts granted his wife a divorce, and later charged him with fraud and perjury. Unscrupulously Charles Taze Russell, in a business venture, advertised and sold so-called 'miracle wheat' at greatly inflated prices to some of his gullible followers.[7]

Walter Martin, in his book *The Kingdom of the Cults*, recounts in detail much of these legal events.

Other curious insights into Charles Taze Russell's character are revealed in his book *The Finished Mystery* in which he taught that the Churches of Christendom were started by bald-headed men who had smoke on their brains. Equally bizarre were Charles Taze Russell's beliefs that if a dog's head were shaped like a man's then the dog could think like a man, and that appendicitis was caused by fighting worms in the colon.[8]

Walter Martin in *Kingdom of the Cults* p.45 sums up Charles Taze Russell's life in a telling manner when he writes,

> As a speaker Russell swayed many, as a theologian he impressed no one as being competent, as a man he failed before the true God.

The fruit of Charles Taze Russell's teaching is enough to prove that its source is not God. Charles Taze Russell and his successors' **new revelations** do not concur with the revelation of the Holy Scriptures.

Jehovah's Witnesses deny the Trinity.

In their own publication *Let God Be True*, pp.100-101 Jehovah's Witnesses deny that God is one substance, in three persons. They claim that God is but one person and they believe this to be a very orthodox assertion. God's Word however, testifies to the opposite: a Triune Godhead.

In Genesis 1:26, God said,

> Let **us** make man in our image. . . .

Jehovah's Witnesses claim here that God was addressing the angels, but, the Bible records that man was not made in the image of an angel, but, in the image of God. In Genesis 3:22 and also in Genesis 11:7 the plural is used for God. Even the name 'Jehovah', is used often in the plural and 'Elohim', is the word for God in a plural form.

In the New Testament in Matthew 28:19 the Lord teaches to baptise in a Triune name. The benedictions within the New Testament, as found in passages such as 2 Corinthians 13:14, and 1 Peter 1:2 also use three names of God, Father, Son and Holy Spirit: not three gods, but God in three persons.

The Trinity is difficult to understand simply because we cannot understand God. One cannot conceive the inconceivable. We are not called upon, as Trinitarians, to explain the inexplicable. However Jehovah's Witnesses must confront and indeed explain away the plain evidence in Scripture for the doctrine of the Trinity. Why are Father, Son and Holy Spirit on separate occasions called God? Study John 6:27, where the Lord Jesus says,

> Labour not for the meat which perisheth, but for that meat which
> endureth unto everlasting life, which the Son of man shall give
> unto you: for him hath **God the Father** sealed.

'God the Father' can be clearly seen as a designation of a person within the Godhead.

How can Hebrews 1:8 be explained except by the Trinity? It reads,

> But unto the Son He (God)[9] saith, Thy throne, O God, is for ever and ever: a sceptre of righteousness is the sceptre of thy kingdom.

Clearly, God the Father has called His Son God. There is no other plausible explanation for this verse.

In the New Testament, the Father is designated God, the Son is designated God, and the Holy Spirit is designated God. Acts 5 records that Ananias and Sapphira had sold possessions and made it look as if they gave the entire proceeds to the work of God. In fact, secretly they kept back some of the money for themselves. God judged them severely by striking them dead. What was their great sin?

In verses 3 and 4 Peter said,

> Ananias, why hath Satan filled thine heart to lie **to the Holy Ghost**, and to keep back part of the price of the land? Whiles it remained, was it not thine own? and after it was sold, was it not in thine own power? Why hast thou conceived this thing in thine heart? Thou hast not lied unto men, **but unto God.**

In verse 3 Peter said that Ananias and Sapphira had lied to the Holy Spirit. However, in verse 4 Peter also says they had lied, but to whom? They lied to God, because the Holy Spirit is a person in the Godhead along with the Father and the Son.

There are many more verses to prove that, in the Scriptures, God is declared as being one substance: God, and yet revealed in three persons: - Father, Son and Holy Spirit.[10]

God, therefore, is not as Jehovah's Witnesses claim; simply Jehovah alone: separate and distinct from the Son, He is not some exalted angelic being, and the Spirit is not an impersonal force that is only the influence of the heavenly Father Jehovah. God is one substance revealed in three persons: the Father, the Son and the Holy Spirit.

The Witness Of Their Christ

Jehovah's Witness theology regarding the person and work of the Lord Jesus Christ is also fatally flawed.

Firstly, the Jehovah's Witnesses witness to a false Christ. The Christ of the Jehovah's Witness Movement is not the Christ of the Bible.

Secondly, the Jehovah's Witness Movement is openly blasphemous regarding the person of the Lord Jesus Christ. They claim that Christ is the archangel Michael who became a man. This doctrine is taught in the *Watchtower* magazine, of 15th May 1963 p.307 and in their publication *The New World* on p.284.

Thirdly, Jehovah's Witnesses teach that Christ was Jehovah's first ever creation: made in the same way as other human beings. They assert that whilst Christ may be superior to the rest, He is a creature: not God.

Scripture warns us in Matthew 24:24 that many false Christs would appear on the world scene. Therefore, we ought to expect false representations of the true. Paul said in Galatians 1:8-9 that if anyone preaches another Jesus let him be anathema. The message Jehovah's Witnesses preach therefore, ought also to be anathema to the true Christian: - there is no other Christ!

The Scriptural Christ is no archangel; He is God the Eternal Son.

In Jude verse 9 we read that the archangel Michael dared not bring a railing accusation against the Devil concerning the bones of Moses for he could not by his own power defeat the Devil, or even reprimand him! Are we to suggest that the Lord Jesus is inept to face the Evil One?

The Scriptures testify to the contrary. Matthew 4:10 records the temptation of the Lord Jesus by the Devil and reports that Christ indeed did rebuke the Devil successfully. We read in verse 11,

> Then the Devil leaveth him.

The Jehovah's Witness Movement claims that He was only a perfect man, not God manifest in flesh yet John 1:1 clearly states,

> In the beginning was the Word (Greek: Logos, referring to Christ)[11]
> and the Word was with God, and the Word **was God**.

The Jehovah's Witnesses have attempted to explain away these and other texts that clearly teach the deity of Christ.

An example of this is how the *New World Translation* changes 'and the Word was God,' to 'the Word was a god' lowercase 'g' to imply Christ was only 'a god.'

Jehovah's Witness teachers assert, incorrectly, that where there is no definite article the indefinite article: a, must be added.

Greek grammar does not warrant the addition in this passage.

John 1:6 reads,

> There was a man sent from God ....

As in verse 1, there is no definite article in the Greek before *God*. Yet the translators of the *New World Translation* do not add the indefinite article.

Similarly in verses 12, 13 and 18 the *New World Translation* translators have translated as 'God', exactly the same expression as is found in verse 1, which they translate as 'a god'.

Why, when neither Greek grammar, nor the context of the passage requires this translation, do they insist upon it in verse 1?

The translation denigrates the person of Jesus Christ.

Fourthly, and paradoxically Jehovah's Witnesses accuse Trinitarian Christians of being polytheistic: believing in more than one God, yet their own theology claims Christ is only 'a god'. Jehovah's Witnesses, therefore, are the ones who believe in more than one God!

The God of the Bible is one substance: God, in three persons, not three Gods. There are so many texts that bear this out. The very name 'Emmanuel', given to Christ at His birth, means 'God with us' and further texts in the New Testament claim Christ Jesus to be the only Saviour. Matthew 1:21 says that He would be called,

> . . . JESUS, for He shall save His people from their sins.

In Revelation 21 God is described there as Alpha and Omega, and in Revelation 22 the Lord Jesus is described as the First and the Last. Can there be two Firsts and two Lasts or two Alphas and two Omegas? There cannot be.

Fifthly, another defective element in the doctrine of the Jehovah's Witnesses is seen in their interpretation of the record of the temptation of the Lord Jesus, Luke 4:1.

The *New World Translation* says,

> You must not put Jehovah, your God, to the test.

Thus Jehovah's Witnesses are translating the Greek word 'kurios', 'Lord' as 'Jehovah'. This ignores that it was the Lord Jesus, who said,

> You shall not tempt the Lord your God.

Who was being tested in the temptation? Was it Jehovah? Or was it Jesus? Jehovah's Witnesses say Jehovah is not Jesus, yet here they translate the word 'Lord' as 'Jehovah'.

Jehovah's Witnesses confuse their readers because Jehovah's Witnesses are confused themselves, not recognising that Jesus is the Lord, Jehovah the Son.

If the Lord Jesus is an exalted angel why does God make the request in Hebrews 1:6, saying,

...let all the angels of God worship Him ...?

The Bible, on several occasions, forbids the worship of angels. John in the Apocalypse fell at the feet of an angel, and the angel lifted him up, for man is forbidden to worship angels.

Sixthly, the Jehovah's Witnesses also denigrate Christ's work of redemption.

According to Jehovah's Witness teaching the merits of Christ's sacrificial death is not enough to ensure heaven; Jehovah's Witnesses must accumulate good works to their credit in order to be one of the 144,000 who they claim will eventually enter Paradise. Jehovah's Witnesses deny the finished work of the Lord Jesus on the cross.

Jehovah's Witnesses also deny the physical resurrection of the Lord Jesus Christ. It is their belief that the Lord Jesus Christ did not rise in body, but that He rose in some kind of spiritual sense. 1 Corinthians 15:15 has this to say,

> Yea, and we are found **false witnesses** of God; because we have testified of God that he raised up Christ, whom he raised not up, if so be that the dead rise not.

Paul is teaching that 'we are false witnesses if Christ is not risen bodily from the dead.' Jehovah's Witnesses must therefore be false witnesses.

The reality of the eternal punishment of hell is denied in Jehovah's Witness theology. It claims that only Jehovah's Witnesses can be saved; an exclusive membership. Jehovah's Witnesses teach that we cannot be brought into covenant relationship with God through a mediator in Jesus Christ. They assert that the 144,000 Jehovah's Witnesses are in the covenant with God and they, alone, must be the mediators to bring us to God. The Jehovah's Witness Movement itself is, therefore, exalted above the Christ in the work of salvation!

However Ephesians 2:8-9 states,

> By grace are ye saved through faith; and that not of yourselves: it is the gift of God: Not of works, lest any man should boast.

Salvation is the gift of God!

First Timothy 2:5 says,

> There is one God, and one mediator between God and men, the man Christ Jesus.

Is there a reader who has got entangled up in the Jehovah's Witness Movement?

On the authority of the Word of Christ: get out, seek a Saviour who will take away all your sins and give you peace with God.

Salvation is not to be found in a society, movement or denomination. Jesus Christ came to men, transcending religion and said,

> I am the way, the truth and the life: no man comes to the Father but by me.

He is God's Son. John 20:28 records that Thomas fell at His feet and cried,

> My Lord and my God.

Thomas realised the reality not only of who Jesus Christ was, but what He had done. The Lord Jesus had died and rose again.

Have you realised that? Will you acknowledge Jesus Christ as the only Lord, the only Saviour, and His work on the cross and His resurrection as the only way that you can get to heaven?

Here are some words of Jehovah's Witnesses who came out of the Movement and found faith in Christ, to the glory of God and to the satisfaction of their souls.

I had no reason to doubt my loving parents who raised me in the organisation. Although I was an honour student, I gave up college and went to Watchtower Headquarters. There I met Bill and we shared many questions and concerns about the organisation during our courtship. We questioned especially the blood issue. We ended up leaving Bethel to get married, and moved to my parent's farm. We were very happy until someone reported our doubts about blood transfusion. We were both finally dis-fellowshipped and disowned by our families. With our inheritance lost and no job training we started our lives over. We researched the organisation and proved they were false prophets, and wrong on doctrine too. We saw that we had put the organisation where Christ should have been. We are determined to serve Christ, not some organisation, and have done so with great joy ever since. Bill is home with the Lord now, and I'm carrying on our ministry with the Lord's help. Although my family still shuns me, I pray that they may one day turn from the organisation to faith in Jesus Christ. Joan Cetnar.

I was converted to Jehovah's Witnesses when I was 18 years old and seeking for God. I gave up earning an honours degree in university to devote myself to the organisation. I'm ashamed now of the control I gave to the organisation over my life. I nearly died refusing a blood transfusion. I let the elders make decisions I should have made. At an assembly in 1972 I stayed with my Christian uncle who immediately set his Church to praying for my deliverance from the Jehovah's Witnesses. As they prayed, and a Christian shared his faith, I finally questioned doctrine - especially about Jesus supposedly being Michael the archangel. I took my concerns to the elders, I found out that you cannot ask honest-hearted questions, nor is there any honourable way out of the organisation. I left early in 1975 causing uproar in the congregation, since Armageddon was expected in a few months. It was the best decision I ever made, other than receiving Christ as my Saviour. My husband, Keith, and I have served the Lord ever since. Lorri Macgregor.

I began studying with Jehovah's Witnesses in the early forties, then after I came out of prison I continued as a Jehovah's Witness until 1970. However I had been reading forbidden Christian books, and also I was not living the life that I should have been. I confessed to the elders, and they dispensed with my 26 years of service in ten minutes. I was out. But then a loving Christian friend put his arms around me and showed me the love of Christ, and I felt more love from him in ten minutes than I felt from the organisation in 26 years. Later, while reading a Christian book, I knew for certain that Jesus Christ is God, and I fell to my knees and received Him as my Saviour. Floyd Erwin.

When I was six months old my parents became Jehovah's Witnesses, and I lived totally for the organisation for 50 years. But I saw so many injustices over the years, and so much unkindness, so little mercy. You know they present a facade of love, but people are really sacrificed for the sake of the organisation. Finally, after they destroyed my family, I began to research the Watchtower organisation and to read the Bible, because I wanted to know if the Watchtower was God's channel, I wanted to know how to get eternal life. Well, I found out that Jesus Christ is the way, the truth and the life - not some organisation - and of course Jesus gives us eternal life. Dan Hall.

I was in my third year of college in 1973, and thinking about law school. At that time my Jehovah's Witness parents told me that Armageddon was due by 1975. I had 18 months to live, so I quit school and went back to the Jehovah's Witnesses - but as God would have it, some wonderful Christian showed me that I was following a false prophet. The facts were right in my own books. Now I don't like being lied to, and when I found out that the Watchtower had deceived me I knew I was in a cult - but then something wonderful happened. I accepted Jesus as my Lord, and He would never lie to me. So many people have accepted the lie by reading the Watchtower. Now I have dedicated my life to showing them the rest of the story, the real story about Jehovah's Witnesses - a non-prophet organisation! My prayer is that Jesus will open the eyes of many Jehovah's Witnesses to see the love of Christ. Duane Magnani.[12]

May all our eyes be opened to see the love of Christ.

Footnotes

1   Jehovah's Witnesses citing Gen 9:3-4; Lev 7:26-27; 17:13-14; Acts 15:28-29; 21:25 claim that the Bible teaches that blood is sacred and therefore blood transfusions are unlawful. Many Witnesses carry a signed card stating that they are not to receive a blood transfusion in the event that they are found unconscious. Such a prohibition goes beyond what is actually written in the Word of God cf. Matt 15:9. Such references clearly prohibit the eating and drinking of blood and not its transfusion for medical purposes. It is also erroneous to reason that because the eating and drinking of blood is forbidden then blood must be sacred. In Acts 21:25 God prohibits fornication as well as the eating and drinking of blood and of course fornication is not sacred but sinful.

2   Added by author for purposes of clarity.

3   Ibid.

4   Ibid.

5   From the video documentary Jehovah's Witnesses: A Non-Prophet Organisation, Jeremiah Films, 1994.

6   Ibid.

7   Ibid.

8   Ibid.

9   Added by author for purposes of clarity.

10   Many more proofs of the biblical doctrine of the Trinity will be presented throughout the following chapters in this book.

11   Added by author for purposes of clarity.

12   From the video documentary Jehovah's Witnesses: A Non-Prophet Organisation, Jeremiah Films, 1994.

Chapter 2
Christian Science And Scientology

Christian Science and Scientology are two separate and distinct movements but here, they are grouped together for this chapter sets out to critique the 'mind sciences'. However under no circumstances could the Christian Science movement and Scientology be defined as true sciences of the mind. In fact, Christian Science and Scientology are two of the most dangerous beliefs prevalent in our world today.

Both secular and Christian observers have agreed that Scientology is having a great impact on today's religious scene. Eugene Methvin wrote in the *Reader's Digest*, May 1980, p.141,

> Scientology is one of the oldest, wealthiest and most dangerous of the major 'new religions' or cults operating today.

Christian Science

Mary Baker Eddy was the founder of the Christian Science movement. She was born in New Hampshire in 1821 in the USA; the daughter of a member of the

Congregational Church. Very early on in her life she rejected the main doctrines of orthodox Christianity.

Biographers tell how Mary Baker Eddy endured a great deal of sickness during her childhood. Mention is made of her having many nervous fits and of manifesting spasmodic seizures of a hysterical nature.[1] Indeed, some writers have concluded that as a result of Mary Baker Eddy's early illnesses and nervous disorders, she became highly neurotic.[2]

In her adult life Mary Baker Eddy dabbled in Spiritism and in the occult. It is reputed that when she fell into one of these trances, people would gather together and seek advice from her, or ask her to contact a dead loved one. Mary Baker Eddy claimed that during the night seasons she was able to hear mysterious tapings and rappings of spirits. She claimed to see spirits of the departed standing by her bedside, and to receive messages in writing from the dead.

In 1862 Mary Baker Eddy suffered another illness, but this time she sought out the help of a quasi-doctor by the name of Phineas Quimby who believed that the mind had power to heal the body.

From his belief that the mind could overpower the body, Phineas Quimby taught a system of healing that dealt primarily with the mind. His claim was that the body could be cured through the 'mental science'.

Phineas Quimby was to influence Mary Baker Eddy immensely. In fact, the teachings she derived from him would later develop into what is now the Christian Science Movement.

In 1866 Mary Baker Eddy had a serious accident and was not expected to live. When she did recover, Mary Baker Eddy maintained her renewed health was due to reflecting on Matthew 9:2

> And, behold, they brought to him a man sick of the palsy, lying on a bed: and Jesus seeing their faith said unto the sick of the palsy; Son, be of good cheer; thy sins be forgiven thee.

This experience, Mary Baker Eddy claimed, enlightened her to the power of exercising 'mind over matter'.

This apparent healing convinced Mary Baker Eddy that healing of the body could be achieved through the mind; hence the foundation of the Christian Science movement was based upon such beliefs. At the age of 54, in 1875, Mary Baker Eddy wrote: *Science and Health with Key to the Scriptures*, which she claimed to be the final revelation of God to humankind.

It is so important when we are studying cults to see this **theological** characteristic in many of the founders of cults and false faiths. Cult founders often make the claim to be a prophet, or to be God's final **revelation** to humanity. Mary Baker Eddy claimed to be such in *Science and Health*; that is why she called it the *Key to the Scriptures*. She believed that this particular book was inspired of God, just like the Bible. Mary Baker Eddy considered herself to be the woman of Revelation 12. Furthermore, she believed that she was the key spoken of by the Lord when He said to the Church of Philadelphia: Revelation 3:7,

> These things saith he that is holy, he that is true, he that hath the key of David, he that openeth, and no man shutteth; and shutteth, and no man openeth.

Mary Baker Eddy described the Bible as a 'dark book'; a book to which apparently she had the key. She claimed that the Bible was full of many mistakes and that her writings in 'Science and Health' had the key to it all. Therefore, Mary Baker Eddy maintained, she could open the great mysteries and secrets of God's Word.

In 1879, four years after writing *Science and Health*, Mary Baker Eddy and some of her students established the 'Church of Christ' in Boston, Massachusetts.

In 1881 Mary Baker Eddy opened a Metaphysical College and like many other cults exhibiting an **overt financial emphasis**, she began to charge for her Christian Science services. She charged $300 for twelve healing sessions, which was a large amount of money in 1881. It is no surprise therefore, that Mary Baker Eddy was a millionaire when she died in 1910!

Is Christian Science, Science?

The definition of 'science' in the Oxford English Dictionary is: 'a branch of knowledge conducted on objective principles.' 'Objective' in the Oxford English Dictionary, is defined as being 'external to the mind, things outside the mind. . . actually existing, things that are real.' The definition of science continues: 'science involves the systematised observation of those things.' It is therefore clear that for something to be science it must be proven as such by experimenting with objective phenomena. Science necessarily involves practical experimentation with the materials and functions of the physical universe.

Science is only true science when proven along these lines.

Does Christian Science satisfy those rigorous demands? Though it claims to be a science of the mind, Christian Science cannot prove the principles that it espouses. Christian Science asserts that pain and sickness are all illusions of the mind. Anyone experiencing sore teeth, an aching head, painful joints, and heart pain, knows full well that it is not an illusion! The fallout from this Christian Science teaching is that Christian Scientists reject the use of medicine, vitamins, nutrition, immunisation, and drugs of every form.

The Christian Science remedy for illness is to correct 'illusions in the mind' by understanding and practising Christian Science principles. Christian Scientists display **exclusivity** in the fact that they assert that if you wish to be healed, you must join them. A measure of **indoctrination** is evidenced in the fact that those desiring healing must start thinking the way Christian Scientists think, doing what Christian Scientists do, and saying what Christian Scientists say.

There are groups of full-time healers called 'Christian Science Practitioners' who claim that people are being restored to health through Christian Science principles. Understandably, there was outrage in the 1990s when it was disclosed by the media that 18 children suffered preventable deaths from the year 1980 because their parents, who were Christian Scientists, chose Christian Science metaphysical healing techniques instead of taking their children to the doctor or phoning for an ambulance.

In the previous chapter we examined the Jehovah's Witnesses and addressed briefly in footnote the blood transfusion issue. Here, however, it is worth noting that both Jehovah's Witnesses and Christian Science display the common **exclusive** characteristic of a cult in that they claim to know more about life and eternity than anyone else. They claim to have an exclusive knowledge of God and the mechanisms of the universe. Therefore, they maintain: they know more than medicine can tell us; they know more than the Bible can tell us; they know more than the Church can tell us; and all because, they claim, they alone truly know God.

It is interesting to note that Mary Baker Eddy wore glasses, underwent tooth extractions and received regular morphine injections when dying even though as a Christian Scientist she was supposed to reject such medical intervention.

Is Christian Science, science? Obviously it is anything but!

Is Christian Science, Christian?

The fact that Mary Baker Eddy's book: *Science and Health*, denies all the essential doctrines of the Christian faith, indicates that this movement is not Christian. If this cult did not use words such as 'Jesus', 'Trinity', 'love', 'grace', and 'sin', it would never be suspected of having any association whatever with Christianity. The use of such words and phrases 'Christianise' the movement: making it appear more acceptable to those from Christian backgrounds.

The following quotations from Mary Baker Eddy's *Science and Health with Key to the Scriptures* show where Christian Science denies the Christian faith.

The first is regarding the substitutionary atonement of our Lord Jesus Christ. Mary Baker Eddy says,

> . . . one sacrifice, however great, is insufficient to pay the debt of sin. The atonement requires constant self-immolation. . . on the sinner's part. That God's wrath should be vented upon his beloved Son, is divinely unnatural. Such a theory is man-made: *Science & Health*, 23:3-7.

The next quote, concerns the precious blood of the Lord Jesus, Mary Baker Eddy says,

> The material blood of Jesus was no more efficacious to cleanse from sin when it was shed upon 'the accursed tree', than when it was flowing in his veins as he went daily about his Father's business: *Science & Health* 25:6-8.

The Scriptures teach that our Lord Jesus Christ made one sacrifice for sins forever, and then sat down at the right hand of the Father on high. From the very beginning of the Old Testament to the end of the New Testament Scripture teaches that without the shedding of blood there is no forgiveness of sin.

According to Mary Baker Eddy this is not true. Mary Baker Eddy believed she had a **new revelation.** In an attempt to explain why the disciples thought Jesus Christ died and rose again Mary Baker Eddy writes,

> His disciples believed Jesus to be dead while he was hidden in the sepulchre, whereas he was alive: *Science & Health* 44:28-29.

This contradicts the following verses of the Bible:

Romans 8:34

> Who is he that condemneth? It is Christ that **died**, yea rather, that is **risen** again.

First Thessalonians 4:14

> ...if we believe that Jesus **died** and **rose** again, even so them also which sleep in Jesus will God bring with him.

First Peter 3:18

> For Christ also hath once suffered for sins, the just for the unjust, that he might bring us to God, being put to **death** in the flesh, but **quickened** by the Spirit.

Is there any power in the blood of Christ? There is in His death, 1 John 1:7

> ...the blood of Jesus Christ his Son cleanseth us from all sin.

These verses are therefore, according to Christian Science, also a delusion.

Christian Science denies also that Jesus is God. Mary Baker Eddy's view that

> If there had never existed such a person as the Galilean Prophet, it would make no difference to me: *The 1st Church of Christ Scientist & Miscellany*, pp.318-319.

ignores John 14.9, where the Lord Jesus Himself claimed to be God,

> ...he that hath seen me hath seen the Father.

We read in John 10:33 that the Jews took up stones to stone Him, saying,

> For a good work we stone thee not; but for blasphemy; and because that thou, being a man, makest thyself God.

Jesus received worship as God because He was GOD.

Colossians 2:9 reads,

> For in Him dwelleth all the fullness of the Godhead bodily.

First Timothy 3:16 reads,

> …great is the mystery of godliness: God was manifest in the flesh.…

Who was that God manifest in flesh? It was, and is Jehovah, the living God in the person of His Son, the Lord Jesus Christ.

Christian Science does not teach the Bible doctrine of the Triune Godhead. Instead it teaches that God is both father and mother. This is not to be found in the Scriptures where the male personal pronoun 'He' is used to designate God.

Perhaps Christian Science thinking on this issue derives from the fact that they believe that God is a principle known as the 'divine mind': that He is not a personality and does not have personhood.

The Christian Science believe that God is 'all in all'. God, to Christian Science, is in everyone and everything and for Christian Science, Christ was not unique; He was a 'way-shower' to God, like many other prophets before Him and after Him. Christ, to the Christian Scientist pointed a way to God. Christian Science claims that Christ epitomised the true principle of what they call 'Christ-consciousness', which dwells in us all. According to Christian Science we are all *Christs*, we are all *gods* and we have all got a divine spark within us.

Christian Science claims that salvation comes by denying sin in your mind.

Unfortunately, the reality of this ignoring of sin is to delude ourselves and, to sin against God. That is the reason God's Word says in 1 John 1:8-10,

> If we say that we have no sin, we deceive ourselves, and the truth is
> not in us. If we confess our sins, he is faithful and just to forgive us our

sins, and to cleanse us from all unrighteousness. If we say that we have not sinned, we make him a liar, and his word is not in us.

In contrast to Christian Science, the Christian gospel calls people to acknowledge their sin, repent and believe in the Saviour who died for sinners: Lord Jesus Christ.

Scientology

Scientology is one of the popular modern cults in our world. Unlike Christian Science, Scientology does not claim to be Christian. It does not claim to follow Christ.

The Bible according to Scientology is no more special than any other holy book in any religion of the world. Scientology does not worship a deity, rather Scientology is a religion about men. Scientologists do not believe there was only one Christ, who was the Son of God but rather they believe the man who died on the cross whist He may have been a little better than most, He was no more of a Christ than anyone else.

L. Ron Hubbard the founder of this cult has stated categorically, 'There was no Christ!' Everything that Christianity is, Scientology denies.

A number of celebrities are members of the Church of Scientology. These include Priscilla Presley, the widow of the late Elvis, their daughter Lisa-Marie and film stars Kelly Preston, Kirstie Alley, Tom Cruise and John Travolta. There is also a seven-storey celebrity centre in Hollywood, California dedicated to Celebrity Scientologists.

In October 1979 there were nine Scientology workers, including the wife of the leader, found guilty in a U.S. court of conspiracy charges.

Raymond Banoun, the Assistant U.S. attorney in charge of that investigation and prosecution, commented upon the guilty saying,

> The evidence presented to the court shows brazen criminal campaigns against private and public organisations and individuals.

The Scientology officials hid behind claims of religious liberty while inflicting injuries upon every element of society.[3]

The Founder - Fiction Author

The biggest fraudster of them all was the founding father of Scientology.

Some biographical facts about L. Ron Hubbard were detailed in a BBC documentary some years ago.[4] The Narrator says,

> In new gurus and religions, none is more powerful or successful than L. Ron Hubbard and the Church of Scientology. L. Ron Hubbard moved effortlessly from writing bestselling science fiction books, like 'Beyond the Black Nebula', or 'The Emperor of the Universe', to founding a new Church 'Scientology', and the writing of a new spiritual guidebook 'Dianetics.' L. Ron Hubbard was a man of astounding abilities and even more astounding claims. He claimed that in earlier incarnations he visited heaven twice. His first visit allegedly took place 43 trillion years ago.

In this television documentary L. Ron Hubbard was quoted as describing heaven as he saw it. He says,

> Heaven is not a floating island in the sky, but a high place in the mountains of another planet. Visitors arrive in a town comprising a trolley bus, some building fronts, a boarding house, a bistro in a basement, and a bank building. Although there seem to be people around - in the boarding house there was a lady in a kimono - these were only effigies. The bank is the key point of interest. Inside was a flight of marble stairs leading to the pearly gates. The gates are well done, well built, an avenue of statues of saints leads up to them. The entering grounds are well-kept, laid out like bush gardens in Pasadena so often seen in the movies.

The Narrator interjects to inform us that L. Ron Hubbard claims to have dropped in on heaven a trillion years later and found it in a sorry state.

L. Ron Hubbard continues with his more recent findings stating,

> The place is shabby, the vegetation is gone, the pillars are scruffy, the saints have vanished and so have the angels. Inside the grounds one can see the excavations, like archaeological diggings with raw terraces that lead to hell. Plain wire fencing encloses the place.

Ron Hubbard Jr., L. Ron Hubbard senior's eldest son, told a *Newsweek* reporter in 1982,

> My father claimed that his theories relating to Scientology were based on 30 years of case histories and research. In fact they were written off the top of his head while he was under the influence of drugs.

Ron Hubbard Jr. continued:

> My father is one of the biggest conmen of this century.

Ron Hubbard Jr. changed his name because he was so ashamed of the unscrupulous reputation of his father.

Despite this damning revelation many high-ranking celebrities are flocking to the shrine of Scientology. There are Scientology Churches in some of the richest cities in the world.

Below is another very revealing transcript of another television programme, ITV's 'The Big Story'. The journalist Dermot Murnaghan examines some further claims of L. Ron Hubbard.

> Dermot Murnaghan (DM): Scientology was created by this man, Lafayette Ron Hubbard, or plain Ron to his followers. From within

Hubbard's inner circle his PR man, Vaughn Young, worked on Ron's chief ambition for 20 years.

Young: Hubbard literally had a plan for world conquest. He actually literally wanted to take over the world, but he had to put it in other terms, and the term he came up with was to clear the planet. This sounds like a very beneficent action, we're going to 'clear the planet', which means rid it of its problems. But really it was more of a case like a Hitler, that he wants to rid the planet of vermin, and the vermin are the people that are stopping him - these were basically the enemies of Scientology.

DM: Scientologists dismiss as propaganda all criticism of Ron Hubbard, the Church or their beliefs from former members, or apostates as they call them. But there are plenty of independent sources too. Science fiction writer Hubbard created a colourful life history for himself, claiming to be a nuclear physicist, explorer and war hero. This was exposed as the myth it was by *Sunday Times* journalist Russell Miller.

Miller: Ron Hubbard was a charlatan, a liar, a confidence trickster, a thief. He invented his whole life, he invented a career to substantiate himself as a Guru for the Church of Scientology.

DM: In 1968 Hubbard was banned from Britain and took to the high seas. The crew of mostly young followers became the elite core of Scientology, the 'Sea Organisation'.

At this point in the programme footage from the past of an interview with L. Ron Hubbard is inserted, where he is asked: 'Do you ever think that you might be quite mad?' L. Ron Hubbard replies: 'Oh yes, the one man in the world who never believes he's mad is a madman.'

Dermot Murnaghan continues:

Hubbard's organisation fought back against bans and adverse publicity worldwide to become a multimillion-dollar empire controlling a myriad of interlocking companies. Hubbard left 650 million dollars when he died in 1986.

What an author of fiction L. Ron Hubbard is! The religion that he founded and formed is fictional itself.

The sad truth is that those who are his disciples actually believe it is true. We know from the truth of God's Word that it is a lie. Satan, subtly, however has given this ridiculous belief an attractive appeal; through both the fictional façade of its founder and also through its celebrity followers.

The Claims - Fictitious Falsehoods

Scientology's fictional author has created a religion of fictitious falsehoods.

The teachings; **new revelations**, of this cult are articulated in two books by L. Ron Hubbard: *What Is Scientology?* and: Clear *Body and Clear Mind.* L. Ron Hubbard apparently believed that the way to Utopia was, as in other mind sciences, to get your mind cleared. This, L. Ron Hubbard declared, was possible through dianetics.

Dianetics is simply a name for Scientology's method of eradicating negative thoughts and negative emotions that have been in our life from our birth. It is claimed that herein lies the way to real deliverance and salvation.

L. Ron Hubbard believed it would take billions of years for this to be realised. This is reflected in the fact that when a person signs up to Scientology they sign a certificate that commits them to a billion years of service. Scientologists believe this is realised through reincarnation.

In 1949 L. Ron Hubbard attributed an improvement in his own health to this discovery of dianetics. He claimed his theory was the modern science of mental health and the psychology of the subconscious mind. It is incredible what this man believed.

Below is another transcript from the same ITV documentary mentioned above. This time Jon Atack, an ex-member of Scientology who has studied their beliefs in depth, is interviewed and details some of their incredible new teachings.

> Dermot Murnaghan (DM): Former Scientologist Jon Atack has collected an enormous archive on the bizarre system of beliefs that Ron Hubbard invented. 'Clearing the planet' means taking everyone to the secret 'OT' or Operating Thetan levels. It can cost Scientologists around £20,000 to discover these inner mysteries.

> Atack: Once you've paid an enormous amount of money, and signed a covenant of secrecy, and you get onto the third OT level, you're told that a galactic prince called Xenu, some 75 million years ago, rounded up the populations of 76 planets averaging 178 billion per planet, and brought them to earth and clustered them together using hydrogen bombs having dumped them in volcanoes.

> DM: The spirit of these exiles, or Thetans, as Hubbard called them, on release from the volcanoes attached themselves to human beings.

> Atack: Scientologists who are doing OT levels come to believe that they are inhabited by thousands of little alien spirits, extraterrestrial spirits, and they're basically seeking to exorcise these spirits which are governing their behaviour and reactions.

Although this account of John Atack's reads like science-fiction it is in fact an authentic account of Scientology beliefs.

The Profits – Fantastic

In L. Ron Hubbard's earlier description of heaven it is significant that 'the bank' was a key feature. It was from the bank that the marble stairs stretched right up to the pearly gates of heaven. Money is a vital factor in Scientology and as a cult it characteristically displays an **overt financial interest**. The profits of the Scientology movement are fantastic.

In August 1986 the headline of the *Daily Express* newspaper read,

> Scientologists adopt daughter worth millions: Elvis heiress cult shock.

The reason for that headline was that Lisa-Marie Presley: Elvis and Priscilla Presley's daughter, on her 18th birthday, was about to inherit two million dollars from her late father's estate. On her 21st birthday she was going to inherit another two million, and when she turned 25 she was to inherit up to 30 million dollars and the Graceland estate where Elvis used to live. It should be no surprise that the Scientologists were so interested in Lisa-Marie! In fact a waitress at the Scientology retreat was reported as saying,

> She (Lisa-Marie) is being handled very carefully. They know she will come into a lot of money and they expect a large chunk of it.

The Scientologists have property across the world that includes expensive properties in the USA and some in Britain. The Scientology Centre in Los Angeles and the Celebrity Centre in Hollywood are but two of their many large buildings. They have had a boat, which was named the 'Apollos' - and in 1976 US tax officials found £1,250,000 in cash aboard it!

L. Ron Hubbard used to charge between £1,700 and £6,300 for consultation for some of his more advanced courses. The estimated gross annual income of the Scientology movement is £45 million.

The Fruit – Fatal

Scientology's profits are fantastic, its claims are fictitious, its founder is a fiction author, and finally: its fruit is fatal eternally. There have been people who have committed suicide because of their affiliation to Scientology.

Below is the text of an interview with a woman called Mary Johnson, perhaps the only person in the whole of Ireland who has been courageous enough to admit that she has come out of the Scientology movement. This interview was broadcast on the RTE chat show, the 'Late Late Show' in 1995.

Read carefully to see an example of how easily a cult can get control of a person's mind and spirit:

> Interviewer, Gaye Byrne: . . .let me tell you about Mary Johnson, OK? Mary Johnson is from Dundalk, a Catholic, she went to school in St Vincent's Mercy Convent in Dundalk. She came first in the town at the Leaving Certificate, and first in Ireland in Italian in the Leaving Certificate. She went to Trinity (Trinity College Dublin)[5], got a degree in Russian and French, she then went to study Marketing at night in the College of Commerce in Rathmines, and did a four-year course in two years. She's an inter-pro squash player for Leinster, and also has coaching qualifications. She plays guitar and sings, and has her own business here in Dublin - she runs a sports shop. Just over two years ago she was introduced to Scientology, the Church of Scientology, by a friend called Tom. Mary, let me just summarise the bare skeleton of what I know about you. You were introduced by Tom, the idea was that Scientology offered you a chance to further your career, your self-fulfilment, your freedom and control over your own life if you took a course; which you did and you paid for. Whether you succeeded in that or not, the idea was that you go to do a second course, and you pay for that, and so on to a third course, and you pay for that. You found yourself being drawn into this organisation, and you began to

get worried about it and concerned about your place in it, and then your family brought pressure to bear upon you, or influence at least to bear upon you to get out. Because of the concern and efforts on their part, and on the part of your friends, you eventually declutched with some difficulty - with some difficulty. Is that a fair sort of summary in broad outline?

Johnson: Yes, in broad outline.

Interviewer: Why are you frightened to be here tonight?

Johnson: I'm frightened to be here, Gaye, because I'm intimidated by the people who are here from the Church of Scientology. The first point I would like to make is that the reason I am here is because I'm the only Irish person who is an ex-member of the Church of Scientology who is prepared to speak out. People. . .ex-members don't speak out, that's the first point. The second point is that it is interesting that the Church of Scientology has seen fit to fly in two people from England today for this show, when I'm Irish. We're dealing with the Church of Scientology in Ireland - are they not happy to have their own members here to speak?

Interviewer: You got out relatively easily, did you not?

Johnson: I did, because my family worked very quickly and very thoroughly to get information on the Church of Scientology, and but for that intervention I wouldn't be here today.

Interviewer: Was there pressure brought to bear upon you when you were getting out, or at any time when you were in, when you first began to voice your reservations?

Johnson: From whom, from the Church?

Interviewer: From the Church, yes.

Johnson: Well, I didn't actually voice my reservations to the Church. By the time my family had intervened I had made a commitment to the Church that I was going to give up my business and move to England and work for the Church for one billion years. Because at that stage I believed in reincarnation, which I don't believe in.

Interviewer: One billion years?

Johnson: Yes, one billion years.

Interviewer: And their influence had got you to the point of almost selling up your business, is that so?

Johnson: Yes, their suggestion was that I would be more fulfilled in Scientology and 'would it not be good idea if I sold my business?'

Interviewer: OK, so you're frightened to be here tonight. When you finally decided to leave, was there pressure and intimidation brought to bear on you?

Johnson: When I left Scientology, the following week I had about 20 phone calls from people in Scientology to find out why I hadn't come back and reported on the intervention of my family, because I was drilled on how to deal with my family by members of the Church.

Interviewer: You were told what to say to your family?

Johnson: I would have a member of the Church of Scientology role-playing my mother, or my sister, or my brother-in-law, and I would answer them, defending the Church of Scientology.

Interviewer: And you did pretty good at that?

Johnson: I was a good student I believe.

Interviewer: Yes, and then eventually you got these phone calls - were they threatening phone calls? Intimidating phone calls? Bullying?

Johnson: Not at that stage, but the problem with them was that they were always - they were to my business, they were to my home, they were invasive. I found them very much invading my privacy. I just... the intimidation, the reason why I feel intimidation is because...I am frightened because the Church of Scientology in the past has revealed personal details given by people like me in confidence to them during counselling sessions. That's why I'm frightened, because they have used details given in confidence to silence their critics.

NOTE CAREFULLY you cannot get out of Scientology easily, and Scientology will not treat you well if you succeed. The movement is strongly **authoritarian** in its leadership and seeks to **isolate** its members from any other dependencies making members completely dependent on Scientology.

Mary Johnson's story revealed that Scientology used **behavioural** techniques of **deprivation** and **indoctrination** to manipulate potential members. Others have testified that after undertaking certain Scientology courses to rid their mind of negative thoughts they found themselves hallucinating before handing over their bankbook, credit card details.

In the 'Big Story' documentary broadcast on ITV mentioned earlier, an undercover journalist joined the Scientology movement. She was given a similar questionnaire to Mary Johnson's. Some of the questions on the questionnaire concerned details regarding any intimate sexual relationships that she had had. The questionnaire asked her to be explicit and specific.

It was felt that the reasoning behind this was the more of this kind of personal information Scientology finds out about members, the greater the hold Scientology has on them. This leads on to the fear that if any member should ever attempt to disclose the dubious nature of what Scientology is doing, Scientology will publish those intimate details and thereby discredit the member.

All should beware of any religious faith that uses manipulative techniques to protect itself at the expense of its members and which motivates men and women to give money in order to gain salvation.

Jesus said,

> You cannot serve two masters, you cannot serve God and money.

Beware of any organisation that says Jesus is 'a way', for in John 14:6 Jesus says,

> I am the way....

He is not one of many truths, but He said

> I am **the** truth....

There is no other way to have life other than Him, because He is the life. He is the only way to the Father, to God. He is the only name under heaven whereby we must be saved: Acts 4:12.

Footnotes

1   See Willa Cather and Georgine Milmine, The Life of Mary Baker G. Eddy and the History of Christian Science (Lincoln: University of Nabraska Press, 1993), p.54 cited by Ron Rhodes in The Challenge of the Cults and New Religions (Zondervan, 2001), p.107.
2   Ron Rhodes, The Challenge of the Cults and New Religions (Zondervan, 2001), p.107.
3   Christianity Today, vol.27, no.4, p.31.
4   The author has been unable to trace the date of the BBC documentary.
5   Added by the author for purposes of clarity.

Chapter 3
Mormonism - The Latter Day Saints

Mormonism, or 'The Church of Jesus Christ of Latter Day Saints', have approximately 11 million members and they are growing at a rate of over 1500 members a day. One baptism occurs in the Mormon Church on average every 1 minute 55 seconds.

Brigham Young University president, Merrill Bateman, predicted in the year 2000 that by 2025 the number of Mormon missionaries will have more than doubled; rising from about 60,000 to 125,000.

These missionaries are sent all around the world and presently they reside in over 150 countries and during the year 2000 alone, there were 35 Mormon temples dedicated. Each temple contains a sight that most Mormons do not see: the Celestial Room, which Mormons view almost like the Holy of Holies in the Old Testament temple.

During the past quarter of a century the Mormon Church has moved to 7th place in the 'top ten' list of USA Church bodies: bypassing the Presbyterians, Episcopalians and Lutherans.

The Origins And Originators Of Mormonism

The founder of Mormonism was Joseph Smith who is heralded as, the Mormon prophet and God's supreme revelation to mankind today. Joseph Smith was born in Vermont in 1805 and was the fourth child of Lucy and Joseph Smith. From his youth Joseph Jnr. was interested in religion, though he was greatly disturbed by the variety of denominations in so-called Christendom. He concluded that all of them could not be right and eventually questioned whether any of them at all were authentic.

In 1820 Joseph Smith determined he would ask God if any of the present-day denominations in Christendom had His true revelation. Some time later the 14 year-old Joseph Smith went into the woods in New York State to pray concerning this very matter. Subsequently he claimed that at the moment he began to pray to God upon James 1:5,

> If any of you lack wisdom, let him ask of God, that giveth to all men liberally, and upbraideth not ... ,

God the Father and the Lord Jesus Christ appeared to him and told him not to join any denomination.   Joseph Smith claimed it was revealed to him that all the denominations were abominations in the sight of God.

As Harold Berry, a Christian commentator on Mormonism has said,

> Thus, Mormons, would have us believe that with one vision given to a 14-year-old boy, God wiped out 18 centuries of historic Christianity.[1]

In claiming that God gave to Joseph Smith a **new revelation** of Jesus Christ Mormons allege that they have **exclusive** possession of the truth. The claim to **new revelation** and **exclusivity** are classic theological characteristics of a cult.

As a result of that revelation Joseph Smith did not join any of his present-day Christian denominations. However, at his own admission, he did not draw near to God from that moment on. In fact, he confessed later in his life that during the next three years he frequently, 'Fell into many foolish errors and displayed the weakness of youth and the foibles of human nature.' Some of his own contemporaries would later list using divining rods, ritual magic and other occultic practices among some of Joseph Smith's youthful errors.

Perhaps, more significant is the fact that Joseph Smith offered at least six different versions of this vision he claimed to receive from God. Within these versions there are many discrepancies; one being that in 1832 only Christ appeared to Joseph Smith in the woods in New York State and then, between the years 1838 and 1839, the version changed to claim that both God the Father and the Son appeared to him there in the forest.

Joseph Smith claimed that three years later in 1823, when he was aged 17, an angel by the name of 'Moroni' appeared to him. This angel was supposedly the son of a man called 'Mormon', who was the leader of the people called 'the Nephites'; inhabitants of America many years ago. It was claimed that Moroni told Joseph Smith that he was chosen to translate the sacred *Book of Mormon,* which had been written by Moroni over 1000 years earlier and that within the *Book of Mormon* was the **new revelation** of the fullness of the true everlasting gospel.

Supposedly the angel told Joseph Smith that the *Book of Mormon* was hidden near where he was living in New York. Joseph Smith subsequently claimed not only to have found the book but also to have been instructed to begin the work of translating the golden tablets through Urim and Thummim, which were stones used in Old Testament times to ascertain the will of God. Urim and Thummim were thus, supposedly used to translate a language written in 'reformed Egyptian characters'.

Linguistic scholars and Egyptologists however, are agreed that 'reformed Egyptian characters' do not exist. Nevertheless, Joseph Smith claimed he used Urim and Thummim like seer-stones, or spectacles, through which God revealed to him the English translation of these reformed Egyptian characters.

During the process of translation Joseph Smith alleged that John the Baptist appeared to him and ordained him to accomplish the divine work of restoring the *true* Church of Jesus Christ by the preaching of the *true* gospel that had been lost from the earth.

Joseph Smith maintained that the golden plates of the original *Book of Mormon* were taken away again by the angel. They have not been seen since. This means no-one can check the validity of Joseph Smith's claims to the existence and content of the original *Book of Mormon*.

The *Book of Mormon* claims to be an account dealing with the history of the Jaredites: the supposed original inhabitants of the American continent, from about 2247 BC to 421 AD. Allegedly these people migrated from the Tower of Babel in the Middle East to Central America, where they perished because of their own immorality. The migration of some of the Jews led by Nephi is also chronicled. Apparently, these Jews fled from persecution in Jerusalem to America where they were divided into two groups; the Nephites and the Lamanites. The *Book of Mormon* traces these groups as they began to fight one another. Having defeated the Nephites in 428AD, the Lamanites apparently lived on and are known today as the American Indian people. The *Book of Mormon* includes an account of the life of the Nephite leader Mormon and a record of the civilisation and culture of the Nephite people.

According to the *Book of Mormon*, Jesus, after His resurrection, came to the Americas to preach to the American Indians; the Lamanites and there He established His Church in the Americas, as He had in Palestine.

After the publication of the *Book of Mormon*, Mormonism began to grow. This new religion was different. Whilst Mormons assert that Elohim is the only god in our universe, they also maintain that there are other gods elsewhere. This new faith had a plurality of gods.

Mormons practiced and condoned polygamy, which immediately raised suspicions in the wider community. Persecution of the Mormons eventually developed and this forced them to move from New York State to Ohio, then to Missouri, and finally to Illinois.

From the inception of the Mormon Church trouble followed the organisation. Atrocities were committed against them but historians clearly tell us that there were also atrocities committed by them.[2]

Trouble dogged the Mormons, not just because of civil unrest, but also because of the rumours regarding polygamy: some of the Mormons were unhappy with this practice. Mormons admit that Joseph Smith was a polygamist. The number of wives he had is unknown; estimates range from 28 to 84, one being as young as 14 years old. His first wife Emma was very hurt and angry when she found out about his polygamous relationships. Joseph's response to her, and his defence of his action, was to claim that he *got a word from the Lord* to the effect that the Lord would kill Emma if she would not submit and cleave to him!

By 1842 some dissident Mormons, so unhappy with the apparent immorality, published a newspaper detailing their grievances against Mormonism and Joseph Smith in particular. The first edition of that newspaper was also the last, because days later Joseph Smith and the City Council decided to destroy the newspaper's printing office. As a result of this action Joseph Smith and his brother Hiram ended up in jail and on June 27th a mob broke into the jail and killed both of them.

Following this the Mormon Church divided into two groups. One group, led by Joseph Smith's widow, went back to Missouri and called themselves 'The Reorganised Church of Jesus Christ of Latter Day Saints'. Maintaining that they were the true Mormon Church, this group laid claim to the legal succession of Church presidency that was subsequently bestowed upon Joseph Smith's son, Joseph Smith III.

Brigham Young led the other Mormons, known today as 'The Church of the Latter Day Saints'. Under Brigham Young's leadership this group went to Utah and eventually ended up at Salt Lake. In 1847, Salt Lake became Salt Lake City, the present day capital of Mormonism.

We have already observed from the studies in our previous chapters that the chief theological characteristics of a cult are the claim of **new revelation**, the declaration of **exclusivity** and the declaration that not to be a member of their group will result in the **loss of salvation**. These characteristics are observed clearly in Mormonism.

Mormonism's claim to be the restoration of the true gospel previously lost from present-day Christendom begs the question: Were Christ's words empty when he said in Matthew 16:18 that He would build His Church and the gates of hell would not prevail against it?

Though Mormons may purport to be Christians: they see themselves as separate from, and superior to Christianity. According to Mormons they, through Joseph Smith, have the true revelation of God and the way of salvation. In fact, the *Book of Mormon* also has, as its subtitle: *Another Testament of Jesus Christ*. In other words, they are announcing that herein you will find another revelation of the Lord Jesus Christ that you will not find anywhere else.

Perhaps one of Joseph Smith's most astounding claims was that of being a human descendant of the Christ himself. Such claims allowed Smith to assert great authority over the early Mormon Church and as we have observed, an **authoritarian leadership** is a structural characteristic of a cult.

Today the Church of Jesus Christ of Latter Day Saints is one of the wealthiest cults in the world, displaying an **overt financial emphasis,** which is another classic structural characteristic of a cult. It possesses between 25 and 30 billion dollars in assets alone. The Church controls at least 100 companies worldwide, including the Marriott hotel chain. It retains 300 million dollars a year in media conglomerates and 3 million dollars a day is generated by the tithes and offerings of their members. In fact, all who join the Church must agree to give a compulsory tithe of their income.

The Teachings And Writings Of Mormonism

The strongest anti-Mormon literature belongs to Mormonism! Contemporary Mormonism is now displaying certain doctrinal divergence from the teachings of the *Book of Mormon*.

One such discrepancy can be found concerning the doctrine of God. The *Book of Mormon* teaches that there is only one God, who is not a man but an unchangeable spirit: Alma 11:26-31; 2 Nephi 31:21; Mormon 9:9-11, 19; Moroni 7:22; 8:18.

Mormon doctrine, however evolved to say there are many gods *'and gods many'*: an incorrect use of 1 Corinthians 8:5. This extract from the video documentary *The Godmakers*, Jeremiah Films, 1982, depicts the Mormon belief that, like Elohim, man can exalt himself to the state of godhood, marry goddesses, and procreate throughout eternity populating planets.

> Mormonism teaches that trillions of planets scattered throughout the cosmos are ruled by countless gods, who once were human like us. They say that long ago on one of these planets, to an unidentified god and one of his goddess wives, a spirit child named Elohim was conceived. This spirit child was born later to human parents who gave him a physical body. Through obedience to Mormon teaching in death and resurrection, he proved himself worthy and was elevated to godhood, as his father before him. Mormons believe that Elohim is their heavenly father, and that he lives with his many goddess wives on a planet near a mysterious star called Kolob. Here the god of Mormonism and his wives, through endless celestial sex, produce billions of spirit children.

Another area of conflict between contemporary Mormonism and the *Book of Mormon* is where the *Book of Mormon* asserts, correctly, that irreversible eternal glory or irreversible eternal punishment is inevitable to all men and women. This teaching is found in the *Book of Mormon* in 3 Nephi 27:11-17; Mosiah 3:24-27; 2 Nephi 28:22-23; Alma 34:32-35.

The Mormon Church however, teaches that according to 1 Corinthians 15:29 baptism is necessary for the dead in order to be exalted to another level of glory in eternity. The Mormon Church, thus become obsessed with baptism for the dead which contrasts with the *Book of Mormon*.

The Mormon Church claims that the *Book of Mormon* is 'the most correct book on earth': even more correct than the Bible! It is interesting to note that H. Michael Marquardt, an ex-Mormon scholar, studied the *Book of Mormon* in detail and found that there are over 200 quotations plagiarised from the Authorised Version of the Bible.

Mormons maintain that an angel made 15 visits from the throne of God to Joseph Smith to ensure that the *Book of Mormon* was correctly printed and translated.

However, the facts do not bear out the claim that it is the most correct book on the earth.

Firstly, considering that the first publication of the *Book of Mormon* was produced 150 years ago there have been almost 4000 changes made to that first publication.

Secondly, archaeology does not substantiate that the Nephite and Lamanite peoples ever existed. Even Mormon archaeologists would have to admit that nothing corresponding to what the *Book of Mormon* describes, has been excavated.

There is no evidence for these ancient people described in the *Book of Mormon*. Neither has evidence been found for the places or the events mentioned. There is also no evidence to prove that the Native American Indians were descendants of the Israelites.

Regarding this latter point, all modern evidence categorically counteracts this fundamental claim of the *Book of Mormon*.

The transcript below from the video documentary, *DNA versus* the *Book of Mormon* demonstrates how DNA technological advances have disproved the claims of the *Book of Mormon* that the Native American Indians were descendants of the Israelites. Indeed, even some Mormon scientists are admitting that the claims of the *Book of Mormon* cannot be substantiated in the light of modern scientific evidence.

> Narrator: Recently new inroads into research on human DNA have allowed scientists to determine the relatedness of different populations around the world. Children inherit a mixture of their

parent's DNA, which is a mixture of their grandparents DNA, and so forth. With each subsequent generation that DNA becomes increasingly mixed and blended with DNA from other ancestors. However, small or isolated amounts of DNA exist in the cells of both fathers and mothers that do not mix when passed to their children. The father's Y-chromosome DNA remains intact as it is passed down to his son, and to his son's son, and so on through multiple generations. In the same way the mother's mitochondrial DNA also remains intact as it is passed down to both her sons and daughters from one generation to the next. Scientists are then able to trace these intact DNA markers back through hundreds of generations to determine ancestry. When the Y-chromosomes or mitochondrial DNA are tested in hundreds or even thousands of individuals from two different populations of people, the results can be compared to see how similar or dissimilar these intact DNA markers are between people groups. Dr David Glen-Smith has spent more than 30 years studying Native American genes. He has dozens of publications to his name; his lab at the University of California Davis is one of the country's leading test-labs of Native American DNA.

Dr David Glen-Smith (Molecular Anthropologist, University of California., Davis): If you look at genes in Native Americans, they came from the ancestors, they had to come from their ancestral populations - those ancestors lived somewhere. You can look for those genes in Jewish populations, but you don't find them. If you look at genes that are commonly, most commonly, found in Native American populations, and those that are most commonly found in Jewish populations, they don't coincide at all.

Dr Denis O'Rourke (Molecular Anthropologist, University of Utah): Recently I've been involved in a number of research projects that have examined DNA variation in ancient populations in the Americas. I don't know of any data that suggests particular similarity of Native American populations to any population of the Middle East.

Dr Stephen L Whittington (Anthropologist, University of Maine): Archaeologists and physical anthropologists have not found any evidence of Hebrew origins for the people of North, South and Central America.

Dr Simon Southerton (Molecular Biologist): Currently on the available evidence there is nothing to suggest any relationship whatsoever with Israelites.

Dr Randall Shortridge (Molecular Biology, University of Buffalo., New York): The overwhelming evidence negates the *Book of Mormon* claim that the American Indian represents a genealogical descendant from Israel.

Thomas Murphy is a Mormon scholar and the chair of the Anthropology Department at Edmonds Community College in Linwood, Washington. His doctorate at the University of Washington is based on the DNA issue that faces his religion. He admits on this issue,

We are in a dilemma now. The genetic evidence shows clearly the American Indians are not Hebrews, they're not the Israelites.[3]

It has been proven categorically that the ancient indigenous American people were not Israelites: rather they came from a gene pool which was spawned somewhere in the eastern part of North Asia, near Siberia. The Mormon Church is attempting to discredit scientists such as Thomas Murphy because he, as a Mormon, is now showing the falsehoods in the *Book of Mormon*. Many other Mormon scientists, though remaining in the Church, are attempting to reinterpret the *Book of Mormon* in the light of these indisputable scientific facts.

Thirdly, the Mormon publication *Doctrine and Covenants* shows how Mormon literature is transformed to suit the present-day. When the 137th section of the *Doctrine and Covenants* was canonised: becoming Holy Writ, over 200 words of the original revelation, supposedly given to Joseph Smith, were omitted. These omissions included the claim that men live on the moon.

The difference between Christianity and the Mormon Church is that the Mormons rework, rewrite, cover up and delete their original scriptures; whereas the Church of Jesus Christ, founded on the Word of God, goes back to the oldest manuscripts it can find in order to find out, with as much accuracy as possible, what the truth of God's Word is.

Beliefs Of Mormonism Set Against The Teaching Of The Bible

Firstly, Mormonism believes in many gods.

Readers of the Bible will discover that the God of the Bible is described as being the only one true God. Deuteronomy 4:35 writes,

> . . . the LORD he is God; there is none else beside him.

Of course a Triune Godhead is revealed in Scripture, but that is not the same as a plurality of gods of which the Church of the Latter Day Saints teaches. The Bible reveals one God in three persons. John 4:24 states very clearly: God is not a man; He is not flesh and blood; God is spirit and they that worship Him must worship Him in spirit and in truth.

First Timothy 2:5 writes,

> There is one God, and one mediator between God and men, the man
> Christ Jesus.

First Timothy 2:5 also teaches that only the Lord Jesus, as mediator, can bring us to God; not Joseph Smith, not Brigham Young, not any other prophet, not any apostle, but the man Christ Jesus. In Malachi 3:6, God says,

For I am the LORD, I change not; therefore ye sons of Jacob are not consumed.

God never changes; He does not become exalted to a heavenly status from a man.

Secondly, Mormons deny the deity of our Lord Jesus Christ; that He is God manifest in flesh.

Early Mormon prophets taught that Elohim and one of his goddess wives came to earth as Adam and Eve to start the human race. To decide their destiny, the head of the Mormon gods called a great heavenly counsel meeting. Both of Elohim's eldest sons were there: Lucifer, and his brother Jesus. A plan was presented to build planet earth, where the spirit children would be sent to take on mortal bodies and learn good from evil. Lucifer stood and made his bid for becoming saviour of this new world - wanting the glory for himself, he planned to force everyone to become gods. Opposing the idea, the Mormon Jesus suggested giving man his freedom of choice as on other planets. The vote that followed approved the proposal of the Mormon Jesus, who would become saviour of the planet earth. Enraged, Lucifer cunningly convinced one-third of the spirits destined for earth to fight with him in revolt. Thus Lucifer became the Devil, and his followers the demons. Sent to this world they would forever be denied bodies of flesh and bone. Those who remain neutral in the battle were cursed to be born with black skin. This is the Mormon explanation for the Negro race. The spirits that fought most valiantly against Lucifer would be born into Mormon families on planet earth. These would be the lighter skinned people, or 'white and delightsome' as the *Book of Mormon* describes them. Thousands of years later Elohim, in human form once again, journeyed to earth from the star base Kolob, this time to have sex with the virgin Mary in order to provide Jesus with a physical body. The Mormon apostle, Orson Pratt, taught that after Jesus Christ grew to manhood he took at least three wives: Mary, Martha and Mary Magdalene. Through these wives the Mormon Jesus, from whom Joseph Smith claimed direct descent, supposedly fathered a number of children before he was crucified.[4]

The Scriptures teach that our Lord was much more than a mere man. John 1:1 writes,

> In the beginning was the Word, and the Word was with God, and the Word was God.

John 1:14 writes that,

> . . . the Word was made flesh, and dwelt among us, (and we beheld his glory, the glory as of the only begotten of the Father,) full of grace and truth.

Again John 1:17-18 writes,

> . . . the law was given by Moses, but grace and truth came by Jesus Christ. No man hath seen God at any time, the only begotten Son, which is in the bosom of the Father, he hath declared him.

God's Word says that grace came by Jesus Christ, not Joseph Smith or any other prophet.

In Matthew 1:18, the angel was heard to say,

> Now the birth of Jesus Christ was on this wise: When as his mother Mary was espoused to Joseph, before they came together, she was found with child of the Holy Ghost.

The angel said that He would be called Emmanuel, God With Us, the Son of the Highest.

Christ was not the son of some unbiblical Adam who had been exalted to be the god Elohim and who then caused the virgin Mary to conceive the Mormon Jesus. This is unimaginable blasphemy. Isaiah 7:14 prophetically writes,

> Therefore the Lord himself shall give you a sign; Behold, a virgin shall conceive, and bear a son, and shall call his name Immanuel.

In other words Mary would remain a virgin after conception by the Holy Spirit.

Thirdly, the mantra of the Mormon Church is, as one of its prophets taught,

> As God once was, man is; and as God is, man may become.

Man, according to Mormonism can achieve his own salvation and god-like status by following the laws and the ordinances of the Mormon Church. This contrasts with what the Scriptures teach in Hebrews 9:22 that without the shedding of blood there is no forgiveness of sin. Brigham Young declared that the blood of Christ was not enough to cleanse us from our sins because he maintained that there were some sins that need the shedding of our own blood!

However, John the Baptist's testimony of Jesus is recorded in John 1:29:

> Behold the Lamb of God, which taketh away the sin of the world.

First Peter 2:24 writes that Christ Himself,

> . . . bore our sins on his own body on the tree, that we, being dead to sins, should live unto righteousness: by whose stripes ye were healed.

Paul in Romans 3:20-25 says,

> Therefore by the deeds of the law there shall no flesh be justified in his sight: for by the law is the knowledge of sin. But now the

righteousness of God without the law is manifested, being witnessed by the law and the prophets; Even the righteousness of God which is by faith of Jesus Christ unto all and upon all them that believe: for there is no difference: For all have sinned, and come short of the glory of God; Being justified freely by his grace through the redemption that is in Christ Jesus: Whom God hath set forth to be a propitiation through faith in his blood, to declare his righteousness for the remission of sins that are past, through the forbearance of God.

Hebrews 10:12 clearly says,

This man (Jesus Christ)[5] after he had offered one sacrifice for sins for ever, sat down on the right hand of God.

The work needed to save men was finished: complete!

Fourthly, Joseph Smith maintained that John the Baptist conferred upon him the Old Testament Aaronic priesthood. Additionally he alleged that later Peter, James and John appeared to him and conferred upon him the priesthood of Melchisedec.

Hebrews 7:24 says,

...this man, (Christ)[6] because he continueth ever hath an unchangeable priesthood.

Christ, alone, is in the order of the priesthood of Melchisedec. 'Unchangeable' in the Greek language of the New Testament can be translated as 'untransferable'. There is only one priest after the order of Melchisedec: the man who died and rose again. Joseph Smith did not rise again Jesus Christ, the Saviour of the world, has the only claim to that. Such an unchangeable priesthood cannot be transferred to another!

Brigham Young said in his Journal of Discourses, Volume 9, p.312, (emphasis added by author),

He that confesses not that Jesus has come in the flesh, *and* sent Joseph Smith with the fullness of the Gospel to this generation, is not of God but is antichrist.

Fifthly, Mormons believes that salvation is achieved through their works.

Romans 10:9 declares that if we confess with the mouth the Lord Jesus, and believe in our heart that God hath raised Him from the dead, we shall be saved! Yet Brigham Young warns in the Journal of Discourses, Volume 3, p.266,

If any of you will deny the plurality of wives and continue to do so, I promise that you will be damned.

The modern Mormon Church has since changed its teaching on polygamy. Does that mean, according to Brigham Young, that all modern Mormons will be damned?

The Holy Scriptures set forth clearly a salvation that is by grace alone, through faith alone, in Christ alone. Ephesians 2:8-9 says,

For by grace are ye saved through faith; and that not of yourselves: it is the gift of God: Not of works, lest any man should boast.

Romans 4:5 says,

But to him that works salvation is not given, but to him that believeth on him that justifies the ungodly, his faith is counted as righteousness.

Sixthly the Mormon Church teaches that continual baptism by proxy for the dead, can redeem those who are lost.

First Corinthians 15:29 clearly mentions baptism for the dead. Even among Christian scholars interpretations of this verse are many and varied. However one of the principal rules of hermeneutics: the method of interpreting the Scriptures, is that the clear passages of God's Word should determine interpretations and doctrines before obscure ones and that obscure passages should be interpreted in light of Scriptures that are clear.

Applying this principle to 1 Corinthians 15:29 we see that there are no other texts in Scripture which mention baptism for the dead. There was however, not far from Corinth a Greek pagan practice of baptising dead people. Paul may have been using this to convince the Corinthians of the reality of resurrection. The sense of Paul's argument could have been 'If pagans are even doing this, how can you Christians not believe in the resurrection from the dead?' He certainly was not claiming that, in contradistinction to everything else in the Scriptures, there is a second chance of salvation after death.

Hebrews 9:27 teaches that

> . . . it is appointed unto men once to die, but after this the judgment.

There is no second opportunity to be saved.

Christ taught this in His story of the Rich Man and Lazarus, as told in Luke 16. This story teaches that in eternity there is a great gulf fixed so that those who desire to pass from hell to heaven cannot; all hope of redemption is past.

The same is echoed in Revelation 20:15 which says,

> . . . whosoever was not found written in the book of life was cast into the lake of fire.

No second opportunities are given after death.

Seventhly, Joseph Smith claims in the *History of the Church*, volume 6, pp.408, 409,

> God is in the still small voice. In all these indictments, (affidavits that were put against him)[7], it is all of the devil - all corruption. Come on!

> Ye prosecutors! Ye false swearers! All hell, boil over! Ye burning mountains, roll down your lava! For I will come out on the top at last. I have more to boast of than ever any man had. I am the only man that has ever been able to keep a whole Church together since the days of Adam. A large majority of the whole have stood by me. Neither Paul, John, Peter nor Jesus ever did it. I boast that no man ever did such a work as I. The followers of Jesus ran away from Him; but the Latter Day Saints never ran away from me yet. . . .

Such a statement is obviously anti-Christ.

Revelation 22:19 tells us that if anyone takes away or adds to God's revelation, God will take away his name from the Book of Life. The Christ of Mormonism is not the Christ of the Bible.

Eighthly, Mormons believe that Elohim, the Mormon god, is an exalted man who has ascended to 'god status'. Satan is said to be the brother of the Lord Jesus Christ and because Jesus' plan of salvation was chosen over Satan's, this exalted man 'Elohim' went to earth and, as Brigham Young claimed, through sexual reproduction with the virgin Mary conceived Jesus! It is the Mormon belief that when Christ returns again to judge the world all men will stand before a panel of three Justices: the Mormon Jesus, Elohim, and Joseph Smith!

Joseph Smith judging the world is not predicted in the Bible, however we do read in Acts 17:31 that God will judge the world

> . . . in righteousness by that man whom he hath ordained; whereof he hath given assurance unto all men, in that he hath raised him from the dead.

The only One who will judge the world is that One who God raised from the dead: the Lord Jesus Christ.

It is obvious that Mormon doctrine contains, in the light of Scripture, what could only be described as blasphemy.

When facing Mormons with some of these facts, which conflict with Scripture, the defence they usually give is heartbreaking. They will often say:'I have prayed to God over the *Book of Mormon*, and He has given me a burning in my bosom that it is true.' Mormons invite anyone to read the *Book of Mormon* and then to ask God to reveal Himself and He, in turn, will give them that same burning in the bosom.

These misguided people fail to see that to rely on a subjective burning in the bosom and to ignore indisputable, objective facts can never lead to truth. Sadly Mormon faith is not rooted in historical facts like Christianity, but upon subjective experience that some Mormons secretly confess never to have known.

However those who diligently examine the facts can be led to the One who is the truth, as experienced by some ex-Mormons. Extracts from their testimonies follow:

> Instead of going back to one of the standard works of the Church, I went to the Bible. I started reading and made up my mind that I was going to go from cover to cover, and in the second chapter of Genesis I studied how Eve was convinced by Satan to eat the fruit, that she could become a god. Then in the 14th chapter of Isaiah, Lucifer was cast out of heaven because he too wanted to be equal to or greater than God.

> I began studying the Bible, I became aware of the real Jesus, the real God, and began to understand that the god of Mormonism was not the God of the Bible.

> We lived the Word of Wisdom, we attended meetings, we paid our tithing, we had Family Home Evening, and we did all the things we were supposed to do. When I became a Christian I suddenly was not the good person I thought I was, because God revealed to us our inner pride, our inner problems, the things that had not been in focus before because we were so concerned in the outward things, we were

so happy with the outward things we were doing that that made us rest, thinking we were OK.

I had been looking all my life for something in the Mormon Church, and I couldn't put my finger on what I was looking for. Then when my Mom accepted Christ into her life, she shared it with me, and I saw a joy in her life that I had never seen before in all of her activity in the Mormon Church. This is what I needed![8]

Let me conclude by saying: Beware of false doctrine, and, if you belong to the Mormon Church, we love you in the Saviour's Name. We would ask you to search the Scriptures and see if these things are so, and may you find the Lord Jesus Christ of the Bible as your Saviour and your Lord.

Footnotes

1   Harold J. Berry, The Truth Twisters, (Back to the Bible, 1992), p.100.
2   E.g. The Mountain Meadows massacre of 1859. Recent evidence on a newly discovered lead sheet appears to directly link Brigham Young to this massacre: Daily Telegraph newspaper, February 27, 2002.
3   From the video documentary DNA versus the Book of Mormon, Living Hope Ministries, 2003.
4   From the video documentary The Godmakers, Jeremiah Films, 1982. See also The Seer, P.172.
5   Ibid.
6   Ibid.
7   Ibid.
8   The Godmakers, Jeremiah Films, 1982.

Chapter 4
Unitarianism

Many famous historical figures were Unitarians. Among them are five past presidents of the United States of America: John Adams, John Quincy Adams, Thomas Jefferson, Millard Fillmore, and William Taft. In the literary world we learn that Henry Wadsworth Longfellow, Ralph Waldo Emerson and Charles Dickens all classed themselves as Unitarians.

No less than eight U.S. Supreme Court Justices have been Unitarians; and some famous women, including 'the lady of the lamp' Florence Nightingale, were Unitarians. There were also several famous Unitarian scientists including Charles Darwin and Alexander Graham Bell. In fact 'Unitarian Universalists' comprise approximately 25% of those who are listed in America's Hall of Fame.

Unitarianism is defined by Paul Murray and Andy Pollock, on the website of St Stephen's Green Unitarian Church Dublin, as follows,

> Unitarians are people of liberal religious outlook who are united by a common search for meaning and truth. Although of Christian origin,

and still following the teaching of Christ as a great and godly leader, Unitarianism today also seeks insight from other religions and philosophies. Individual beliefs within our religious community are quite diverse, and personal religious development is seen as a continuing process. Unitarianism has no set doctrines or dogmas.

The broad beliefs of the Irish Unitarians are summed up, in the introductory statement of the Dublin Church's monthly calendar, under the three central Unitarian principles of freedom, reason and tolerance. The statement reads,

Love is the doctrine of this Church, the quest for truth is its sacrament, and service is its prayer. To dwell together in peace, to seek knowledge in freedom, to serve mankind in fellowship, to the end that all souls shall grow in harmony with the Divine; thus do we covenant with each other and with God.

Unitarianism can be seen as the epitome of historical Christian liberalism. Both morality and truth appear relative in Unitarianism. Practically speaking, therefore, this form of liberal Christianity tolerates various alternative lifestyles, as found in our contemporary culture, such as homosexuality. Views such as radical feminism and practices such as abortion on demand are condoned. In addition, Unitarianism recognises all religious beliefs as equally legitimate.

Unitarianism is practised in Ireland through the denomination known as 'The Non-Subscribing Presbyterian Church of Ireland'. In Ireland alone there are several denominations of the Presbyterian strain. There is the Presbyterian Church of Ireland, the Evangelical Presbyterian Church, the Reformed Presbyterian Church, and the Free Presbyterian Church. Many have therefore wrongly assumed that the 'The Non-subscribing Presbyterian Church of Ireland' is another of the same.

Though they may take the name 'Presbyterian' the Non-Subscribing Presbyterian Church are far from being orthodox Christians as their liberal stance on moral and theological tolerance demonstrates.

The Roots Of Unitarianism

The Church in Europe in the first half of the 18th century developed an increasing reluctance to accept the doctrine of the Trinity: that God is one in essence, but revealed in three persons. This began to express itself in the religious thought and writing of some Presbyterians. As yet this viewpoint was not yet called 'Unitarianism', but that eventually would become its name.

This thinking regarding the Godhead was not new. It is found in embryo, back in the early Church in the teaching of Arius who taught, along with others like Origen, that the Lord Jesus Christ was not God, did not claim to be God and was not one substance with the Father.

The Nicene Creed was developed at the Council of Nicea in AD325 when the Church categorically rejected Arius' teaching on the non-deity of the Christ.

This idea that the Lord Jesus Christ was not God, did not gain any real impetus until the time of the Reformation when a Spaniard named Servitus began expounding his Arian views. Servitus lived from 1511-1553 and is considered by many as the founder of Unitarianism in continental Europe. He denied that Jesus Christ was the Son of God, and in 1531 Servitus published a strong polemic against the doctrine of the Trinity entitled: *On the Errors of the Trinity in Seven Books*. In it Servitus writes,

> Your Trinity is the product of subtlety and madness, the Gospel knows nothing of it.

During the time of the Reformation such statements brought swift condemnation from the religious authorities of the day. Servitus, had to change his name and flee in exile to France. For several decades he escaped inquisition, only to be later executed in 1553.

Faustus Socinus who lived from 1539-1604 contributed also to this early Unitarian doctrine. He believed that the Scriptures should be interpreted rationally and it was his belief that the Father could only be God and not Jesus Christ as well.

The History Of Unitarianism In Ireland

The term 'Unitarianism' did not come into common usage until 1770. Then, a former Anglican minister named Theophilus Lindsey began to teach that there was no Trinity and, that the divinity of Christ was some doctrine that had developed in the Church in later years.

Once more, Arian doctrine was openly espoused in the Church. Consequently Theophilis Lindsey founded a Unitarian chapel in central London. One of the earliest members of that Church was the scientist Joseph Priestley; the discoverer of oxygen.

Many Irish Presbyterians, like most orthodox Christians, were astounded and alarmed at these heretical views concerning the person of Christ and the authority of the Holy Scriptures. They were even more alarmed when they discovered that these heretical doctrines were being taught in some of the oldest Presbyterian Churches in County Antrim and County Down.

Many Unitarian Churches still exist there today.

Irish Presbyterian leaders met together to deliberate over this matter of false doctrine. In response, they decided that a new subscription to the Westminster Confession of Faith was necessary.

The Westminster Confession of Faith is the document from which came *the Longer and Shorter Catechism with scriptural proofs*. It was authored at Westminster Abbey in 1643. Here the English Parliament decided that 'learned and godly judicious divines' should meet together in Westminster Abbey to provide advice on issues of worship, doctrine, government and Church discipline.

Despite it being authored by many Church of England divines, the Church of England did not adopt the Westminster Confession of Faith. Many dissenting Protestant congregations, however, did adopt it; as the confession of doctrine and belief.

The liberal ministers espousing Arian views were appalled when these Presbyterian leaders in Ulster felt there was a need for re-subscription to the Westminster Confession of Faith. In 1726 John Abernethy, who was also the leader of the so-called 'New Light Movement', along with sixteen other ministers refused to sign the Westminster Confession of Faith. Subsequently they, and their congregations, were expelled from the Presbytery of the Synod of Ulster.

It is worthy of note at this point that the claim to possess 'new light' is often a classic characteristic of a false cult. Unitarians claim to own **new revelation** enhancing our understanding of God, particularly concerning the person and work of Christ. They claim that Jesus Christ was a mere man and that everyone ultimately will be saved.

Irish Unitarianism was strengthened also by the influence of an American Unitarian, William Ellery Channing. He was a preacher and writer in Boston, Massachusetts and was one of the greatest influences on Unitarianism in the USA, where it still thrives more than anywhere else in the world. William Ellery Channing impacted greatly Harvard Divinity School and other Protestant seminaries in the USA with his liberal thinking.

The battle against Unitarianism in the Presbyterian Church of Ireland may have been a lost cause had it not been for the valiant voice for truth, in the person of the conservative Ulster Presbyterian leader, the Rev. Henry Cooke. During the 1820s and 1830s Henry Cook took it upon himself to fight Arianism in Irish Presbyterianism. Henry Cooke said that he wanted to rescue Irish Presbyterianism from,

> The bog of indifference and moral laxity.

Henry Cooke's energies were not limited just to the North of Ireland; he fought this heresy also in the whole of Ireland.

His labour against Arianism in the South was so successful that there are only two Unitarian Churches in the South of Ireland today: one in Dublin at St Stephen's

Green, and the other in Cork. In recent times however, the congregation in Dublin claims to have experienced something of a revival. Unitarian Sunday morning congregations have risen from 15-20 to 60-80 in number, and Unitarians testify that many young Roman Catholics and people from non-religious backgrounds

> ...are searching for a new form of spirituality in Ireland, the Ireland of the Celtic Tiger.

There are currently 32 Non-Subscribing Presbyterian Unitarian Churches in Northern Ireland. In both the North and South of Ireland there are approximately 4000 members and 20 clergy, both male and female.

Unitarianism Worldwide

Though individual Unitarian Churches are autonomous they are linked together by a General Assembly; a united group called 'The Unitarian Universalist Association'. In 1995 there were approximately 195 of these congregations in Britain. In the Commonwealth countries, Australia, New Zealand, and South Africa, there were an estimated 15,000 Unitarians. As many as half a million Unitarians are thought to be in America today. Unitarianism can also be found in Romania, Hungary, the Czech Republic, Germany, and even in India. It is reported that the movement is growing at a 4% rate annually. The Church in Britain is a member of the 'British Council of Churches', and Unitarianism worldwide is a member of the 'World Congress of Faiths'.

The Beliefs Of Unitarianism Set Against the Claims of the Bible

Though the Unitarian Church do not have a set group of doctrines and taught dogma; they do have beliefs and general tenets of faith to which Unitarianism worldwide adheres.

An official publication of the General Assembly of Unitarianism defines itself as,

> . . . a liberal religious movement arising out of Christianity, expressing itself largely but not wholly in Christian forms and terms, and in the spirit of the man Jesus. It is liberal in rejecting the idea of a unique and final revelation of truth and in trusting men to discover and believe as much as they can for themselves; it is a religious movement inasmuch as it has Churches and a ministry and ways of worship. . . . It is glad to remain Christian where it can but glad also to discover other truth and beauty and goodness in other faiths and other lives. Unitarians know of no better man in religion than Jesus of Nazareth but they believe that there have been others like him in the past, and that there will be others like him again.

Today many Unitarians no longer claim to be Christians in the traditional and biblical sense. They are content, as stated above, to express themselves 'largely, but not wholly in Christian forms and terms and, in the spirit of the man Jesus.' Unitarians choose not to restrict themselves to the definitions and doctrines of Christianity.

God

In their very name, Unitarianians confess that they believe in one God who exists in one person and whose personality is expressed in the Father. Today, however, Unitarianism is so liberal that some have even found it helpful not to use the word 'God' at all. Unitarians are not sure who or what God is, so they reason it is better to leave God out of religion altogether!

In previous chapters of this book Genesis 1:26 has been cited as evidence of the Trinity at the beginning of creation.

Additionally Genesis 11 tells of the account of what took place at the building of the Tower of Babel where man, like Unitarians today, was attempting to get to God on his own terms. In verses 7-8 God uses the plural of Himself as in Genesis 1:26 and says,

> Go to, let **us** go down, and there confound their language, that they may not understand one another's speech. So the LORD scattered them abroad....

God said, *'let us'*, in the plural.

In the New Testament we have, recorded for us in Matthew 28, what has been commonly called the baptismal formula of the Christian Church. The Lord's instruction, clearly taught in verse 19, says,

> Go ye therefore, and teach all nations, baptizing them in the name of the Father, and of the Son, and of the Holy Ghost.

Note that the Lord commands to baptise in the 'name': singular, one name, yet that name is expressed in three persons: Father, Son and Holy Ghost. That is the essence of the Trinity: one substance, all God, but expressed in three persons.

Many other Scriptures teach the doctrine of the Trinity. One easy way to remember three of these crucial passages is by recalling that they are to be found in the first chapters of the books of John, Hebrews and Revelation. John 1:1 says,

> In the beginning was the Word, and the Word was with God, and the Word was God.

The Word speaks of Christ with God and as God. In verse 14 John, describing how God was incarnate in Christ, says,

> ....the Word became flesh and dwelt among us....

In Hebrews 1, God says,

> . . . unto the Son, Thy throne, O God, is for ever and ever. . . .

In Revelation 1, God is described as Alpha and Omega, and further down that chapter and later on in that book, the Lord Jesus is also described as the Alpha and the Omega: the First and the Last. There cannot be two Firsts and two Lasts.

These Scriptures ascribe divinity to the Lord Jesus Christ.

Thomas, the disciple, recognised this truth as he fell at the feet of the risen Christ, confessing,

> My Lord, and my God!

Paul in 1 Timothy 3:16 says,

> . . . great is the mystery of godliness: God manifest in the flesh. . . .

Colossians 2:9 teaches that the fullness of the Godhead bodily dwells in Christ.

Recorded in Matthew 4 is Christ's baptism where, a dove-like form comes down from the sky, and the voice of the Father is heard from heaven saying,

> This is My Beloved Son, in whom I am well pleased.

Three evident persons are present and yet only one God.

Moses taught the Israelites to say in Deuteronomy 6:4

> Hear, O Israel: The LORD our God is one LORD.

Many other Scriptures teach that this one God is revealed in three persons.

The Bible

Unitarians teach that man is to be guided by his individual conscience rather than the revelation of God. Though this is not **new revelation,** as is normally found in many cults, Unitarians advocate the search for guidance from some source other than God's revelation: the Scriptures. Unitarians advocate the human conscience as superior to the Scriptures in the matter of guidance.

This is a dangerous deception for, as Jeremiah records in Jeremiah 17 9, the heart is deceitful above all things and desperately wicked.

Indeed, the whole Bible teaches how the fall of man has depraved the human nature. Yet, Unitarians teach that man is to be guided by, and rely on, his own human reason.

Whilst Unitarians admit that the Bible is a helpful guide, and that it does contain religious insights and wisdom, they reject the fundamental truth that the Bible is the divinely inspired Word of God. To Unitarians, the Bible is only one of many divine books; it is not unique as a holy book. The writings of Buddha, Mohammed, Confucius, and many others are purported to be equally holy.

Unitarians espouse an idea of universal inspiration of life when they assert that God is continuing to reveal His truth today to good people of all religions. God, according to the Unitarian, speaks in some kind of abstract way: in the order and beauty of nature, in moral standards, neighbourliness and the charitableness of mankind.

The problem with such teaching is that it contradicts with what Scripture teaches.

Isaiah 8:20 says,

> To the law and to the testimony: if they speak not according to this word, it is because there is no light in them.

God's Word is clear: there is no light in what is contrary to the Holy Scriptures.

In John 17 the Lord Jesus prays for the Church and, in verse 17, He says,

> Sanctify them through thy truth. . . .

What is God's truth? The answer is given in the same verse. Jesus says,

> . . . thy word is truth.

God's Word is the only truth.

We read in 1 Corinthians 1:20-21 that the wisdom of this world: the wisdom of reason, rationale and intellectual aptitude, is not the means whereby God reveals His truth to men. God reveals His truth through the foolishness of the message preached: that is, Christ and Him crucified, foolishness to the Greek and a stumbling block to the Jew: 1 Corinthians 1:23.

Many to whom Paul preached could not understand the message of the gospel because their religious wisdom and intellectual rationale prevented them.

First Corinthians 2:14, also confounds what Unitarianism teaches and says,

> . . . the natural man receiveth not the things of the Spirit of God: for they are foolishness unto him: neither can he know them, because they are spiritually discerned.

The Person Of Christ

In previous chapters it has been observed that one chief characteristic of a cult is its view of Christ. Cults characteristically have denigrating view of our blessed Lord.

Unitarianism teaches that the Lord Jesus Christ was only a man and as such should not be worshipped. To the Unitarians, the Lord Jesus Christ was only a good example of showing what man can be: Christ is not unique but rather, only one of the many great leaders in the world.

John Mendelsohn, a respected Unitarian minister, has stated,

> I am willing to call myself Christian only if in the next breath I am permitted to say that in varying degrees I am also a Jew, a Hindu, a Muslim, a Buddhist, a Stoic, an admirer of Zoroaster, Confucius and Socrates.[1]

Dr Carl M Chorowsky, another Unitarian minister, says,

> Unitarians do not believe that Jesus is the Messiah either of Jewish hope or Christian fantasy.[2]

What does God's Word say about the Lord Jesus?

In John 14:6 Jesus claimed,

> I am the way, the truth, and the life: no man cometh unto the Father, but by me.

Matthew 16:16 recorded the foundational truth upon which the Church was built.

When Jesus asked as to whom Peter believed Him to be, Peter replied,

> Thou art the Christ, the Son of the living God.

In verse 17 Jesus answered and said to Peter,

> Blessed art thou, Simon Barjona: for flesh and blood hath not revealed it unto thee, but my Father which is in heaven.

Christ commended Peter for his declaration that He was indeed God's Son.

Clearly the Lord pointed out that divine revelation, and not Peter's own human reason or intellectual ingenuity, brought Peter to this conclusion about Jesus.

The Jews understood that, when Jesus was claiming to be God's Son, He was claiming to be in essence God! John 5:18 states

> Therefore the Jews sought the more to kill him, because he not only had broken the sabbath, but said also that God was his Father, making himself equal with God.

In John 10:30 we see this claim again. Christ said,

> I and my Father are one.

C.S. Lewis was astute when he deduced,

> A man who was merely a man and said the sort of things Jesus said would not be a great moral teacher. He would either be a lunatic – on the level with the man who says he is a poached egg – or else he would be the Devil of Hell. You must make your choice. Either this man was, and is, the Son of God: or else a madman or something worse.[3]

The Work Of Christ

Unitarianism does not believe that man needs a mediator or Saviour because it believes that man is intrinsically good. Unitarians do not believe, as the Bible teaches, that man is born in sin but rather, that children are born in innocence. For the Unitarian an atoning sacrifice or substitutionary Saviour is not necessary. This is why many Unitarian congregations do not observe the Lord's Supper and for those who do, it is a mere remembrance of the life and teachings of the Christ.

Yet Romans 3:20 tells us man does need a Saviour and Redeemer. Paul says,

> . . .for by the works of the law shall no man be justified.

Also Ephesians 2:13 writes,

> But now in Christ Jesus ye who sometimes were far off are made nigh by the blood of Jesus.

In Christ's life He fulfilled all the law and He had to do such if He was going to be our Saviour, but the atoning work was accomplished at Calvary, where He shed His precious blood for us. Ephesians 2:18 writes,

> For through him we both have access by one Spirit unto the Father.

First Peter 3:18 tells how He, as the just, justified the unjust, and brought us to God by His death. For the Unitarian there is no value in the precious blood. Yet the Scriptures teach clearly that without the shedding of blood there is no forgiveness of sins.

The Resurrection

Unitarians interpret the resurrection of Christ as the resurrection of His deeds, thoughts and teachings, living in the lives of other people. When Unitarians think about Him, talk about Him, and teach about Him they believe that Christ's resurrection is manifest.

Unitarians teach that there is no physical or spiritual resurrection of the body of the Lord, or indeed, of our own. Yet in Luke 24:5-6 the angel is recorded as saying,

> Why seek ye the living amongst the dead? He is not here, He is risen as He said!

First Corinthians 15:4 continues

> ...He was buried, and that he rose again the third day according to
> the Scriptures.....

In verse 17 Paul tells us of the consequences if Christ was not physically resurrected

> ...if Christ be not raised, your faith is vain; ye are yet in your sins.

In verses 18-20 Paul says,

> Then they also which are fallen asleep in Christ are perished. If in this
> life only we have hope in Christ, we are of all men most miserable. But
> now is Christ risen from the dead, and become the first fruits of them
> that slept.

The Holy Spirit

Unitarian belief in the Holy Spirit is varied.

One view held by some Unitarians is that the Holy Spirit is the influence of Christ's teaching in the world today. Another belief is that the Holy Spirit is the way God reveals Himself in our lives thus viewing the Holy Spirit as revealing Himself in a strange abstract way; through the joys and sorrows of life.

Some Unitarians understand the Holy Spirit to be the power beyond us: that source of divinity that is moving behind everything in the universe.

Whatever Unitarians believe the Holy Spirit is; they are clear in their teaching that He is not a person.

However in John 16:7, Jesus is recorded as referring to the Holy Spirit as a personality saying,

I tell you the truth; It is expedient for you that I go away: for if I go not away, the Comforter will not come unto you; but if I depart, I will send **him** unto you.

Acts 5:3-4, referred to in a previous chapter of this book, records that Ananias and Sapphira lied to the Holy Ghost, yet it also says that they lied to God because the Holy Ghost is God, and He is a person to whom you can lie.

Salvation

It must be asked of Unitarians as to why they believe the Spirit's ministry is needed at all, if, as they claim, man does not need salvation. If man is essentially good, he does not need to be regenerated, changed, made a new creature, and sanctified, which are all aspects of the Holy Spirit's ministry.

Unitarians are called 'Unitarian Universalists' because they believe that everyone ultimately will be saved. This is the logical conclusion if one believes, as Unitarians do, that all faiths are equally valid systems to bring us to God.

The Bible, however, teaches that there is only one way to God, and that is through the Lord Jesus Christ. He is much more than simply one of the great Saviours of mankind. He is the one and only Saviour.

Scripture clearly teaches that man does need salvation because he is a sinner. Psalm 51:5 says,

> Behold, I was shapen in iniquity; and in sin did my mother conceive me.

Christ says of all men in Matthew 15:19,

> Out of the heart of mankind proceeds evil thoughts, murders, adulteries, fornications, thefts, false witnesses, blasphemies.

The same truth is taught in Romans 3:10, 23,

> As it is written, There is none righteous, no, not one...For all have
> sinned, and come short of the glory of God.

Scripture also declares that Jesus Christ is the only Saviour for sinners. In John 10:9
Jesus is recorded as saying

> I am the door: by me if any man enter in, he shall be saved, and shall
> go in and out, and find pasture.

In Acts 4:12 Peter preached,

> Neither is there salvation in any other: for there is none other name
> under heaven given among men, whereby we must be saved.

Paul's reply to the desperate Philippian jailer who had asked what he should do to be
saved is recorded in Acts 16:31

> Believe on the Lord Jesus Christ and thou shalt be saved....

Unitarian minister John Mendelsohn comments on Paul's answer to the Philippian
jailer remarking,

> Here was the trap of authoritarianism on which orthodox Christianity
> would run from Paul's day to our own. It did not occur to Paul that the
> jailer might have some thoughts and insights of his own worth
> probing and nurturing. Paul saw no reason whatsoever for
> encouraging the man to think, to use his own mind, to exercise his
> reason, to ponder the experiences of heart and conscience for
> satisfying religious answers. Paul said none of the words that might
> have moved Christianity in the direction of freedom and personal
> responsibility. Instead he uttered a dogma. He said, in effect, this is

> not something to discuss, to weigh, to test by the experience. No, this
> is something you simply accept.[4]

John Mendelsohn was perceptive when he observed that the Gospel Paul spoke of was not to be doubted: it was not to be discussed, human wisdom was not to augment it. It was simply to be accepted! The sad reality of the Unitarian position becomes clear when John Mendelsohn concludes,

> Unitarian Universalists will have none of it![5]

The Future

Some Unitarians believe in personal immortality, some believe we live on in the deeds and thoughts that we have left behind in the memories of others and some, simply do not know. It would appear that Unitarians do not believe in heaven or hell. Yet Hebrews 9:27 teaches,

> . . . it is appointed unto man once to die and after this the judgment.

There are many other Scriptures that teach these truths regarding the future.

In John 5:28-29 Jesus tells of the future resurrection of the just unto life, and of the resurrection of the damned unto eternal perdition. Job, in Job 19:26, rejoiced in the hope that one day, his flesh that had been eaten by worms would stand again in a new form and he would see his Redeemer.

Prayer

Unitarians believe that prayer is something that only affects us; changing us so that we become better people, and then our examples may even affect a change in others. This belief contradicts what the Bible teaches when it declares that prayer not only changes people but also things.

Unitarians do not like to pray in Jesus' name because they say they do not need a mediator. Yet Scripture says that is exactly how we ought to pray. The Lord Jesus, in John 16:23, said whatever you ask in His name according to the Father's will, He would give. First John 5:14 writes that our confidence that the Father hears us, is in the fact that we pray through the Lord Jesus.

Though many Unitarians are extremely charitable, full of kindness, and fight for the freedom and rights of others, they belong to a non-Christian cult with liberal humanistic values.

The only way 'true light' can be obtained is through the Holy Scriptures, which reveals the 'Light of the World': the Lord Jesus Christ. In the written Word, God has made Himself known. Through Christ's death man's sin can be forgiven and through His resurrection eternal life and hope can be given to all. To know salvation and intimacy with God we must repent and come to Him, by faith through His Son Jesus Christ, who is only revealed in the Holy Scriptures.

Scripture makes plain that the Gospel of Jesus Christ is not based on human wisdom or any other mutable foundation but on the immutable revelation of God declared in His Word.

> For the preaching of the cross is to them that perish foolishness; but unto us which are saved it is the power of God. For it is written, I will destroy the wisdom of the wise, and will bring to nothing the understanding of the prudent. Where is the wise? where is the scribe? where is the disputer of this world? hath not God made foolish the wisdom of this world? For after that in the wisdom of God the world by wisdom knew not God, it pleased God by the foolishness of preaching to save them that believe. For the Jews require a sign, and the Greeks seek after wisdom: But we preach Christ crucified, unto the Jews a stumblingblock, and unto the Greeks foolishness; But unto them which are called, both Jews and Greeks, Christ the power of God, and the wisdom of God. Because the foolishness of God is wiser than

men; and the weakness of God is stronger than men. (1 Corinthians 1:18-25)

Footnotes

1   John Mendelsohn, Why I am a Unitarian, p.68.
2   Carl M. Chorowsky, What is a Unitarian? An article in Look magazine 8th March 1955.
3   C.S. Lewis, Mere Christianity, p.26
4   John Mendelsohn, Why I am a Unitarian, pp.29-30.
5   Ibid.

Chapter 5
Spiritism

Spiritism uses the occult practices of:

Séance - a group communication with the dead.

Telepathy - communicating thoughts, ideas and pictures from one mind to another without verbal communication.

Astrology – guidance from the study of the stars.

Clairvoyance - perceiving the future.

Audiovoyance – the ability to hear spirits speaking.

Ouija Board - a style of alphabet or circle of symbols through which the spirit world communicates.

Pendulum - used to divine the future, to find lost objects or even to discern the sex of an unborn child.

Fortune-telling – predicting future events in another's life using various means.

Automatic Writing – handwriting directed by spirits to communicate messages.

Table Rapping – spirits communicating through 'rapping' and 'tapping' noises.

Walter Martin, author of *The Kingdom of the Cults*, calls Spiritism 'The Cult of Antiquity.' He maintains that Spiritism is the oldest religious cult in existence and also one of the deadliest.

Spiritism In Modern Times

Spiritism came to the fore in Ancient Babylon and ever since has been found in every culture. The book of Exodus records that Pharaoh's magicians in Ancient Egypt displayed occultic powers in their replica miracles. It is this same ancient force that operates through Spiritism today.

The revival of Spiritism as an 'organised religion' began in 1848, in Hydesville, New York, in the home of the Fox family. On moving to a new house in Hydesville, two of the three Fox daughters, Margaret and Kate, claimed to hear 'rappings' around the home. The girls believed that those 'rappings' were supernatural phenomena. Later when the Fox family moved from Hydesville to Rochester, Margaret and Kate testified to the same experience in their new house. The girls believed that these noises were communications from the unseen spirit world and they sought to devise a method of communication to converse with the dead.

News of this phenomenon in Hydesville travelled rapidly: séances were subsequently being held across the USA and much of Europe.

In contrast to many founders of other religious cults, the Fox sisters did not die rich but in abject poverty, having experienced great suffering and pain in their lives. One biographer says,

> In time they became victims of the drink menace, nothing could satisfy their craving for alcohol, and they lost all sense of moral responsibility.

Late in Margaret Fox's life, at an anti-spiritualist gathering in 1888 and in the presence of her sister Kate she is said to have testified,

> I am here tonight as one of the founders of Spiritualism to denounce it as absolute falsehood, the most wicked blasphemy the world has ever known.

Such a statement from one of the founders of Spiritism should cause us to doubt the claims of this movement.

Despite this, there are an increasing number of people who believe in the ability to contact the dead and as a result they are turning to Spiritism for meaning, comfort and guidance.

Is it all pure fantasy?

The Daily Mail newspaper, Thursday September 23rd 2004, carried the headline on an article: 'Is There Anybody There?' Beneath the headline was a picture of a séance across which in bold capital letters was written the answer - 'NO!' The subtitle that summed up the article's content read: 'Messages From The Spirit World Are Based on Guesswork Says Professor.'

Professor Richard Wiseman of the University of Herefordshire had completed experimental research and concluded that, in modern Spiritism, people were being deceived. Many other competent professionals have exposed Spiritism as being fraudulent.

Walter Martin, in *The Kingdom of the Cults*, cites some classic exposés of modern Spiritism. These include an exposé by Houdini and Dunninger in 1967 called 'Magic and Mystery'; another performed in 1976 by a former psychic M. Lamar Keene called 'The Psychic Mafia'; and a joint investigation in 1980 called 'Fakers'[1] was performed by two Christians; a Christian physician called Paul Meier and a 'Christian magician' called Danny Korem. All three of these exposés conclude that a great deal of what passes as Spiritism is fraudulent.

Although this is undoubtedly the case it must be asserted that not all Spiritistic phenomena are fraudulent: there is a real spiritual realm. There is the danger that when the fraudulent elements of Spiritism are rejected so too is the belief that a supernatural realm exists. This perhaps is one of the Devil's greatest coups.

The Kingdom of the Cults also gives some independently verified instances of proven Spiritistic phenomena.[2] Many universities worldwide have established departments for study of ESP (Extra-Sensory Perception).

Christians believe in a spiritual realm because the Bible testifies to it. The Christian wrestles not against flesh and blood, but struggles with principalities and powers, and the rulers of the darkness of this world - spiritual wickedness in high places: Ephesians 6:12.

Spiritism In General

Several famous names in history were Spiritists. Arthur Conan Doyle; the author of Sherlock Holmes was a Spiritist, together with Harriet Beecher Stowe author of 'Uncle

Tom's Cabin'. So too were William E. Gladstone, once Prime Minister of Great Britain and Ireland, and Daniel Webster the U.S. statesman.

It is amazing to discover how many individuals believe Christianity to be compatible with dabbling in Spiritism.

The Spiritist movement does appear to have similarities to the Christian Church. The Spiritualist Church and its ministers often advertise its activities on Church announcement pages of local newspapers. Some 'congregations' meet in homes, some in community halls and some in buildings that look just like any Church building. The Spiritualist Church even has their own hymnbook and many of their hymns are set to well known Christian tunes and some even resemble Christian hymns in their content.

Below is an example of one Spiritualist hymn obviously similar to a well known Christian hymn. It is, upon close examination that the subtle satanic differences are observed:

Just as I am, without one plea,
But that, O God, Thou madest me
And that my life is found in Thee
O God of Love, I come, I come.

Just as I am, nor poor, nor blind
Nor bound by chains in soul or mind;
For all of Thee within I find
O God of Love, I come, I come.

Just as I am, Thou wilt receive
Tho' dogmas I may ne'er believe
Nor heights of holiness achieve
O God of Love, I come, I come.

Verse one of this hymn shows that the Spiritualist believes in a transcendent 'god of love' who would never damn any of his creation but, who will save everyone in the end. Verse two shows that the Spiritualist does not believe that man is poor and blind as a sinner but, instead has self-worth and has spiritual sight to see into the unseen spirit world. Verse three shows that the Spiritualist does not value doctrinal truth or holiness of life but rather acceptance with the Spiritualists' god is based on the oneness of the whole universe.

Spiritualist Church buildings have pulpits, where their ministers pray and supposedly communicate healing messages from the spirit world.

These and any other similarities between the Spiritualist Church and the Christian Church are however, only cosmetic. Regardless of how Spiritism dresses itself in Christian clothes Spiritualism/Spiritism remains occultic in its origin and practice.

Occult simply means something hidden; secret knowledge for the select few. It is the opposite of overt. Spiritism is an occult movement that believes it has the secret to eternal realities that are only discovered by tapping into the hidden spirit world. Spiritism therefore exhibits the classic **theological** characteristics of a cult claiming **new revelation** and **exclusivity**.

The Occult And The Bible

In Ephesians 2:1-2 the Apostle Paul reminds the believers in Ephesus of their spiritual condition prior to conversion,

> ...you...were dead in trespasses and sins; Wherein in time past ye
> walked according to the course of this world according to the prince
> of the power of the air.

The 'prince of the power of the air' is Satan. Satan was Lucifer, probably the greatest angel ever created. Ezekiel 28 and Isaiah 14 record that Lucifer's pride caused him to attempt a revolt against God's rule. Consequently God cast Lucifer from glory down to the outer parts of this earth, and to this day, Satan still inhabits the air. He inhabits the earth as well but the air is his chief domain.

Satan is the god of this world, not Jehovah. Jehovah is the God of the universe in the sovereign sense but the god who is served by man on earth, whether consciously or unconsciously, is Satan. Scripture tells us that this world lies in the lap of the Wicked One: 1 John 5:19.

In Ephesians 2:2 Paul elaborates by describing Satan as,

> . . . the spirit that now worketh in the children of disobedience. . . .

The Amplified Version renders *spirit*,

> . . . the demon spirit that still constantly works in the sons of disobedience . . . ,

suggesting that those who are not converted to Jesus Christ are controlled by the demonic powers resident in this world system. This does not mean that everyone who is not a Christian is demon possessed but it does mean that they are under the influence of the Evil One.

Ephesians 6 explains that the Lord Jesus through the cross has defeated sin, death, hell and the Devil. This means that although the Devil has not finally been put down yet in an operative sense, his doom is sealed and therefore in Christ, the Christian has the victory!

In Ephesians 6:10 Paul writes,

> Finally, my brethren, be strong in the Lord, and the power of His might.

No one has the power and authority to face Satan alone. Jude records that even the great archangel Michael dared not bring a railing accusation against the Devil. Jude 9 records, Michael simply said,

> The Lord rebuke thee.

Michael had no personal power over Satan in this face-to-face confrontation. The only power that Michael had was in the strength of the Lord, and this, is the only power that the Christian has. Therefore Paul exhorts us in Ephesians 6:11-13 to,

> Put on the whole armour of God, that ye may be able to stand against the wiles of the Devil. For we wrestle not against flesh and blood, but against principalities, against powers, against the rulers of the darkness of this world, against spiritual wickedness in high places. Wherefore take unto you the whole armour of God, that ye may be able to withstand in the evil day, and having done all, to stand.

It is not the aim of this chapter to glorify the works of Satan or to satisfy an unhealthy preoccupation with the occult. However it is important to be aware of the spiritual dangers in addressing this subject and the Christian should ensure that, by faith, they are clothed with armour of God for their protection.

'Spiritism', or 'Spiritualism', is essentially the pursuit of seeking to communicate with the dead spirits in the spirit world. Spiritism is fuelled by a desire to obtain hidden information that God has not declared in the Bible: His revelation to humanity.

Deuteronomy 29:29 reads,

> The secret things belong unto the LORD our God: but those things which are revealed belong unto us and to our children for ever, that we may do all the words of this law.

To explore the dark secrets of occultism that God has not revealed for our benefit is to transgress His law to our eternal detriment.

Spiritist Practices In Scripture

Occult practices are condemned in Holy Scripture as an abomination in God's sight. An abomination is something that God detests.

When the children of Israel were about to enter the Promised Land they were commanded by God to drive out all the inhabiting nations along with their cultures and religions. This was to prevent Israel from being contaminated with idolatry and Devil worship. God said to the prophet Moses in Deuteronomy 18:9

> When thou art come into the land which the LORD thy God giveth thee, thou shalt not learn to do after the abominations of those nations.

In Deuteronomy 18:10-12 there are nine abominations mentioned:

> There shall not be found among you any one that maketh his son or his daughter to pass through the fire, or that useth divination, or an observer of times, or an enchanter, or a witch, or a charmer, or a consulter with familiar spirits, or a wizard, or a necromancer. For all that do these things are an abomination unto the LORD: and because of these abominations the LORD thy God doth drive them out from before thee.

1. Passing Through the Fire

Deuteronomy 18:10,

> There shall not be found among you any one that maketh his son or his daughter to pass through the fire.... .

Several ancient false gods, including 'Molech', the god of the Ammonites, were worshipped by human sacrifice: Lev 18:21; 20:2-5; 1 Kg 11:7; 2 Kg 23:16; Jer 32:35. The worshipper would take their son or daughter and feed them to the flames as a pecuniary sacrifice to their angry deity. Human sacrifice is still practised in some parts of the world today.

In a spiritual sense this abomination is widely practised in false religions and cults. Offering to the Lord a sacrifice that He has not prescribed is what the Bible calls 'strange fire'. Everyone who does not worship God through the *new and living way* of the Gospel of the Lord Jesus Christ is approaching Him in a way He has not approved.

2. Divination

Deuteronomy 18:10b,

> ... or that useth divination ....

A simple definition of 'divination' is the practice or the art, as some see it, of discovering hidden knowledge. This may manifest itself in the ability to foretell the future.

This is practised today through phenomena such as psychics; fortune-tellers; the ouija board; reading the crystal ball or various crystals and tarot card reading. Cutting a deck of ordinary playing cards in a particular way is another form of foretelling. Many do not realise that ordinary playing cards have an occult symbolism of their own, also used to divine the future.

Some diviners believe they can divine the future through reading tealeaves. Other diviners believe that, through use of the pendulum, lost items can be retrieved. Some individuals, especially in rural Ireland, believe they have the gift of water divination. Many who have experienced this testify that, at times, the force with which the branch turns could almost break an arm! Examples could be given of farmers who have had difficultly getting a water source on their farm and in turn have sought the help of a 'water diviner' to locate some water.

Joseph Smith the founder of Mormonism, was a crystal gazer: he sought to divine hidden knowledge through the reading of crystals. Indeed, he claimed to have interpreted the *Book of Mormon* by this means. It is disturbing to note that several founders of religions and cults were in some way engaged in seeking out this secret hidden knowledge of the occult.

3. Observer of Times

Deuteronomy 18:10c,

> ...or an observer of times....

An observer of times is someone who engages in astrology. Signs of the horoscope and the relation of the planets are used to divine knowledge of the future.

Superstition is involved in this abomination of observing the times. Many believe superstition to be a harmless occupation. The fact of the matter is, superstitions can bring people into mental and even spiritual bondage.

There are those for whom superstition shrouds their every movement. Some folk, because it is Friday the 13th, will not take a flight or travel even in a car. Others, when they do travel will not carry red and white pyjamas because red and white, they think, symbolises death.

To believe in luck or fatalism is to put your faith in something other than God. It is the declaration that you are looking to another source other than the Sovereign God of the universe to determine the outworking of your affairs. Whatever the forces, rules, and principles of your superstition, they are understood to be apart from God and thus you actively take your life out of His hands and put them into the hands of these 'times'.

The reason God does not want man to look into the future is because He desires to be trusted with our lives. God, and not any earthly diviner of the future, has exclusive knowledge and therefore, He should be trusted exclusively.

4. Enchanter

Deuteronomy 18:10d,

> . . . or an enchanter. . . .

An enchanter is a magician or a sorcerer who casts spells and bewitches people. The clear teaching of God's Word is that the child of God must avoid anything that is associated with magic.

The problem today, especially among the young, is the popularisation of magic.

Children are spoon-fed a diet of magic, through novels, magazines, rock-songs and even computer games, which can desensitise the young to the occult though a seemingly innocent veneer.

Consider, as someone has called it, the 'Hollywoodisation of the occult' through films like 'The Exorcist', 'Carrie', 'Devil's Advocate', 'The Craft', 'The Sixth Sense', 'The Blair Witch Project', 'Halloween', 'Friday The Thirteenth', and 'Nightmare on Elm Street'. In more recent years such horror has moved from the cinema screen to the TV screen at home through series such as 'Buffy The Vampire Slayer', 'Angel', 'Dark Angel', 'Charmed', 'The X-Files', 'The Dead Zone', 'Millennium' and 'The Witchblade'. Some people may regard this type of entertainment as harmless but young and impressionable minds are being influenced for evil and not for God.

Under the category of enchanting comes another two modern practices: 'yoga' and 'reiki'. Yoga encourages the participant to empty their mind of everything but, to open their mind to anything!

Reiki is arguably more sinister. It originates from Japan and does not simply encourage the emptying of the mind but it encourages also, the contacting of a great force from outside of us and, allowing it to enter us.

'Meditation' is another enchantment. This often comes in the form of repeating mantras in vain repetition, as the Saviour said the heathen do: Mt 6:7.

'Hypnotism' is another enchantment, as is the use of subliminal tapes, which encourage a person to become unconscious to themselves, and yet open their mind to other external phenomena.

A few years ago Paul McKenna, the hypnotist entertainer, was involved in a TV programme that explored some of the phenomena that are witnessed in certain branches of the Charismatic Movement today. He was able to reproduce the same effect through hypnosis. Paul McKenna's concluding remarks cautioned people about opening their minds to external phenomena.

The 'Martial Arts', though widely accepted, involve some techniques relating to the mind and heart that are equivalent to enchantment.

'New-age medicine' is also a form of enchantment. The origins and principles behind some practices of aromatherapy, homeopathy and Feng Shui make them enchantments.

5. Witch

Deuteronomy 18:10e,

> . . .or a witch. . . .

A witch is a person who practices magic; specifically dealing with demonic spirits.

Black and white magic are equally demonic. Yet today, many witches portray 'white witchcraft' or 'wicca' as benevolent. Witchcraft is now repackaged as the religion of Paganism. Whatever it is named, it is still the practice of witchcraft and God condemns it as an abomination.

6. Charmer

Deuteronomy 18:11a,

> Or a charmer....

A charmer is a person who casts a spell on another in order to change circumstances. They may chant magical mantras, verses or formulae in order achieve a desired end.

There are charms for many physical ailments from warts to whooping cough. There are even charms that use the name of the Trinity: Father, Son and Holy Spirit and so some people accept these as legitimate because of the use of the name of God.

Many people are completely pragmatic about charms concluding that if it works then that is all that matters: if the result is good it must be from God. However, pragmatists fail to realise that the Devil is not only instrumental in the bad things of life but, as an angel of light, he can also affect good things, if it is in his interest. He is a master of masquerade! Just because something works does not mean it is right in the sight of God.

Objects that are often used by charmers for magic purposes are crystals and various pieces of jewellery. Christians should beware of owning or wearing occult symbols, talismans, amulets, crystals etc.

7. Consulter with Familiar Spirits

Deuteronomy 18:11b,

> ...or a consulter with familiar spirits....

A consulter with familiar spirits is essentially a medium who asks the assistance of an evil spirit. In this way, the medium purports to contact the dead.

In reality the dead cannot be contacted. A medium is in cooperation with a counterfeiting spirit who impersonates the deceased. Through corroboration with 'seducing spirits': 1 Timothy 4:1, the medium simulates contact with the dead.

Many poor, bereaved souls are deceived into believing they can communicate with their loved ones who have passed on but, in reality, Satan is praying on their vulnerabilities in order to get them hooked into the occult world.

8. Wizard

Deuteronomy 18:11c,

> ...or a wizard....

A wizard is the male version of the witch.

Similarly the wizard knows a great deal about these hidden things and is in touch with the demonic spirit realm. He uses magic to control others, using potions and spells that today can be freely purchased on the open market.

Wizards are involved in visualisation, sorcery, mantras, astral travel, projection, levitation, clairvoyance, and audiovoyance.

9. Necromancer

Deuteronomy 18:11d

> ...or a necromancer.

A necromancer is one who claims to speak to the dead for the purpose of fortune telling.

Like a medium, the necromancer is in league, not with the dead, but with evil spirits who pretend to be the deceased.

Despite the warnings of Deuteronomy 18, God's Old Testament people, on many occasions, dabbled in these abominations.

On one occasion God, through Isaiah the prophet in Isaiah 8:19, said,

> When they shall say unto you, Seek unto them that have familiar spirits, and unto wizards that peep, and that mutter: should not a people seek unto their God?

Saul in 1 Samuel 28 was in a state of disobedience to God when he contacted the Witch of Endor. The prophet Samuel however, did not appear by the conjuring or in response to the witch. In fact 1 Samuel 28:11 says.

> Then said the woman, Whom shall I bring up unto thee? And he said, Bring me up Samuel. And when the woman saw Samuel, she cried with a loud voice.

There is no room between verses 11 and 12 for any of the incantations of this witch or for her medium séance to be used properly. It seems Samuel appeared to her immediately and in verse 12 the medium is obviously shocked. This appears to be something that did not often happen. We read,

> And when the woman saw Samuel, she cried with a loud voice: and the woman spake to Saul, saying, Why hast thou deceived me? for thou art Saul.

Later the medium speaks of seeing gods and spirits coming out of the earth and going into the earth. This was obviously something that she did not experience in her everyday profession. Something real appeared to be happening here before the medium had an opportunity to use her chants and incantations.

It seems that God allowed Samuel to appear for Saul's judgment but not, in response to the medium-ship of the witch. This is borne out in the fact that Samuel carried a message, from the Lord, of more condemnation upon Saul.

God was using this event to judge Saul for his constant unfaithfulness and disobedience.

Note too, that it *was* Samuel who appeared: his name is mentioned six times and not a reference to an impostor spirit.

God condemns all who engage in these abominations because there is a God in heaven whom men ought to seek! God hates Spiritism.

It is clear from all Scripture that hidden things, occultic things, are not to be explored by Christians.

The gospel was for the purpose of opening the eyes of the blind: turning men from darkness to light and from the power of Satan unto God! Why would someone dabble in dark things when they have seen the light?

Some people perceive such divine prohibitions as being restrictive. Some may even conclude that God is a killjoy; seeking to keep all the secrets to Himself. It is however, important to realise that God does not want to stunt our intelligence, rather He wishes to protect us from all harm.

Even before occult exploration occurred in Ancient Babylon, the desire for hidden knowledge was expressed in the Garden of Eden. Genesis 3:4-5 records that Satan said to Eve,

> Ye shall not surely die: For God doth know that in the day ye eat thereof, then your eyes shall be opened, and ye shall be as gods, knowing good and evil.

Satan was implying that God was hiding something from His creatures: a secret knowledge that would advance them. This intrigued Eve. Cults, as we have observed, can attract the supernaturally curious. Genesis 3:6 records Eve's response,

> And when the woman saw that the tree was good for food, and that it was pleasant to the eyes, and a tree to be desired to make one wise, she took of the fruit thereof, and did eat, and gave also unto her husband with her; and he did eat.

Such hidden knowledge was hidden for a reason: it was irrevocably harmful.

Eve's disobedience to God ushered in the Fall into Sin of all mankind and the consequential spiritual death. God was only protecting Eve when He forbade her to take of the 'tree of the knowledge of good and evil.'

Sadly Spiritists still believe what Satan expressed to Eve in Genesis 3:4,

> Ye shall not surely die . . . .

For the Spiritist, death is not to be feared: the spirit simply goes to another world, another realm where, they believe, we will be as gods and thus, have a true knowledge of spiritual realities.

Freedom From The Darkness

How can someone involved in the occult be free?

First Peter 1:18-19 says,

> Forasmuch as ye know that ye were not redeemed with corruptible things, as silver and gold, from your vain conversation received by tradition from your fathers. But with the precious blood of Christ, as of a lamb without blemish and without spot.

The blood of Christ shed for you at Calvary can defeat sin, hell, death and Satan. You can be delivered!

What you must do is **come by faith to the Lord Jesus Christ**. He has all power in heaven and on earth: He is God!

Satan is very powerful, and in and of ourselves we have cause to fear him but,

> Jesus is stronger than Satan, and Satan to Jesus must bow!

When the name of Jesus Christ the Lord is spoken, Satan must bow. This great power is witnessed in the record of Mark 5; the story of the man possessed with many demons. He came and fell at the feet of Christ because Christ had the power to cast the demons all away. What a transformation! We then read of this man sitting clothed and in his right mind and all because he came to the Lord Jesus.

John 8:36 says,

> If the Son therefore shall make you free, ye shall be free indeed.

We see the power of Satan as recorded in Acts 19:13-17,

> ...certain of the vagabond Jews, exorcists, took upon them to call over them which had evil spirits the name of the Lord Jesus, saying, We adjure you by Jesus whom Paul preacheth. And there were seven sons of one Sceva, a Jew, and chief of the priests, which did so. And the evil spirit answered and said, Jesus I know, and Paul I know; but who are ye? And the man in whom the evil spirit was leaped on them, and overcame them, and prevailed against them, so that they fled out of that house naked and wounded. And this was known to all the Jews and Greeks also dwelling at Ephesus.

These Jewish exorcists were trying to cast out demons in their own power. Though they used the name of Jesus Christ, the Lord Jesus was not in their life and, as a result they were overcome by the Devil.

Significantly, later on in this portion of Scripture we read that,

> …the name of the Lord Jesus was magnified. And many that believed
> came, and confessed, and shewed their deeds: Acts 19:17-18.

Acts 19:19 records that they brought the instruments that they had used in the arts of occult and also their books and

> …burned them before all men: and they counted the price of them,
> and found it fifty thousand pieces of silver. So mightily grew the word
> of God and prevailed.

They did not only **believe** and **confess** but they also **renounced** their sinful lifestyles and all things associated with them. Then, complete freedom was theirs and the Word of God grew mightily and prevailed.

Believe on the Lord Jesus Christ for salvation and then renounce any sinful practices in His name and you will prevail in the victory of the cross! If you do not, you will remain hindered in spiritual bondage.

Footnotes

1   Walter Martin, The Kingdom of the Cults, pp.228ff.
2   Ibid., pp.233-239

Chapter 6
Church Of Christ

The 'Church of Christ' or the 'International Church of Christ' is also known as the 'Boston Movement', 'Multiplying Ministries' and the 'Discipling Movement'.

The International Church of Christ originated in the USA as a splinter group from the more mainstream Church of Christ denomination. Subsequently the leader of this new movement, Kip McKean, founded his own Church the 'Boston Movement' in Boston, Massachusetts and worldwide all the International Churches of Christ emanate from this.

The Central London Church of Christ was founded in 1982 and there are other congregations across the United Kingdom and Ireland. The Church of Christ maintain that the Scriptures record that the Apostles established only one Church per city and they further claim that the Church of Christ is the only true Church in any city. To the Church of Christ all other denominations are sinful and apostate. In 2001 it was estimated that there were over 400 Churches of Christ across the globe with a membership of 130,000 worldwide in 150 countries.

The Church of Christ's commitment and devotion to the study of the Word of God is very impressive, as is their strong emphasis on obedience. Their friendliness is extremely winsome and their desire to convert others to their faith is almost insatiable. It has to be said that, as with many other religious groups, these standards would put many evangelical Christians to shame.

The Church of Christ also displays great zeal and devotion in its beliefs and religious practices, which has been welcomed, by many, as refreshing when contrasted with the lifelessness and lack of conviction in much of present day Christendom.

The Church of Christ believe in the Trinity; the deity of Jesus Christ; the deity and personality of the Holy Spirit; the bodily resurrection of Jesus Christ; the Bible as the Word of God and rule of faith for the Church; a literal heaven and hell; and the personality of Satan as a literal fallen angel. These orthodox beliefs lead some people to accept the Church of Christ as another mainstream Christian denomination.

This is perhaps the most dangerous aspect of the Church of Christ.

When the Church of Christ is examined in further detail regarding their methods, techniques, practices and beliefs the discrepancies with orthodox Christianity becomes evident.

Some years ago BBC Breakfast News broadcast a six-minute cameo of some of the beliefs and practices of the London Church of Christ. The late Jill Dando introduced the piece by stating,

> There has been increasing criticism of the teaching methods used by one group, and that is the London Church of Christ.

During the programme journalist Anastasia Cook interviewed several ex-members of the Church, some parents who were concerned about children involved in the organisation, and a psychiatrist. Below is the transcript of some the interview that gives a first hand insight into the subtle dangers of this movement.

Cook: An ex-member told us how her parents kidnapped her from the group because they felt she was being brainwashed. Two years on, she's still trying to come to terms with her experiences.

Ex-Member: Whilst you're with the group . . . you're not encouraged to be responsible, you have no independence basically. You've lost the ability to think for yourself, because whatever you do you always have to seek help, seek advice.

Cook: You say you've met a lot of friends in the Church, do you know what has happened to them now?

Ex-Member: One young lady comes to mind, she has only been with the group for a short while, but she became very, very disturbed and confused about the teachings and what she had learned before joining the group, to the point of being psychologically disturbed - in fact, very suicidal.

Cook: We asked the country's leading cult psychiatrist if she had come across any similar cases during her many dealings with ex-members.

Psychiatrist: The phone calls I've had . . . I've had a lot of phone-calls about the London Church of Christ, and I haven't recorded them all - but they've been from psychiatric hospitals in the London area, and they've been about the fact that somebody who was admitted on section with an acute psychosis, talking unintelligibly and very distressed - either very high or very withdrawn. The relatives have told the psychiatrist concerned that the breakdown had something to do with the London Church of Christ.

Ian Haworth, an ex-cult member who dedicates himself to informing people of the dangers of cults, said during the programme,

> I was a victim of mind control and psychological coercion in a matter of four days, in fact they had me by Saturday mid-day, just after two … Cults grow exponentially: each person that becomes a victim becomes a victimiser; each person that's recruited becomes a recruiter and so they can grow rather rapidly unless people are warned.

From these testimonies it would appear that cult-like behaviour is evident in the Church of Christ.

The Church of Christ denies that it is a cult. In fact the Church of Christ in Singapore took a newspaper to court for designating them as such. The Church of Christ won the case.

However, there are some frightening similarities between the Church of Christ and cult behaviour.

The Church of Christ seemingly exhibit the **theological** characteristics of the claims to **new revelation**, **exclusivity** and a **loss of salvation** in the event of leaving the group. **Structurally** the Church of Christ is seen to exhibit an **authoritarian leadership** while encouraging their members to be **financially** and **socially isolated**. **Behaviourally,** it appears that the Church of Christ expose their members to **indoctrination** and at times food and sleep **deprivation**.

In Steve Wookey's, *As Angels of Light* the London Church of Christ is described in this way:

> You might meet them in the underground, or outside a station, or on the street. They will ask you if you would like to join a Bible study or come to a meeting. They will be friendly but a little insistent. You may already be a member of a Church, but somehow their Church has so

much more to offer, so you really ought to try their Church. They will get hold of your telephone number and then call you often, sometimes everyday, to encourage you to come along to their meetings. Before you know it, you are caught up with them. You have questions, but somehow you never get the chance to ask them. Your timetable is just too full, and the commitment expected of you is simply too demanding. You find yourself with a discipler, who begins to make all your decisions for you - what job you should do, what course you should take, where you should live. Your parents or friends appear worried by the amount of time that you are spending with the Church, so your discipler points out that they are a bad influence, and you ought not to see them too much....

This description highlights certain trends that worryingly correspond to some classic characteristics of a cult.

Discipling

In November 2002 Kip McKean resigned as the leader of the Church, somewhat shaking the **authoritarian leadership** structure of the movement.

Kip McKean was unquestionably the head of the Church of Christ. In fact one member of the Church said,

> He is the greatest living treasure that God has ever given the Kingdom on the face of the earth today.

The next level of authority is the elders who serve under the leader's authority and wisdom. Beneath the elders there are evangelists and women's ministry leaders for the major city Churches. Next in the hierarchy are the zone leaders; then the house Church leaders who are obsolete in most congregations; and then the assistant Bible-talk leaders.

This leadership structure illustrates the system of tight control operated by the Church of Christ. Kip McKean once said,

> I'm the one who gives them direction.

Al Baird, an important Boston Church of Christ elder, was quoted in *Time* magazine 18th May 1992, p.62 as saying,

> It is not a dictatorship, it is a theocracy with God on top.

However, Baird also said in *What Does the Boston Movement Teach?* P.7,

> In questions of spiritual leaders abusing their authority, it is not an option to rebel against their authority.

Later in the same article he went as far to declare that,

> When we are under authority we are to submit to and obey our leaders even when they are not very Christ-like.

Some who have left the Boston Church of Christ have testified that,

> The advice which members are expected to obey may include such details as where to live, whom and when to date, what courses to take in school, even how often to have sexual relations with a spouse: *Time*, 18th May 1992, p.62.

The Church of Christ is renowned for 'evangelising' on university campuses, where, at times, there are people known to be emotionally, spiritually and even financially vulnerable.

Upon recruitment a member enters immediately into the authority structure of the Church of Christ. They are discipled, having been allocated a discipler. This discipler chaperones the member and is consulted regarding all of their personal decisions. Of course discipleship and making disciples is a biblical concept, but the Bible does not teach that one disciple has authority over another. One-to-one discipleship that seeks to bring instruction is very different from one-over-one discipleship that primarily seeks control.

It is often as a result of such discipling that friction is caused in other personal relationships, which the member has outside the Church. The member can become eventually more dependent upon the Church than upon their friends and family. Whether or not this is the Church's intention, **isolation** is often the result, as members, through various processes of mind control, are weaned away from every other dependency and association. Relationships are to be with the Church and the Church alone. Some families have attempted to abduct and reprogram their loved ones in order to get them out of the group.

Some years ago Ulster Television in their documentary programme 'UTV Insight' addressed the issue of the Church of Christ's activities in the Queen's University area of Belfast. In the course of the programme Tim Hendy, a student from the Republic of Ireland, shared his personal experience of how, having moved to Belfast, he was recruited by the Church of Christ in only three weeks. He recounts,

> I was baptised by full immersion in Belfast Lough in November, so as you can imagine it was very cold! But it was a very good experience, I enjoyed it, and this was the moment that I was inducted, this is the moment that I was brought in, this is the moment that I was saved to receive the Holy Spirit....There was a strong sense of 'This is what the Church should be doing', and that includes each individual sort of participating fully in the life of the Church, which basically has a very busy schedule. There's not really much free time to go to do something, if you want to be on your own for a couple of hours - you know - it is really out of the question.

Interviewed in the same programme was Ayman Akshar, a former senior member of the Church of Christ, who spoke in more detail of how the movement sought to control its members. Specifically, his job was to oversee the lives of married couples under his care, and his control was absolute. He says,

> The level of influence is almost every aspect of their lives, for example in their finances they have to know each and every detail, how they spend, where they spend their money. I will tell them when and when not to spend their money, I will have to make sure that I get the maximum amount of money into the cult. When it comes to their marital relationship I will have to tell them when and when not to have sex, when and when not to have kids - what position they should have, the frequency, we used to give them weekly goals - again to know if there is any weakness in the relationship. The purpose of all that, if you ask, [is][1] to use sex as means to control people. If you know the weakness of people, you will be able to control them.

Teaching

As already established, most of the Church of Christ's doctrines are orthodox. Sadly, however their doctrine of Baptismal Regeneration is not biblical. The Church of Christ believe that salvation results from the act of baptism. To the Church of Christ, exercising faith in Christ is not sufficient to save; a person must also be baptised by total immersion and only then do they receive the gift of the Holy Spirit. In other words apart from water baptism, sins cannot not be forgiven.

This false doctrine is deepened further by the Church of Christ's insistence that true baptism can only be administered in the confines of, and by a leader of, the Church of Christ. If an individual has already been baptised by immersion outside the Church of Christ they must be re-baptised by the Church of Christ. In addition all baptismal candidates must understand and believe that the moment of baptism is also the moment of their regeneration and reception of the Holy Spirit.

Baptismal Regeneration is a denial of the fundamental Christian doctrine of justification by faith alone. The Church of Christ does believe in justification by faith, but the Bible teaches justification by faith **alone**! Sola fide, faith alone, was the clarion cry of the Reformation. During the Reformation men began again to read the Bible and in doing so rediscovered that salvation is not to be found in a particular Church or through priests and sacraments but in Christ and Christ alone! The Bible teaches that justification is the legal act whereby God declares the sinner innocent: no sin attributed to him! God has declared him innocent in His sight.

How does the Bible say this occurs? The Apostle Paul in Romans 5:1 says,

> Therefore being justified **by faith**, we have peace with God through our Lord Jesus Christ.

Romans 5:8-9 continues,

> But God commendeth his love toward us, in that, while we were yet sinners, Christ died for us. Much more then, being now justified **by his blood**, we shall be saved from wrath through him.

These texts are clear; baptism is not mentioned at all. To make the matter even clearer Paul in Romans 3:28 says,

> Therefore we conclude that a man is justified **by faith, without the deeds of the law** (meaning - apart from the deeds of the law).[2]

The Bible teaches that works cannot save, even if that work is baptism.

Paul makes the same point in Romans 4:5,

> But to him that worketh not, but believeth on him that justifieth the ungodly, his faith is counted for righteousness.

And in Romans 11:6 Paul says,

> And if by grace, then is it no more of works....

You can not have grace and works; it is one or the other or as Paul says,

> ...otherwise grace is no more grace. But if it be of works, then it is no more grace: otherwise work is no more work.

God's Word testifies clearly that salvation is by faith in Christ alone, not of ourselves; it is the gift of God lest any of us should boast; Ephesians 2:8-9.

It is not unusual for new converts in the Church of Christ to undergo home Bible studies in the book of Galatians. Significantly the Galatian controversy was over a group of false teachers, called Judaisers, who told the Christians in effect: 'You believe Jesus died for you, and you put faith in Him, but that's not enough; you need to be circumcised as well, you've got to adhere to the Old Testament Law in addition to belief in Christ's death.'

Paul declared, inspired by the Holy Spirit: that is not the Gospel! Paul maintained that such a gospel was anathema! Therefore, any gospel that requires baptism as an essential to salvation is to be considered anathema.

Paul says in Galatians 2:16,

> Knowing that a man is not justified by the works of the law, but by the faith of Jesus Christ, even we have believed in Jesus Christ, that we might be justified by the faith of Christ, and not by the works of the law: for by the works of the law shall no flesh be justified.

Galatians 2:21 says,

> I do not frustrate the grace of God: for if righteousness come by the law, then Christ is dead in vain.

If water can wash away my sin, why did Christ need to die?

There are approximately 150 passages in the New Testament that state clearly and without reference to baptism, that salvation is by faith and faith alone in Christ. Proponents of Baptismal Regeneration often quote Bible texts that, at a casual glance may appear to teach this doctrine. This, however is a failure to recognise that there is a far greater weight of textual evidence to prove that salvation is by faith in Christ and nothing more.

Remember a rule of Bible interpretation highlighted in a previous chapter: always interpret difficult passages of Scripture in the light of clear ones and not vice versa. The cults have a tendency to take texts out of their context and make them a pretext for false doctrine. A common verse cited by proponents of Baptismal Regeneration is Mark 16:16 which says,

> He that believeth and is baptized shall be saved; but he that believeth not shall be damned.

Though this verse links believing and being baptised, it does not state that condemnation results from *not* being baptised. Clearly damnation is the result of unbelief. Otherwise the verse would read 'He that believeth and is baptised is saved; and he that does not believe and is not baptised shall be damned.' In fact this verse actually teaches that condemnation comes through not believing and not as a result of a rejection of baptism. Therefore, the verse agrees with the rest of the Bible record in maintaining that the essential matter by which salvation is realised is belief and not baptism.

It is worthy of note that this verse is part of our Lord's Great Commission. He is informing the disciples what will occur when they go and preach to every creature: 'People will savingly believe and be baptised; and others, because they do not believe, will be damned.'

Another text used in support of Baptismal Regeneration is John 3:5. The Lord Jesus Christ says that those who are born again are,

> . . . born of water and of the Spirit.

There are many interpretations of what 'the water' is in this verse. The Church of Christ says it is baptism. Other interpreters, because of the context, believe that the Lord is talking about physical birth because He goes on in verse 6 to say,

> . . . that which is born of the flesh is flesh; and that which is born of the Spirit is Spirit

This is plausible.

There is another interpretation that understands 'the water' as the Word of God because often in Scripture water is used as a picture of the Word. Therefore, the meaning could be that the new birth is affected by the Word as well as the Spirit. This, too, is a plausible explanation. A third, and perhaps more likely interpretation is that the word 'and' in the verse can be translated as 'even' to read, *'except a man is born of water **even** of the Spirit, he cannot enter the kingdom of God.'*

The figure of water in Scripture is also a representation of the Holy Spirit and therefore this is another very possible and plausible understanding of the verse that correlates with what the rest of the Bible teaches.

However, here is the salient point: whatever is uncertain about this verse, it is abundantly clear that 'water' does not mean baptism. Why? When taking the text in context, baptism is not mentioned nor alluded to in the whole passage; the new birth is the subject.

Acts 2:38 is a favourite text of the Church of Christ. It says,

> Then Peter said unto them, Repent, and be baptized every one of you in the name of Jesus Christ for the remission of sins, and ye shall receive the gift of the Holy Ghost.

If this verse is taken in isolation from its biblical context it does seem obvious that it teaches the need to be baptised in order to be saved. However we must read all that the Apostle Peter said. Verse 21 says,

> And it shall come to pass that whosoever shall call on the name of the Lord shall be saved

It does not say *whoever is baptised shall be saved*; baptism is not mentioned. The intrinsic ingredient for salvation is faith. Acts 3:19 declares,

> Repent ye therefore, and be converted, that your sins may be blotted out, when the times of refreshing shall come from the presence of the Lord.

Repentant belief is the point at which forgiveness of sins is bestowed, yet it would appear in Acts 2:38 that baptism is another requirement. Are these contradicting one another?

The word 'for' in the Greek is also the word 'because'. It is translated that way in Matthew 12:42 referring to the conversion of the Ninevites - 'because of the preaching of Jonah.' Therefore a valid translation of verse 38 would read,

> ...be baptized **because** of the remission of sins that you receive through faith in Jesus Christ.

What *is* clear is that it cannot mean that baptism washes sins away.

Another Scripture often cited in favour of Baptismal Regeneration comes from Acts 22:16. Before commenting on the verse, it is worth stating how dangerous it can be to build Church doctrine solely from material found in the book of the Acts of the Apostles. Acts is primarily a book of history recording events in the early Church rather than a book of instruction relating to either Church doctrine or practice.

Acts 22:16 reads,

> And now why tarriest thou? arise, and be baptized, and wash away thy sins, calling on the name of the Lord.

Paul tells how he was instructed to be baptised to wash away his sins.

A search of Scripture will establish that the only time 'washing away sins' is spoken of in relation to baptism is when a Jew is being addressed. This is significant.

It was the Jews who cried at the crucifixion of the Lord Jesus, 'Let His blood be upon us and our children's children'; Matthew 27:25. Their cry was an outward sign that they were prepared to be counted guilty of the blood of the Lord. Baptism is an outward sign of salvation, showing to others what God has done for us and, specifically, in relation to the Jew, it was showing that the sin of crucifying Christ was being washed off them publicly. It was testimony that they, as a Jew, were not guilty of this sin any more.

Paul's testimony as recorded also in Acts 9:17 is helpful in understanding the role of baptism.

> Ananias went his way, and entered into the house; and putting his hands on him said, Brother Saul, the Lord, even Jesus, that appeared unto thee in the way as thou camest, hath sent me, that thou mightest receive thy sight, and be filled with the Holy Spirit.

How could he call him 'brother' if he was not saved? The fact is he was saved even though he was not yet baptised.

Another verse used to substantiate this false teaching is 1 Peter 3:21. First Peter 3:20 says,

> ...once the longsuffering of God waited in the days of Noah, while

the ark was a preparing, wherein few, that is, eight souls were saved by water.

The Greek word 'by' can also be translated 'through', which means the verse could read *'saved through water.'* This makes sense as Peter has already stated that Noah and his seven family members were saved because they were in the ark.

Peter goes on,

> The like figure whereunto even baptism doth also now save us.

The New King James Version translates the verse this way,

> There is also an antitype which now saves us.

The word 'like figure' in 1 Peter 2:21; Authorised Version, is therefore rendered in the New King James Version as *'an antitype which now saves us.'* An antitype is simply the fulfilment of a type[3]. The key question is: if it is this antitype which saves us, what is the type being spoken of here? Is it the water? It cannot be for Noah was not saved by water; he was saved *through* water that was a type of judgement.

It was the ark that saved Noah and therefore Christ is the antitype of that ark that now saves us. If we are in Christ we have been saved through the judgement of God, which He sheltered us from on the cross. We are saved through the waters of God's wrath that the Saviour underwent for us. True baptism is identification with Christ's death and resurrection that saves us. We trust in Christ, not in water. Paul in 1 Corinthians 1:17 is unambiguous when he pronounces

> Christ sent me not to baptize, but to preach the gospel.

Paul clearly states that baptism was not his primary ministry. It would be strange, as well as completely inconsistent, to propound a gospel that requires baptism in order to be saved, and then only baptise a few, as Paul claims to have done: 1 Corinthians 1:14, 16.

In Acts 16:31, the Philippian jailer said,

> What must I do to be saved?

Paul answered 'Believe on the Lord Jesus Christ.' The Philippian jailer was baptised after conversion, and his family after their conversion.

First Corinthians 15:1-5 declares the gospel that Paul preached, and baptism is not mentioned once.

Categorical proof of the fact that baptism is not instrumental in salvation is found recorded in Acts 10:44-48,

> While Peter yet spake these words, the Holy Ghost fell on all them which heard the word. And they of the circumcision which believed were astonished, as many as came with Peter, because that on the Gentiles also was poured out the gift of the Holy Ghost. For they heard them speak with tongues, and magnify God. Then answered Peter, Can any man forbid water, that these should not be baptized, which have received the Holy Ghost as well as we? And he commanded them to be baptized in the name of the Lord Jesus.

They received the Word, they believed, they received the Holy Spirit, they spoke in tongues, which is only a gift given to a believer, yet they were not baptised.

It must be affirmed that baptism is a non-negotiable command of the Saviour to the believer, and therefore all Christians are obliged to obey. It is however, a false gospel that makes obedience to this command a saving act. It is significant that the Saviour of the world, the Lord Jesus Christ did not baptise any - John 4:2,

> ... Jesus himself baptized not, but his disciples.

If baptism is the essential act that saves then it would follow that the Saviour, who came from heaven to bring salvation, would baptise. The thief on the cross did not have time to get baptised, yet Christ promised that He would take him to paradise; Luke 23:43.

The Church of Christ denies several other truths. These omissions include original sin and the eternal security of the believer. It is sad that there is no assurance of salvation in the Church of Christ. The Lord Jesus Christ taught in John 10:27-28,

> My sheep hear my voice, and I know them, and they follow me: And I give unto them eternal life; and they shall never perish, neither shall any man pluck them out of my hand.

First Peter1:3-5 also declares with great assurance,

> Blessed be the God and Father of our Lord Jesus Christ, which according to his abundant mercy hath begotten us again unto a lively hope by the resurrection of Jesus Christ from the dead, To an inheritance incorruptible, and undefiled, and that fadeth not away, reserved in heaven for you, Who are kept by the power of God through faith unto salvation ready to be revealed in the last time.

This inheritance is 'reserved'; booked by faith in heaven for the believer in Christ.

All, who depend on self, baptism, or a Church, will be lost and lost for eternity! Reader, whatever you are relying on other than Christ, throw it to the wind and take by faith the Lord Jesus Christ and His cross alone for salvation.

It has been said 'Baptism will make you wetter, but no better'; that is true. Baptism is an outward sign of an inward reality. It is an act of obedience to Christ that will bless you. Baptism displays your salvation in the eyes of men. It is a demonstration of how you have been brought from the Kingdom of darkness into the Kingdom of light. Baptism is a vital part of Christian discipleship and it does appear that when the gospel was preached in the early Church, baptism was the public confession of faith in Christ. Baptism then, immediately followed belief.

Whatever baptism is, however, it does not and cannot save one soul. Christ must save, and He alone!

Footnotes

1   Added by author for purposes of clarity.
2   Added by author for purposes of clarity.
3   A foreshadowing in the Old Testament of a person or event of the Christian dispensation.

Chapter 7
Christadelphianism

Christadelphianism claims to be the Christian Church preaching the Christian gospel and, as such, they claim to be the true followers of Christ in the world today.

Christadelphianism is a small religious group with less than 19,000 people among its 282 congregations in the United Kingdom. England has the largest number of Christadelphians in the world with Birmingham as the central hub of power for each of the independent and autonomous congregations in England. From here counsel and guidance is given to Christadelphians.

Though the Christadelphians are small in number they are very active wherever they are found. Often they will advertise their meetings in the announcement page of the local press, usually giving their subject, which is often prophecy related.

Much of the helpful material dealing with cults comes from the USA, where Christadelphianism is not of great concern. Many writers on the subject of cults have ignored Christadelphianism but it is vitally important, however, that Christadelphians are not overlooked as their teachings are very dangerous.

The founder of the Christadelphians, Dr John Thomas, states in *We are the Christadelphians* p.3

> ...we repudiate the popular Churches...and affirm that there is no salvation within the pale of any of them.

Christadelphian History

The group's original name was the 'Thomasites', or 'Thomasism' after the founder Dr John Thomas. When Civil War broke out in the USA 'Thomasites' were called upon to enlist but, because of their conscientious objection, they refused. However, as only recognised religious groups were allowed to refuse conscription, they needed to change their name. Dr John Thomas duly named them 'The Christadelphians'.

In Greek 'Christ' means 'the anointed one', and 'delphos' means 'brother'; hence Christadelphians means 'Christ's Brothers', 'Christ's Brethren'. The name 'Christadelphian' betrays one of their fatal errors; the belief that Christ was only human and therefore we are His brothers.

Dr John Thomas was born in London 12th April 1805. Like several other founders of cults he had a Christian upbringing; the son of a Congregational minister. After qualifying as a physician, he decided in 1832 to emigrate to the USA to further his studies. On his way to New York the ship experienced some terrible storms. Everyone on board thought the ship would be wrecked and that all aboard would die.

Apparently at that moment, Dr John Thomas lifted his heart to God and promised that if God spared his life he, in turn, would devote his life to the study of religion; Dr John Thomas' life, along with the others, on the ship was preserved. Resolving to keep his promise to God, Dr John Thomas joined a religious group called the 'Campbellites', which was also known as 'the Disciples'.

Before long Dr John Thomas began to differ with some of the biblical interpretations of the Campbellites. Eventually he left them, taking with him many of their members. This was the beginning of the Christadelphian movement, though as yet that was not the group's name.

Dr John Thomas began to publicise his doctrinal views in 1834 in a magazine called *The Apostolic Advocate*. Ten years later he published another magazine called *The Herald of the Future Age*. In these publications he concentrated particularly on the subject of eschatology: the study of the End Times and the Second Coming of Jesus Christ.

The fundamental New Testament doctrine of the Second Coming of the Lord Jesus Christ is a truth in which all Christians should rejoice in and for which they should prepare.

However, this overemphasis on eschatology to the detriment of other equally important subjects and, the tendency to add to the details revealed in Scripture regarding this truth are notable characteristics of many of the cults.

The magazine *The Herald of the Future Age* later became known as *The Christadelphian* and it eventually became the official publication of Christadelphianism. In 1848 Christadelphianism was established as a religious movement in the USA.

Dr John Thomas returned to England to preach and teach his doctrine. When he arrived there, he found that as a result of his writings, a number of people had embraced his teachings.

While Dr John Thomas was in the United Kingdom, he wrote his book: *Elpis Israel*. The meaning of *Elpis Israel* is 'The Hope of Israel'. The book includes a study of prophetic

Scriptures relating to the future of the nation of Israel. *Elpis Israel* also contains Dr John Thomas' teachings on creation, God's Law, sin, death, immortality, religion, and the coming Kingdom. It became one of the most important books for the Christadelphian movement. After writing *Elpis Israel* Dr John Thomas returned to the USA.

Dr John Thomas was a tireless worker who sought, as he understood, to study God's Word. He felt he was attempting to come to the true meaning and interpretation of the doctrines of Holy Scripture. Dr John Thomas was deeply sincere, which is typical of many of the founders of these cults. However Dr John Thomas, like many other cult founders, made the grave mistake of despising the counsel and wisdom of those who were more learned than he. He ignored the whole of Christian history.

Dr John Thomas had what many call 'the Messiah complex': thinking he was God's new man, anointed more than others. He believed he had rediscovered, single-handedly, the true gospel that had been lost from the earth or perverted by established Christendom. This is one of the major characteristics of any cult: the **theological** claim to **new revelation**, **exclusivity** and **no salvation** outside of their group. Whether it is Joseph Smith of the Mormons, Charles Taze Russell of the Jehovah's Witnesses, L. Ron Hubbard of Scientology, Mary Baker Eddy of Christian Science, or any other founder of a cult, the personal views of a mortal man have claimed to have a **new** and **exclusive revelation** that restores the true gospel to the earth.

However 2 Peter 1:19-20 states,

> We have also a more sure word of prophecy; whereunto ye do well that ye take heed, as unto a light that shineth in a dark place, until the day dawn, and the day star arise in your hearts: Knowing this first, that no prophecy of the Scripture is of any private interpretation.

This does not mean that individuals cannot interpret God's Word because the Spirit has promised to lead us into all truth. Nor does it mean, as the Roman Catholic Church teaches, that only Roman Catholic clergy can interpret the Scriptures. What it does mean is that no particular man can tell you what is God's revealed will.

God's revealed will has been known to men: men were inspired by the Holy Spirit to write the Apostle's doctrine. We have in the New Testament the sure word of prophecy.

2 Peter 1:21 writes,

> For the prophecy came not in old time by the will of man.

This was not by one man, but by several Apostles. Those Apostles wrote down the teaching that God gave them. They were, as 2 Peter 1:21 writes,

> ...holy men of God...moved by the Holy Ghost.

Peter declares that God's true gospel is not to be found in man; it is given by God's Spirit. It was not just given to one Apostle or one prophet but it was given to several. That is why we need to recognise and be wary of any one who claims to be God's sole revelatory medium to men today. A false gospel is thereby being preached. When someone claims to know more about the Bible than anybody else, alarm bells ought to be ringing in our heads!

It is also noteworthy that many of the cult founders were, at one time, influenced by orthodox Christianity. Many were born into Christian homes, even manses. However, at some point, they willingly turned from biblical Christianity, which the Scriptures warn us is a sure sign of false prophets.

Regarding false prophets 1 John 2:19 writes,

> They went out from us, but they were not of us; for if they had been of us, they would no doubt have continued with us: but they went out, that they might be made manifest that they were not all of us.

According to 2 Timothy 4:4 the Apostle Paul forewarned that the time would come when men would turn their ears from the truth and be turned to fables. The dictionary states that a fable is a falsehood, a fairytale, a fiction, or a myth, especially in a religious sense. Christadelphianism, like all other cults, is based upon fables. Cults and false religions have erred primarily in their understanding of the person and work of our Lord Jesus Christ. In the New Testament, any error concerning Christ's person and work is equal to a turning away from the truth and a turning to fables.

Christians must maintain the faith, once and for all, delivered to the saints; Jude 3. Christian history did not start in the 1800s by Dr John Thomas but began in the Lord Jesus Christ, continued on in the Apostles who followed Him and then in all who have responded by faith to that same message of Christ.

Christ's promise, in Matthew 16:18, of

> …I will build my Church, and the gates of hell shall not prevail against it

declares that Christ's Church will not cease to exist.

Is Christadelphian Doctrine, Christian Doctrine?

The answer is categorically no!

Any movement, which denies one or more of the essential doctrines of Christianity can not be considered as Christian.

What are the essential doctrines of Christianity?

The first essential doctrine in Christianity is that of the **deity of Christ**. That means that Christ is God's Son and also He is God the Son. This doctrine also includes the acceptance of the doctrine of the **Trinity**: the belief in one God who is revealed in Scripture, in three distinct persons.

The second essential doctrine is that **salvation is by grace through faith alone in Christ:** not through a Church, sacraments, good works, religious rites or practices but by grace; undeserved favour, imparted by faith in Christ alone.

The third essential of Christianity is the doctrine of the **resurrection of Christ**. In 1 Corinthians 15:19 we read that we are, of all men, most to be pitied if Christ's body is still in the grave. If Jesus Christ did not rise again, our faith is vain, and our message is a fairytale.

Christadelphianism denies the first two of these essential doctrines of Christianity. Our appraisal of Jesus Christ: what we believe about who He was, where He came from, how He was born, where He is now and what He is doing now, determines whether we are truly Christian.

The Bible teaches that the Lord Jesus existed before creation; this is called the pre-existence of Christ.

John 1:1 says,

> In the beginning was the Word, and the Word was with God, and the Word was God.

'The Word' in Greek is 'logos', which speaks of the expression of God to men: the Lord Jesus. John says Jesus Christ was *with* God, but He also *was* God, and John 1:14 reads,

> And the Word was made flesh, and dwelt among us, (and we beheld his glory, the glory as of the only begotten of the Father,) full of grace and truth.

Colossians 2:9 is another verse that proves that Christ lived in pre-existence as God,

> For in him dwelleth all the fulness of the Godhead bodily.

All the fullness of the Godhead bodily dwelt in the Lord Jesus Christ. This truth is also taught in Philippians 2:5-6 which reads,

> Let this mind be in you, which was also in Christ Jesus: Who, being in the form of God, (meaning 'in very nature God')[1], thought it not robbery, (something to be grasped at)[2], to be equal with God.

Christ was equal with God but during His time here on earth He did not grasp after the free use of many of the divine attributes which He possessed. Rather, Philippians 2:7-8 writes that Christ,

> . . . made Himself of no reputation, and took upon Himself the form of a servant, was made in the likeness of men, and humbled Himself and became obedient unto death, even the death of the cross.

In Hebrews 1:8 we read of God the Father speaking to His Son as God and saying,

> But unto the Son God saith, Thy throne, O God, is for ever and ever: a sceptre of righteousness is the sceptre of thy kingdom.

It cannot be over-emphasised that the Lord Jesus Christ is God of very God, begotten not created. There is a difference! The Greek word 'begotten' designates more than simply the birth of Christ; it conveys that Christ is eternally begotten of the Father, not created.

Christadelphians accept the virgin birth as Christians do but they will not accept that Jesus is God the pre-existent Son. They teach that at Jesus' baptism He became the Christ and that He was in some way divine. However there is only one God and that is the Father and none other.

Harry Tennant in *The Christadelphians: What They Believe and Preach*, 1986 p.85 claims,

> There is no hint in the Old Testament that the Son of God was already existent or in any way active at that time.

In the same publication p.86 Harry Tennant also claims,

> Jesus Christ, the Son of God, was first promised, and came into being only when He was born of the virgin Mary.

In other words Christadelphians believe that Christ did not pre-exist Bethlehem.

At a Christadelphian Exhibition in the Ulster Hall in Belfast in July 1989 a number of display stands clearly outlined what the Christadelphians believe. Referring to the birth of Jesus, one statement, quoting Isaiah 7:14 read:

> …a virgin shall conceive, bear a son, and shall call his name Immanuel

Placed in brackets was the comment that Immanuel was 'a name for Jesus.' Immanuel is indeed a name for Jesus however, it also carries with it 'God with us'! Christadelphians appear to ignore this very important fact.

Another quote, referring to Revelation 1:18 read,

> These prophecies were fulfilled when Christ was raised from the dead, after three days in the tomb, He declared later: I am He that liveth and was dead and behold, I am alive for evermore…and have the keys of hell and of death.

The Christadelphians fail to quote what the resurrected Christ said in His full statement, for Revelation 1:17 writes,

> Fear not; I am the first and I am the last.

That is a direct quotation from Isaiah 44:6, where God says,

> I am the first and I am the last.…

The Christadelphians have dropped these inspired words that would make a case for Jesus being divine.

Concerning the life the Lord lived, another Christadelphian quote stated,

> Jesus never sinned. He conquered the temptations which arise from
> our sinful nature - a nature that he too shared, for only thus could he
> be a Saviour. God cannot sin. But Jesus could have sinned, though he
> never did. Such a Saviour, provided by God, was central to His loving
> purpose.

Christadelphians teach that Christ had a sinful nature. In affirming that God cannot
sin Christadelphians infer that Jesus is not God.

In *The Christadelphians: What They Believe and Preach* p.74, Harry Tennant explained
this teaching of the sinful nature of Christ

> ...we conclude that it is not only that Jesus was called a sinner at his
> trial by his enemies or that he was 'numbered with the transgressors'
> when he was crucified between two thieves, but more particularly
> that he shared the very nature which had made a sinner out of every
> other man who had borne it.

Such a statement is blasphemous in the light of Holy Scripture. The Bible teaches that
men are among Adam's fallen race: humans are depraved and are liable to sin both
internally and externally. Though Christ came in the likeness of sinful flesh; Romans
8:3 and was subject to some of the restrictions borne by all humans, He had no sinful
nature. Christ was not vulnerable to sin; He did not lust after sin. In fact, the Lord
Jesus in John 14:30 said,

> ...the prince of this world (the Devil)[3] cometh, and he hath nothing
> in me.

When the virgin Mary conceived she was overshadowed by the Holy Spirit and the
angel said to her,

> That holy thing which shall be born of thee, shall be called the Son of
> God.

Contrast these truths with the teaching espoused by the Christadelphians.

In *Christadelphian Answers*, compiled by Frank G. Jannaway, p.24 we read, in reference to Christ,

> He saved himself in order to save us...it was for that very reason that the Lord Jesus himself needed salvation.

All that Satan needs to do, to damn people eternally, is to get them to believe in a false Christ. This is Satan's strategy in spawning these confusing cults and false faiths. The Saviour in Matthew 24:24, Himself warned us that this would happen.

> For there shall arise false Christs, and false prophets, and shall shew great signs and wonders; insomuch that, if it were possible, they shall deceive the very elect.

Only the true Christ can reveal to us the true God. The Lord Jesus claimed that He would reveal the Father and taught that He and the Father were one. Those who had seen Him had seen the Father.

In John 14:6 He said,

> I am the way, the truth and the life; no man cometh unto the Father but by me.

It follows that if you deny the divine nature of Christ, if you ascribe a sinful nature to the spotless Son of God, if you believe that He needed to be saved; you are serving a false god and following a false Christ. Paul the Apostle said to the Galatians that if any man preaches another Jesus unto you let him be anathema; Galatians 1:8-9.

The second essential doctrine of Christianity denied by Christadelphianism is the substitutionary atonement of the Lord Jesus Christ on the cross. This truth of salvation by grace through faith alone in Christ is perverted. Christadelphians tamper with God's provided way of salvation. Christadelphians claim Christ did not bear our sins; rather He simply represented sinful fallen humanity.

However, to the contrary 1 Peter 2:24 states

> …who his own self bare our sins in his own body on the tree.…

And Isaiah 53:5 writes,

> He was wounded for our transgressions, He was bruised for our iniquities, the chastisement of our peace was upon Him, and with His stripes we are healed.

When 2 Corinthians 5:21 states that Christ was made sin for us, Christadelphians interpret this as meaning that Christ required a sin offering to be made on His own behalf. Christadelphians teach that Christ needed a sin offering to be saved!

However 1 Peter 2:22 states that Christ,

> …did no sin, neither was guile found in his mouth.…

He knew no sin, He was the impeccable Christ, He could not sin! Yet here is what Christadelphianism teaches,

> The second secret of the cross is that it is the source of the forgiveness of sins. It is not a debt settled by due payment. It is not a substitutionary offering whereby someone has paid a price so that others might then go free: Harry Tennant, *Christadelphians: What They Believe and Preach*, p.71.

Tragically the Christadelphian cannot sing:

> Bearing shame, and scoffing rude;
> In my place, condemned, He stood.
> Sealed my pardon with His blood,
> Hallelujah! What a Saviour!

There is no Saviour without a substitutionary atonement! Yet interestingly, Harry Tennant remarks concerning the way of salvation that,

> The Bible approach is much simpler and much more satisfying. Forgiveness comes to the man who believes the Gospel, repents, and is baptized in the name of Christ: *The Christadelphians: What They Believe and Preach* p.71.

Like the Church of Christ considered in the previous chapter, Christadelphianism claims that baptism is essential to salvation.

Another quotation from the Christadelphian display at the Ulster Hall in 1989 revealed their view on baptism,

> Without true baptism our sin will not be washed away.

The Bible does not teach this. In 1 Corinthians 1:17 the Apostle Paul stated that he did not come to baptise, but to preach the gospel.

In John 4:2 we read that Jesus did not baptise anyone. As the Saviour of the world, would He not have baptised men if that was the means whereby their sins were washed away?

Only the blood of Jesus Christ can cleanse from sin; 1 John 1:7. Baptism is important as a command of the Lord Jesus Christ and ought to be obeyed by every believer but it will not wash one sin away. In fact, the Bible clearly teaches that it is only to be undergone by those who have had their sins forgiven.

The Christadelphian exhibition in the Ulster Hall in Belfast, July 1989 also demonstrated that Christadelphians believe sin is synonymous with Satan. In other words, Satan is not a literal person. Referring to Christ's temptation the exhibition stated that Christ was,

...tempted and engaged in the fight against SIN (which the Bible calls the DEVIL).

A further statement on this display spoke of Christ destroying the Devil and states,

By this means SIN (the DEVIL) could be destroyed.

Christ, however, spoke of the Devil as a personality when He said in Luke 10:18,

I beheld Satan as lightning fall from heaven.

Another board in this exhibition conveyed that Christadelphians believe in only one God, but they define Him as the Father. This is very similar to Mormonism. Robert Roberts, the successor of Dr John Thomas, claimed that the Father is a tangible person. The reason for this is that Christadelphians believe that if the Lord Jesus is the express image of God as Hebrews 1 writes, then God must have a body, God must have a form; yet, John 4 tells us that God is spirit.

Christadelphians believe that 'The Holy Spirit is God's power': He is not a personality but He is God the Father's influence in our lives. However, it is evident throughout Scripture that the Holy Spirit is a person. Ananias and Sapphira lied to Him and, He as a result was grieved; Acts 5 and Ephesians 4:30.

Robert Roberts states that there is no manifestation of the Spirit in these days.

Significantly, 1 John 2:22 writes,

Who is a liar but he that denieth that Jesus is the Christ? He is antichrist, that denieth the Father and the Son.

This verse applies to those who deny the deity of our Lord Jesus Christ and the doctrine of salvation by grace through faith alone in Christ. John the Apostle was dealing with similar heresies in his day.

The implications of John's words are that anyone involved in any cult or religious group that denigrates the personality and the deity of our Lord Jesus Christ and His essential work on the cross, are involved in an anti-Christ movement.

Christadelphians teach a salvation by works: the faithful alone will inherit eternal life. Like so many other cults and false religions in our world today, Christadelphianism gives the sinner no hope or assurance of salvation. They believe that if the soul is lost it will just be blown out like a candle; annihilated because of unfaithfulness. Yet the Lord Jesus clearly contradicts this in Matthew 25:46,

> And these shall go away into everlasting punishment: but the righteous into life eternal.

God's Word states clearly that because of our Lord Jesus Christ and His perfect life, His peerless character as God's Son, His purging work on Calvary's cross as the sinner's substitute and His powerful resurrection, we can be sure that we are saved eternally.

First John 5:13 says,

> These things are written have I written unto you that believe on the name of the Son of God; that ye may know that ye have eternal life. . . .

Hallelujah! Reader, do you know that you have eternal life? Not 'Do you hope so', or 'You would like to think so', or 'You are trying your best to get there': do you know for sure?

The only way to know is to come to the cross of Calvary, to admit that the One hanging there is in your place, to admit that He is none other than God the Son and to acknowledge that your sin is upon Him. Take, by faith, that gift of salvation purchased for you at the cross; embrace it and the power of His resurrection will flood your soul!

Then, believing in Christ and Christ alone, you will know that you are saved.

Footnotes

1   Added by author for purposes of clarity.
2   Ibid.
3   Ibid.

Chapter 8
Buddhism

Our attention now turns from the cults that could be classified as coming out of 'Christendom', to the faiths that do not class themselves as Christian, in that they worship a different god or gods.

One of these faiths is 'Buddhism' whose founder was Buddha.

For many Buddha is, as his copious pictures portray him, a large, fat man who sits in the lotus position with his arms often held out in a meditative fashion. Buddha, however is not a religious figment of the imagination, but was in fact a real man whose name was Siddhartha Gautama. However, when studying Siddhartha Gautama's life it is often difficult to distinguish between history and legend. Even scholars cannot come to agreement on the dates for Siddharta Gautama's life, but it is probable that he was born in a village near Benares in India around 560 BC and died at about the age of 80 years.

Interestingly Siddhartha Gautama was born a Hindu. The son of a wealthy Hindu Raja, Siddhartha Gautama would have had a privileged upbringing in palaces. His father was reported to have been keen to protect him from the evil and suffering of the outside world.

However, when he was a young married man with a son of his own, Siddhartha Gautama was curious as to life beyond the palaces. Venturing out into the unknown he encountered four scenes that changed his life.

The first phenomenon he saw on his travels was that of an old man. Siddhartha Gautama was struck by how frail the man was and, of the tragic affects of age on the human form. Secondly, Siddhartha Gautama saw a sick and diseased man. The effects of illness and disease were apparent on the human form. The third sight Siddhartha Gautama witnessed was a dead man in a funeral cortege. Siddhartha Gautama saw the horrors of what death did to human beings. After questioning the significance of his revelations, Siddhartha Gautama was reportedly given the answer that all that he had witnessed was the common fate of mankind.

There was, however, a fourth sight which Siddhartha Gautama observed and that was of a religious man. This was a positive experience for the Siddhartha Gautama because although this religious man was a begging monk, he seemed to have a joyful aura about him.

Siddhartha Gautama was convinced that this inner happiness had nothing to do with external pleasures but rather, was associated with living a fulfilled life. He saw some unspecified meaning in religion and was thereby won over by it. As a result Siddhartha Gautama decided to leave the palace, counting all his palatial benefits of birth as worthless. He even left his wife and his child, and embarked on a new existence as a monk.

The next night, we are told, Siddhartha Gautama sat in the lotus posture and fought an inner battle that sacred writings of Buddhism have described as the 'temptation of Mara'. Siddhartha Gautama was understood to have wrestled in mediation, with the personification of change, death and evil in this world.

After this event Siddhartha Gautama spent the next six years as a Hindu holy man with very few possessions and little food. One day, ill from having no food at all, he collapsed and then came to the realisation that what he was doing, as a Hindu holy man, was of little benefit. According to the story, on Siddhartha Gautama's 35th birthday, as he was meditating under a fig tree, which Buddhists call 'the tree of wisdom', he came to learn new truths that would revolutionise not only his life, but would spawn a major world religion.

Like the cults, the false religions of the world claim to have discovered **new revelations** of truth that the world has never known before. Their founder is usually a self-styled prophet who purports to impart **new revelation** to mankind. Siddhartha Gautama, under the new name of 'the Buddha' 'the enlightened one' was one such prophet.

This story of the origins of Buddhism contains the core beliefs of the Buddhist faith; namely that everyone in the world is suffering, trapped in a life of physical or emotional turmoil and pain. Buddhists maintain that the reason for our pain and suffering is because of our material goods and our consuming desires and appetites for pleasure.

This is the reason why Buddhist monks abstain from killing, stealing, forbidden sex, lying and the use of drugs and alcohol. They believe these matters will cause suffering, and of course there is a measure of truth in this. The problem is the idea behind Buddhist abstention: the belief that all matter, and especially that which is associated with our human senses, is intrinsically evil.

According to the Buddha, suffering was unavoidable but the way to salvation had been revealed to him, as the Enlightened One. Buddha believed he had received the knowledge of 'the four noble truths'. He claimed to have the answers to the age-old question 'why?' and also to have discovered a way to eradicate suffering. These practical guidelines for living were called 'the eightfold path'.

Buddha taught that if man could understand why he was suffering, and then followed the eightfold path to avoid suffering, he may then achieve a state called 'Nirvana'. 'Nirvana' literally means 'blowing out'; the idea of a state of non-existence.

What Buddha was teaching was that there is a level of transcendent, permanent obliviousness to suffering. Man, according to Buddha, can reach this position.

The Four Noble Truths Of Buddhism

According to Buddhism these four noble truths explain the reasons why people suffer. The first is obvious: 'the fact of suffering'. This is the acknowledgement of the existence of suffering in our world in all its shapes and forms. The second gives a little bit more insight into the noble truths of Buddhism, because it tells us that 'the cause of suffering is craving and desire'. The reason why humans suffer is because they desire that which is harmful for them. The third noble truth is that 'suffering stops with the cessation of desire': stop wanting material objects and sensual pleasure and suffering will cease. The way this can be achieved is by following 'the eightfold path of Buddhism', which is itself the fourth noble truth.

The Eightfold Path Of Buddhism

First of all man must have 'the right viewpoint' which, is the Buddhist viewpoint. The second path is to have 'the right aspiration', right ambitions and right desires that are not physical, material, or sensual. The third is 'right speech'; fourth, 'right behaviour'; fifth, 'right occupation'; sixth, 'right effort'; seventh, 'right mindfulness' and eighth, 'right meditation'. The emphasis in this eightfold path is that man has to *be* right, to *do* everything right, to *say* everything right, to *think* everything right, and then, man may possibly achieve the state of 'nirvana' where suffering is a thing of the past.

Buddha began his spiritual journey as a Hindu, and therefore it should not be surprising that there are certain similarities between Hinduism and Buddhism. Some even view Buddhism as a reformation of Hinduism. The Dali Lama actually calls Buddhism and Hinduism 'natural twins'.

One of the similarities between Hinduism and Buddhism is the belief in reincarnation. The modern New Age movement has popularised the belief that man lives in the cycle of life, and at death, humans are reincarnated into another existence. The form of this other existence is determined by 'karma', which is effectively merit achieved by doing good.

In Buddhism karma is gained by 'the Eightfold Path'. Buddists believe that if a man can obtain credit as a good person then reincarnation will be beneficial; perhaps being reincarnated as a 'better' human being. However 'bad karma' can result in reincarnation that may bring them back as a cow, or even a flea!

Some disciplines of Buddhism are derived from Hinduism, particularly yoga as a form of meditation. As Christians we must beware of the non-religious branding of these practices; realising their origin and potential danger. Similar dangerous forms of meditation are also found in Reiki and the Martial Arts.

The meditative disciplines of Buddhism are exercised in order to achieve the eradication of personal suffering and eventually 'nirvana'; a state where suffering is completely excluded from life because all cravings, desires, and ambitions have disappeared. Once nirvana is achieved, reincarnation is no longer necessary: a transcendent state of permanent oblivion has now been reached.

An interesting fact is that not even Buddha could say what nirvana really was; indicating the obscure nature of the Buddhist faith and the lack of a sure foundation.

The development of this religion is also of interest. Obviously it spread in India where it originated, but it spread abroad even in Buddha's lifetime. After Buddha's death Buddhism was unable to hold ground in India, and that is why today the majority of Buddhists are found in countries such as Sri Lanka, and beyond India into Burma and Thailand. There are an estimated 500-600 million Buddhists in the world today and their religion has evolved different branches. One of the most famous branches is Zen Buddhism, which originated in China and today is practised in Japan.

Buddhism is common now in the West. A film recently was released entitled 'Seven Years in Tibet' starring a Bollywood celebrity and the Hollywood star Brad Pitt. This film is about 'the Lord Buddha', the Dali Lama of the day, and traces the story of his life. Brad Pitt claims to have been greatly affected by the film. Another interesting fact is that Richard Gere, a devout Buddhist, wanted to produce the film. This shows a greater awareness and acceptance of Buddhist beliefs. Gaynor Faye, a British Television actress, is also Buddhist.

The celebrity factor obviously popularises Buddhism. In a *New York Times* article by Gustav Niebuhr published on 3rd June 2001 it was reported that Buddhist meditation was practised in USA prisons and that it was having positive results. This positive outcome, however, may be as a result of the practice of mediation preoccupying the inmates!

Buddha's understanding of reincarnation was not that there is a soul to be born, but rather there is to be a rearrangement of the elements of a person's identity: 'the self'. It could therefore be said that Buddhism is, in this respect, a 'self-centred' religion. This impression is further confirmed when it is understood that there is no divine being in Buddhism: no God. Belief in God is perceived as ignorance. Rather than 'God-focused', Buddhism pursues the 'search for the hero inside yourself.'

Below is an interview with the 'Most Venerable Dr M. Vajiragnana', from the London Buddhist Vihara, in which he expresses, in very clear terms, how the Buddhist does not believe in God.[1]

> Interviewer: You can be certain that whoever thought up these programmes was not a Buddhist, for no Buddhist would put God first. No Buddhist would put God anywhere. Speculation about eternity is discouraged in the most basic forms of Buddhism, concentration is on the here and now, the need to penetrate who we are, what tight corner we find ourselves in, and how we escape the wall-to-wall craving that equals human life. The one who woke up to an understanding of these things is the Buddha. The path of the Buddha bypasses God as one of the 1001 distractions that serious wayfarers do without.
>
> Dr Vajiragnana: According to Buddhism there's nothing created, everything comes as cause and effect.

Interviewer: How is it that the idea of God has arisen in the world?

Dr Vajiragnana: As we Buddhists believe, purely due to the fear and also due to ignorance.

Interviewer: Fear and ignorance?

Dr Vajiragnana: Yes, fear and ignorance. Ignorance means the not understanding things as they really are, because when natural things happened they didn't know how to tackle it, and how to handle it, and how to realise it; and they thought that there was a powerful being who does these things, or there was a powerful being behind of [sic.] all those things. To prevent any danger from that powerful being they started venerating or praising or praying to that unseen being whom they have created by themselves as a god.

Interviewer: How did we emerge?

Dr Vajiragnana: Absolute first cause is not to be found, because it was in the dim past.

Interviewer: And there's no point spending energy trying to go back to the first cause?

Dr Vajiragnana: No point at all, because it doesn't help us to solve the problems in the modern, in the present-day life.

Interviewer: Does anything come to our rescue when things go rough in Buddhism?

Dr Vajiragnana: Nothing from outside. Again we have to go back to say cause and effect, and we have to think about what is in the popular language 'karma' and results.

Interviewer: Sorry, I didn't get that...

Dr Vajiragnana: Actions and results.

Interviewer: Actions and results - and you have to look into that to explain the position you are in.

Dr Vajiragnana: Yes, and our position will be explained by karmic theory.

Interviewer: Karmic theory?

Dr Vajiragnana: Yes, karmic theory, and those who have done good things are happy, and they are enjoying; and those who have done bad deeds in the past, they are not happy, or they are unhappy, or sometimes we can say they are suffering.

Interviewer: We sometimes need, as human beings, a parental hug or a shoulder to cry on - now where does a Buddhist find that sort of comfort?

Dr Vajiragnana: We don't have anybody to hug for comfort, as man has created God to have that comfort. In Buddhism we don't have something of that nature, and we are born of our karma or actions, and we are dependent on our actions, and it is our own actions that will do everything for us.

Interviewer: Where does compassion come in? There's no God to give compassion, where does compassion come from?

Dr Vajiragnana: Compassion is not coming from outside, it is a human feeling. It is like not only compassion, love, compassion, kindness, sympathetic joy, equanimity - these are human feelings and human emotions, they're not coming from outside. We can create them, and we can be comforted by ourselves thinking about our own lifestyle or way of living. When we do good things we can be comforted by ourselves:'Oh, I have done good things. Oh, I have done something good' - and that gives comfort.

When Dr Vajiragnana was asked,

What then is the source of compassion that you have in your life?

Dr Vajiragnana replied,

Well, we do not need compassion from God, but can receive this from ourselves.

Buddhism, then, is a religion that could be classified as centring on self:'God is not in any of their thoughts'; Ps 10:4. One paraphrase renders Ps 10:4:'He seems to think that God is dead.' How sad that this appears to be the view of the Buddhism.

Buddhism Versus The Bible

What is the Christian message, and how does the Christian message compare with what the Buddha taught?

The Christian message is found in the Bible and Christians believe the Bible is the truth, the whole truth, and nothing but the truth. The Bible's supreme message is first about God, and then secondly, it tells us about ourselves. Unlike the message of Buddhism, the Bible tells us that God does exist and that He can be known. The God of the Bible is more than a force or life that is reincarnated through various cycles and through generations. He is a personal God who can be known personally. Indeed the whole reason for the existence of human life, according to the Bible, is that we might come to know God.

The Bible is the revelation of God: how God has revealed Himself. The Book of the Apocalypse, at the end of the New Testament, has been entitled the book of the

Revelation; but the whole Bible has been classified as 'revelation', because in it God reveals Himself to mankind. As we read the New Testament we find that the Old Testament Scriptures were pointing to the day when there would be a Messiah born to declare God to the human race. Hebrews 1:2-3 records that in these last days, God has spoken to us by His Son.

The author of Hebrews goes on to define who His Son is and says,

> ...whom he hath appointed heir of all things, by whom also he made the worlds; Who being the brightness of his glory, and the express image of his person, upholds all things by the word of his power.

God is personal, and the Bible teaches that God is knowable through His Son, Jesus Christ, who made the worlds and who upholds all things by the word of His power. He is God the Son and John 1 says that He is the Word of God: 'logos', 'the expression of God's mind.'

Therefore, if man wishes to know what God is like, he must look to the Lord Jesus Christ in whom God is fully declared. God is knowable personally, through the Lord Jesus Christ, the Son of God.

The Bible also tells us that God is the Creator, Genesis 1:1 writes,

> In the beginning God....

God as Creator pre-existed all of creation, the universe and all matter. Not only does the Bible tell us that God is our Creator, but it tells us also that as His creatures we are answerable to Him. Hebrews 9:27 writes,

> ...it is appointed unto man once to die, and after this the judgment.

Revelation 21 speaks of the judgment: how one day men and women, without Christ, will stand before a Great White Throne, and God will open the books and judge them.

We will be held responsible and judged for our deeds because there is a Creator God.

The Bible tells us also that our very lives depend on God. Job could say, in the Old Testament, that his very breath was held in the hand of God; Job 12:10. In Acts 17:28, Paul the Apostle, preaching to the Greeks reinforces the truth that in God,

> . . . we live, we move, we have our being. . . .

Our very existence, the next breath we take, is a gift from God and we ought to be thankful to Him for it.

Buddhism contradicts what the revelation of the Bible teaches.

The Bible also teaches about man, and it does not paint a pretty picture. It tells us we, by nature, are sinners and totally depraved. This does not mean that humans are as evil and wicked as they could be, but it does mean that the stain of sin taints everything in our lives. Even our good works, the Bible says, are like filthy rags in the eyes of God; Isaiah 64:6.

The Psalmist David, in Psalm 51:5, said,

> Behold, I was shapen in iniquity; and in sin did my mother conceive me.

We know from this verse that life begins at conception and so does, life as a sinner!

Romans 3:23 is very clear; Paul said there is no difference in humanity,

> For all have sinned, and come short of the glory of God.

We are all lawbreakers. God has given us His good laws: thou shalt not kill, thou shalt not steal, thou shalt not commit adultery and thou shalt have no other gods before

Him. We have broken these laws and the reason we have transgressed is because we want to please ourselves rather than God!

John 3:19 writes,

> And this is the condemnation, that light is come into the world, and men loved darkness rather than light, because their deeds were evil.

We are sinners and we can not escape from that truth.   We please ourselves intrinsically and deserve to be judged. Our self-pleasing condemns us as guilty in the eyes of God. God declared in Ezekiel 18:4 saying,

> . . . the soul that sinneth, it shall die.

Romans 6:23 also writes,

> ...the wages of sin is death. . . .

Our sins and our iniquities have separated us from our God and our sins have hid His face from us; Isaiah 59:2. Hell, originally prepared for the Devil and his angels; Matthew 25:41, will also be the place of punishment for sinners.

Man is guilty, and the fact of the matter is, man is hopeless. *This* is the reason for human suffering. The human race is hopeless; there is no *'hero inside us'*! Nothing in us can commend us to God, and we cannot change our nature! Our nature is fallen, separated from God.

Jeremiah 13:23 writes,

> Can the Ethiopian change his skin, or the leopard change his spots? Then may ye also do good, that are accustomed to do evil.

The Buddha taught that evil comes from without, that evil comes from suffering, but if we read Matthew 15, the Lord Jesus Christ taught that evil comes from within. Matthew 15:18-19 writes,

> . . . those things which proceed out of the mouth come forth from the heart; and they defile the man. For out of the heart proceed evil thoughts, murders, adulteries, fornications, thefts, false witness, blasphemies.

The acts man commits externally may be sinful, but the motivations for those acts are not external, they are internal. We sin when we follow the lust that is in our heart; James 1:14-15.

John records in John 2:25 that the Lord Jesus Christ,

> . . . needed not that any should testify of man: for he knew what was in man.

The Lord Jesus knew that man had a fallen nature.

The Buddhist, as we have observed, does not claim to need deliverance from any external source but rather derives help from 'the self'. The wonderful message of the New Testament gospel is that despite humanity being hopeless, God has so loved the world that He did something about this hopeless, lost state. The Bible says that He sent His Son, His only begotten Son, into the world.

John 3:16 writes,

> For God so loved the world, that he gave his only begotten Son, that whosoever believeth in him should not perish, but have everlasting life.

The Son of God came to earth as a man in human flesh, and went to the cross to take the punishment for all the wrongs of humanity.

The solution to 'bad karma' is not 'good karma', but Calvary, the cross, and the blood of Jesus Christ.

Who can claim, honestly, to have delivered themselves from evil? Who can escape its symptoms? Who can quench its cravings and its desires, its selfishness, its pride, its envy, its jealousy, its covetousness and its anger? The truth is, we cannot escape what is in our hearts and in our nature. We live as fallen creatures in a fallen world: that is why there is suffering!

In the beginning God told Adam and Eve not to take the fruit of the tree of the knowledge of good and evil, but they took from it, and from that moment death and sin came upon the world; Romans 5:12.

Buddhism maintains that by following the eightfold path suffering will be eradicated.

Do you know what the sad news is? Desires cannot be eliminated: the sinful behaviour that we manifest is because there is a sinner's heart in our breast. It is impossible to stop this behaviour; but even if you could, what about everybody else in the world? What about the man who crashes into your car, or the man who steals your wife? That is not a craving that *you* had and for which you are suffering: someone else is guilty. Therefore, even if we could reach nirvana, and we cannot, nirvana would not prevent others causing us suffering.

Buddhism is not the answer to sin and suffering. In fact Buddhism has no answers for suffering sinners!

Christians do not claim to have an answer to every question asked in this life. However, God has given us the answers to life's greatest questions in the Bible. He has told us that suffering is because of sin. This does not mean that specific sins in our lives necessarily cause specific sufferings, but rather that the sufferings in this world today are as a direct result, not of bad karma, but of original sin.

God has told us that it is impossible to change what we are inside, however hard we might try. Buddhism, like every other false religion and cult in this world is, man's attempt to lift himself up by his own bootlaces! It is man's effort to get to God. Contrast this with the Gospel where God is coming to man, as man, to bring him to God!

Buddhism is sure to fail because it suppresses the symptoms of sin, and therefore does not solve the problem of its source.

Jesus Christ by taking our sins on Himself and becoming cursed for them by God on the cross, gives us in return, through our act of faith, His own goodness! The Lord Jesus gives us a new heart, a new nature: old things pass away, behold all things become new; 2 Corinthians 5:17. Peter says we are given the divine nature, the very life of God in us by the Holy Spirit; 2 Peter 1:4.

What could be better than that? God deals with the source!

Buddhism versus the Bible is the issue of Buddhism versus the truth!

In John 14:6 Jesus says,

> I am ... the truth ... no man cometh unto the Father but by me.

Do you doubt that Jesus Christ is the only truth? Can I give you four reasons why He is the truth, and why you should believe in Him?

First, the Lord Jesus Christ's **biography was written before His birth**. We read in the Old Testament, in the book of Micah that Christ would be born in Bethlehem Ephratah Micah 5:2: the very town where He was born; Matthew 2:5-6. Isaiah 7:14 tells us, that Christ's birth would be to a virgin; Matthew 1:23. Also Isaiah 7:14 records that Christ would be called Immanuel: the same name that the angel announced to Mary; Matthew 1:23.

Second, the Lord Jesus Christ's **life is unique**. Nicodemus, commenting on Christ's miracles, could say, 'No man can do these things except God be with Him'; John 3:2. Look at His wonderful words! Who could teach like Christ?

Third, the Lord Jesus Christ's **death was unique**. Christ lived a perfect life, no one at His crucifixion could point the finger and say, 'This is a sin that I saw Him do, this is a wicked word I heard Him speak': yet they crucified Him! Christ said that no man could take His life from Him; He laid it down Himself; John 10:18. Christ prophesied His own death when He said that He would go into Jerusalem and die at the hands of wicked sinners, and would rise again the third day. Christ did die, and He died for sinners.

Fourth, the Lord Jesus Christ's **resurrection was unique**. Three days after Christ's death He was raised to life again; and it has been proven, as historical fact, that He is raised, and He is alive! Buddha is dead, but Christ lives, and He is coming again.

May I conclude with a double challenge? A challenge first of all to the Christian: there are 500-600 million Buddhists in our world; how shall they hear without a preacher? Will you go and tell them? Right across the Asiatic world there are people who only know the mistaken beliefs of Buddhism. The Truth, the Lord Jesus Christ, who alone can bring them to God, is unknown to them. Have they even ever heard the name of Jesus?

What about you? Are you a Buddhist? Have you been imbibing Buddhist teaching? All false religions are trying to get to God in their own strength. It is not only a characteristic of religion, but of proud mankind. God's Word to you is: change your mind about your sinful self and by faith, embrace the Saviour! Will you do that now? Will you come to Christ?

Footnotes

1   From a Channel Four British TV documentary on Buddhism, Faith, Hope and Charity, 1991.

Chapter 9
The Baha'i Faith

The Baha'i Faith originated in Iran and it presently has a worldwide membership of approximately 5 million.

The Baha'i Faith grew out of the religion of Islam and it is like its despised stepchild. Most Muslims consider the Baha'i Faith as apostate because it believes their founder; Baha'u'llah to be a greater prophet than Mohammed; the highly esteemed prophet of Islam.

The Baha'i Faith presently suffers a reign of terror and persecution from its Muslim brothers. Today hundreds are imprisoned for their Baha'i Faith: thousands lose their possessions and homes and they are under continuous persecution.

Whilst we are engaged in this biblical examination of religious cults and world faiths we must, as Christians, defend and maintain the right of all everywhere, at home and abroad, regardless of culture and race, to worship in freedom and peace according to their conscience.

The Origins Of The Baha'i Faith

The Baha'i Faith first appeared in Persia over 100 years ago. At that time, many Persian Muslims felt that their religion was so corrupted that the arrival of the promised one was imminent.

In the 1840s, a young Persian merchant calling himself 'the Bab' announced that he, indeed, was the promised one: the purifier of the faith. According to the Bab he was the herald of a greater one yet to come. 'The Bab' means 'the gate', thus portraying how the Bab would prepare the way for the great prophet.

This merchant maintained that Islam and indeed, all of society, must be reformed by new spiritual and social teachings. The Bab's message was radical, even militant: followers must be prepared to shed their blood for the cause.

Not surprisingly the authorities saw the 'Babi' movement as a threat. Three thousand followers were put to death: often after violent clashes with government troops. The Bab himself was imprisoned and subsequently charged with heresy. In July 1850 the Bab was shot. With most of its leaders dead or sent into exile the 'Babi' movement began to fade.

A resurgence however came about under the leadership of Mirza Husayn Ali: the Baha'u'llah, a follower of the Bab. Whilst languishing in a Persian prison, Baha'u'llah maintained that a vision inferring new status on him was revealed.

In 1863 the Baha'u'llah announced himself as the new messenger of God. He claimed to be the promised one of all religions: the Second Coming of Christ, the Jewish Lord of Hosts, and the Mahdi awaited by the Muslims. It apparently had been revealed to Baha'u'llah that until his time, all the great religions of the world were true but, the time had now come for him, as the latest messenger from God, to reveal a new message of peace and unity in the one faith: the Baha'i Faith. The Baha'u'llah was to be the promised one and the fulfilment of everything that every religious system and belief has ever sought.

As Baha'u'llah's message spread the authorities exiled him further and further away from Persia. He and his family were shunted around the Ottoman Empire, arriving finally in 1868 at the prison city of Akká on the West Coast of Palestine. It is said Baha'u'llah's followers camped underneath the windows waiting for a glimpse of their messiah.

Inside his cell, despite the harsh and cramped conditions, Baha'u'llah developed the principles of his new Baha'i religion. He sat down a new code of laws and social teachings, which he said would transform mankind: racial equality, the abolition of poverty, the creation of a universal language, and for the future a Baha'i world government under one god.

Baha'u'llah sent letters to the kings and rulers of the earth, calling on them to set up an international tribunal to stop all wars. No one replied although it was rumoured that Queen Victoria looked kindly on his message.

Baha'u'llah spent the last 20 years of his life in a mansion on the outskirts of Akká, having convinced his jailers that he and his teachings were not a threat. There he completed his writings; nearly a hundred volumes of spiritual and social teachings, which provided a foundation for the growth of the religion. Baha'u'llah appointed his eldest son Abdul Baha to lead the faith.

Baha'u'llah's kindly disposition attracted many indeed, many thought the Baha'u'llah was Christ returned to earth.

Pilgrims from the West began to visit: attracted by this gentle mystical religion of the Baha'u'llah.

The attraction was mutual, for just as the West had come to Abdul Baha, so in 1911 Abdul Baha decided to go to the West.[1]

What Is Baha'ism?

'Baha'u'llah' simply means 'the glory of God' and 'the Baha'i' are the 'followers of that glory of God'. In J.E. Esslemont's book *Baha'u'llah and the New Era: An Introduction to the Baha'i Faith* 1980 p.71, Abdul Baha, the Baha'i Faith leader explains that:

> To be a Baha'i simply means to love all the world; to love humanity and try to serve it; to work for universal peace and universal brotherhood.

The Baha'i Faith believes in one God; in a unity of all the prophets from all religions and in a principle of the oneness of the entire human race. In this excerpt from *Uniting the Human Family: The Baha'i Faith* 1998 p.5 this idea of unity is communicated,

> If you imagine all people as the leaves on one tree, though we are of different size, shape, and hue, the same sun warms us and the same rain nourishes us. Imagine us all as drops in one ocean or waves of the one sea. Your souls are as waves on the sea of the spirit; although each individual is a distinct wave, the ocean is one, all are united in God.

In the Baha'i Faith there is no room for anything that divides humanity. The Baha'i Scriptures teach,

> Love ye all religions and races with a love that is true and sincere and show that love through deeds.

We, as Christians, also believe that we should live together in harmony and that regardless of culture or religion we should love one another in the fashion that Christ exemplified and taught. However, as Christians we can not deny the exclusive claim of the gospel: Christ is the only way to God. It is contradictory to say a person can be a Christian yet believe that there are other ways to reach God apart from Christ.

Herein, lies a fundamental misunderstanding of the Christian position. Often it is perceived that Christians are bigoted and against other cultures because they take issue with a particular religion. However, to preach that there is only one way to God through Jesus Christ His Son is not racist or bigoted. In fact, the terms Christian and racist from a biblical perspective are mutually exclusive. According to the Bible you cannot be both.

Contradiction is found in the Baha'i Faith, which attempts, without realising it, to deny the obvious cultural, racial and religious differences of humanity. Those who retain racial, cultural or religious distinctions are viewed as an obstruction to the Baha'i. All religionists are deemed intolerable unless they accept the Baha'i Faith's assessment that there are essentially no contradictions in religion. The Baha'i Faith is **exclusivist** in its claims.

From my experience I have found the Baha'i Faith tolerant only when its beliefs are embraced, but if one should agree to differ the tolerance ends. As a consequence of this critique on the Baha'i Faith I was reported to the authorities and accused of Incitement to Racial and Religious Hatred.

Further expression of the Baha'i Faith's teaching regarding religious unity is found in *Gleanings from the Writings of the Baha'u'llah* p.217,

> There can be no doubt whatever that the peoples of the world, of whatever race or religion, derive their inspiration from one heavenly source, and are the subjects of one God. The difference between the ordinances under which they abide should be attributed to the varying requirements and exigencies of the age in which they were revealed. All of them … were ordained of God, and are a reflection of His Will and Purpose.

This unity principle under-girds all the other doctrines of the Baha'i Faith. In all there are 10 doctrines. Briefly summarised they are:

there is one God,

major faiths come from God and are one religion,

humanity is one family,

prejudice is destructive, so to disagree with any other particular religion or to have any sectarian bias at all, is the true evil in the Baha'i Faith,

everyone must receive an education,

a world government is needed to uphold world peace,

science and religion must agree,

there ought to be an international auxiliary language,

essentially God's creation is good,

and

the faith of God is progressive in nature.

The Baha'i Faith believe that God, through the many faiths, has revealed various stages of truth down through the ages. Baha'i's believe that there are between nine and twelve divine manifestations in history. The first was an unknown prophet, then there was Krishna, then the patriarch Abraham, followed by Hud, Salih, Moses, Zoroaster, Buddha, Christ, Mohammed, the Bab and then the final prophet, Baha'u'llah.

This is a classic **theological** characteristic of a cult or false religion: the claim to reveal a **new revelation** from God that is **exclusively** found in their group or particular **anointed prophet**.

In *Baha'i World Faith* pp.20-28 the Baha'u'llah himself wrote concerning the various manifestations of God through the world religions,

> If thou wilt observe with discriminating eyes, thou wilt behold them all abiding in the same tabernacle, soaring in the same heaven, seated upon the same throne, uttering the same speech, and proclaiming the same faith.

This allows the Baha'i Faith to legitimise all religions as emanating from God.

The distinctive temples of the Baha'i Faith reflect the teaching of the Baha'i. The nine sides represent the nine major international living religions in our world. Even the architecture reflects this unity: a synagogue, a mosque and a cathedral. Whilst the Baha'i Faith has no living prophet today, it does have a council, a ruling body of nine individuals who rule from the 'temple of justice'. The religious backgrounds of these nine represent the nine international religions of the world.

The Baha'i Faith Versus The Bible

Are the gods of every religion really the same, single God? Are all the nine major world religions really one? Should we ignore the 'petty' theological differences in various religions and come together as one world faith?

The Baha'i Faith claims they are compatible with Christianity and that their members are as 'Christian' as anyone To be more specific we must ask, from our perspective, if Christianity is compatible with the Baha'i Faith.

In the light of the Holy Scriptures let us analyse some of these Baha'i teachings.

From the first book of the Bible and right through to the last book of the Bible, God has said it is foolishness to attempt to unite world religion.

God has clearly expressed His opposition to any attempt on the part of mankind to unify world religions. It is utterly futile. It will fail. It must fail! Why? Unity, if it is to be true unity in God's eyes, must be unity based on truth. To deny the obvious differences between all world faiths and then to say that we can in some way bridge those differences by claiming unity, is irrational and unreasonable.

There is incredible diversity in world religion. There are religions that believe in an impersonal God. Yet others, like Christianity, Judaism, and Islam believe in a personal knowable God but, they disagree on how to worship and approach that God.

Some religions are polytheistic. Hinduism has millions of gods, yet Judaism, Islam and Christianity are monotheistic religions. The Baha'i Faith claims to be monotheistic yet it also claims to have the same faith as the polytheistic religions that worship many gods.

Some religions believe that God is able to beget and others do not believe that God has begotten a Son. Others believe that their God is transcendent to the extent that He is unconcerned about humanity, whilst others believe that God is intrinsically involved in human lives, day by day.

It is absurd to say that all religions stem from the one faith when such contradictions exist.

Ankerberg and Weldon in the *Encyclopaedia of Cults and New Religions*, p.66, articulate the Baha'i Faith's view as to how Christianity has erred:

> Today, Christians make the same mistake the Jews made 2,000 years ago. They are so concerned with their own ideas of what Christ is that they cannot see the spirit of Christ in Baha'u'llah.

The Baha'u'llah is perceived as another **revelation** of God, in the same vein as Christians claim Christ is, or Muslims claim Mohammed was. The Baha'i Faith claim that Christians cannot see past the historical Christ, and in not doing so fail to recognise that the 'Christ spirit' is with us today in the Baha'u'llah and the Baha'i Faith.

Below is a quotation from Dr Keith Munro, a medical doctor from Londonderry, Northern Ireland who is a member of the Baha'i Faith. He claims that he could be classed as a Christian because he is following in Christ's steps by believing the Baha'i Faith and following the Baha'u'llah in the world today.

> I believe that mine (Dr Keith Munro's Baha'i Faith)[2] is the same as Christianity, which is the same as the others. In other words, there has always been one religion, it happens to have had a different name in each age. I am now obeying Jesus Christ by turning to Baha'u'llah. One could say that it is like the days of the week, in other words: the sun rises on a Monday, Tuesday, Wednesday, Thursday, Friday, we know it is the same sun - but we can also say that it is the sun of Monday, it is the sun of Tuesday. It is coming up on the horizon at a slightly different spot each day as the year goes through. So you could say that the sun - s-u-n - of Christ arose in Judea, the sun of Mohammed arose in Arabia, and so on and so on. So that, to us - and Baha'u'llah makes this very categorical - he says 'Make no difference between any of the manifestations of God', he calls them manifestations, the prophets of God. Now beyond that, Baha'u'llah says that, 'Every fixed star out there in the universe hath its planets, and every planet its forms of life whose number no man can compute' - interesting word he used 100 years ago, 'compute', for they had no computers then, but it is very apt today. Now that, you see, has broadened my consciousness to realise that, my goodness, this almighty loving God who has created the human race here on this little piece of dust in this little part of the galaxy, in one galaxy amongst millions, also has made human beings on other planets, in other systems, in other galaxies, and they're all unique.[3]

The Baha'i Faith believes that other galaxies have life forms with their own Christs and prophets. Many in the Baha'i Faith use this illustration that Dr Keith Munro used of the days of the week. In the same way they claim: that in the day of Islam, Mohammed reflected the light of God and that in the day of Christianity, Christ reflected the light. The Baha'i Faith believes that from the 1800's until today the mirror reflecting the glory of God is the Baha'u'llah.

In this politically correct age such teaching is very popular. However, when the Scriptures are examined we find that this is far from what God says is true.

According to Dr Keith Munro, Christians have got it wrong, expecting Christ to return again to the earth when He has already come. Dr Keith Munro says, 'Christ has come in the Baha'u'llah!' and he challenges Christians to examine the evidence.

Let us do that.

The Bible does not once mention the Baha'u'llah. If the Baha'u'llah is the epitome of all faiths, and particularly the Christian faith, and if he is the actual Second Advent of the Lord Jesus Christ; it would be expected that the Bible would mention his name.

This is not the case.

Indirectly, however there are a few references to a Baha'u'llah. One is found in Matthew 24:4-5,

> And Jesus answered and said unto them, Take heed that no man deceive you. For many shall come in my name, saying, I am Christ; and shall deceive many.

The Baha'u'llah in claiming: 'I am Christ who has come; I am the Matraiya of Buddhism; I am the 'Day of God' for Muslims; I am the same spirit that was in Mohammed for the Islamic religion; I am the epitome of every religion that has ever lived and every prophet that has ever prophesied,' is deceiving.

Another Bible reference that could be applied to the Baha'u'llah is in 2 Corinthians 11:13-15 where Paul said,

For such are false apostles, deceitful workers, transforming themselves into the apostles of Christ. And do not marvel; for Satan himself is transformed into an angel of light. Therefore it is no great thing if his ministers also be transformed as the ministers of righteousness; whose end shall be according to their works.

The Lord Jesus in Matthew 24:4 and the Apostle Paul in 2 Corinthians 11:13-15 foretold that others would come and claim to be Christ, even Christ in His Second Advent but, we were not to believe them, for they would be anti-Christs!

The Baha'i Faith claims that the Baha'u'llah has fulfilled many of the prophecies concerning the coming of Messiah as foretold in the Old and New Testament. This is impossible.

First of all, the Baha'u'llah was of Iranian descent, whereas the Messiah was to be Jewish; Matthew 1, Genesis 12:1-3, 2 Samuel 7:12-13.

Of even more significance is the fact that the New Testament tells us that the fulfilment of all Old Testament prophecies are to be found in Jesus, who was born in Bethlehem's manger. Hundreds of Old Testament prophecies have been fulfilled in the New Testament Jesus. Isaiah 7:14 foretold that He would be born of a virgin and would be called Immanuel. Isaiah 9:6-7 spoke of His government and how it would be without end. Isaiah 53, described His death and His propitiation through the cross for the sins of His people. Jesus the Nazarene was the fulfilment of all of these prophecies.

The Baha'u'llah does not fit any of these prophecies: he was not born in Bethlehem, he was not called Immanuel, he did not die on a cross and he did not rule in Jerusalem.

Like many other false religions and cults, the Baha'i Faith interprets the Scriptures using 'isogesis'. 'Exegesis' is correctly dissecting the Scriptures, dividing up the Word of Truth to find out what God is communicating through the Bible. 'Isogesis' is forcing subjective conjecture upon Scripture. It is to bring something foreign, from outside of Scripture and then to impose it upon the biblical account.

At Christ's ascension He spoke regarding the nature of His Second Coming. Acts 1:9-11 records,

> And when he (Christ)[4] had spoken these things while they (the disciples)[5], beheld, he was taken up; and a cloud received him out of their sight. And while they looked steadfastly toward heaven as he went up, behold, two men stood by them in white apparel; Which also said, Ye men of Galilee, why stand ye gazing up into heaven? this same Jesus, which is taken up from you into heaven, shall so come in like manner as ye have seen him go into heaven.

Note that the two angels did not say 'This same Christ... shall so come' but 'This same Jesus'. This is noteworthy because the Baha'i Faith believes in the 'Christ principle', which means that all religions have the 'logos', the Christ: some kind of light and word from God. The Baha'i believe that this spirit of Christ is in all nine world religions and that today this Christ has come in complete fulfilment in the Baha'u'llah. This belief has no basis in Scripture.

Again, note the detailed accuracy of the Scriptures: not 'This same Christ,' but 'This same Jesus will come in like manner as ye have seen him go into heaven.' This confirms that the 'Christ principle' will not return upon the Baha'u'llah but it will be *Jesus* Christ who will return.

Zechariah 14:4 prophecies that at Christ's return His feet will touch the Mount of Olives and there will be great sights for everyone to see.

Revelation 1:7 says,

> Behold, he cometh with clouds; and every eye shall see him, and they also which pierced him: and all kindreds of the earth shall wail because of him.

Did the Baha'u'llah come on a cloud? Was the Baha'u'llah crucified? Did he have nail-prints in his hands and on his feet, and a scar in his side? Did the nations of the world wail when he came?

The Jesus of the Baha'i Faith is not the biblical Jesus of whom Paul and the other Apostles preached. As far as Paul was concerned, Jesus Christ was God's final revelation to man: there could not be another 'Jesus'.

The Apostle Peter in his sermon recorded in Acts 4:12, concurred that Jesus Christ was the only way to God,

> Neither is there salvation in any other: for there is none other name under heaven given among men, whereby we must be saved.

Again Paul declared with equal certainty to Timothy in 1 Timothy 2:5,

> For there is one God, and one mediator between God and men, the man Christ Jesus.

A 'Christ principle' is not mentioned, but 'the man Christ Jesus' is. The Baha'i Faith preaches a false Christ because Jesus claimed to be God and claimed to be God's unique Son.

John 3:16 tells us that,

> For God so loved the world, that he gave his only begotten Son....

Jesus Christ is the only Son that God begot in this unique way: the Greek word for 'begotten' carries the idea of 'one-of-a-kind'. Jesus is one-of-a-kind, and always will be. He had the same nature as His Father; divine, and He claimed to be the Son of God. The Jewish people of His day understood what Jesus was attributing to Himself. In John 5:18 we read that the people realising that Jesus was claiming to be God picked up rocks to stone Him to death. Many other instances in the Gospels show clearly that Jesus claimed to be God's unique Son.

Paul in Colossians 1:16 shows that the Lord Jesus is also the Creator of the universe,

> For by him were all things created, that are in heaven, and that are in earth, visible and invisible, whether they be thrones, or dominions, or principalities, or powers: all things were created by him, and for him.

John 1:3 also declares that,

> All things were made by him; and without him was not any thing made that was made.

Therefore the Bible teaches that the Lord Jesus Christ was the incarnation of God and He was also the Creator. The Baha'i Faith believes that Christ was just one of these 'Christ spirits' and that Jesus had this 'Christ spirit' within Him revealing something of God. In the Baha'i Faith Jesus was not unique; Mohammed also had the Christ spirit within him and it now resides in the Baha'u'llah. The Scriptures show how false this teaching is when it declares plainly that Christ, the Creator of the universe, did not come to reside in a man or on a man but He became a man!

John 1:14 says,

> And the Word was made flesh, and dwelt among us....

The Bible teaches that to deny either the humanity or the deity of Christ is heresy; 1 John 4:2-3. Jesus is 'Immanuel'; 'God with us'; Matthew 1:23. He is the greatest and only revelation of God.

John 1:18, reads,

> No man hath seen God at any time; the only begotten Son, which is in the bosom of the Father, he hath declared him.

In John 12:45 the Lord Jesus taught the truth,

> He that seeth me seeth him that sent me.

In John 13:20 the Lord Jesus declares,

> Verily, verily, I say unto you, He that receiveth whomsoever I send receiveth me; and he that receiveth me receiveth him that sent me.

The writer to the Hebrews is emphatic regarding Christ's unique position as God's revelation when he states in Hebrews 1:1-2,

> God, who at sundry times and in different manners spake in time past unto the fathers by the prophets, Hath in these last days spoken unto us by his Son, whom He hath appointed heir of all things, by whom also He made the worlds.

God has spoken in the incarnation of His Son and to deny that is error. To deny Christ's humanity is error. To deny Christ's deity is error. Jesus Christ had two natures in one person: the nature of God and the nature of man. It is erroneous to deny either of these natures and the fact that both were together in one personality.

Jesus Christ is the only one who has revealed God and it is through Him that God has chosen to reveal Himself. This is the explanation for God opening the heavens and revealing to humanity, 'This is My beloved Son.'

The Bible exalts the Lord Jesus Christ from beginning to end. Both His humanity and His deity are extolled; His humanity is as important as His deity. If Jesus Christ was not human He could not die for us and if He could not die for us He could not save us!

From the beginning to the end of Scripture the Lord Jesus Christ's name is lifted high, so much so that Philippians 2:9-11 tells us that after accomplishing salvation by His death and resurrection,

> …God has highly exalted him, and given him a name which is above every name: That at the name of Jesus every knee should bow, of things in heaven, and things in earth, and things under the earth; And that every tongue should confess that Jesus Christ is Lord, to the glory of God the Father.

In keeping with this we read in Ephesians 1:20-21 that now Christ is raised from the dead and God has,

> …set him at his own right hand in the heavenly places, Far above all principality, and power, and might, and dominion, and every name that is named, not only in this world, but also in that which is to come.

God has given the Lord Jesus Christ centre stage of heaven and earth, above all for evermore - Hallelujah!

The Baha'u'llah lived a mere 75 years, died in 1892, and today his skeleton lies in the grave. This does not fulfil the prophecies concerning the resurrection of the Christ.

The only common ground for unity that Christians can have with anyone is upon the truth of the Bible. The truth is the only basis for fellowship because Christ is the truth and Christ is God's revelation.

Jesus said in John 14:6,

> I am the way, the truth, and the life: no man comes unto the Father, but by me.

People ask, 'How can we know truth today?' In John 17:17 Jesus prayed to His Father,

> …Thy word is truth.

The Lord Jesus says that the written Word is truth! That same written Word teaches us that God is knowable through the intimate revelation of the incarnate Son. The record of that life is found in the written Word of God that testifies that the Saviour who lived among men, who died on the cross for man's sins, and who rose again victorious, is ascended and is coming again! The Gospel of the Bible declares that through personal faith, the Lord Jesus Christ can be known in an intimate way because of His redemption and salvation. The Bible teaches that man is fallen, man is a sinner therefore He must be saved.

Contrary to the Baha'i Faith the Scriptures teach that there is a literal hell for those who reject Christ; and similarly there is a literal heaven gained by those who put faith in Christ alone.

The Baha'i Faith, as with all other false faiths and cults, gives no assurance of salvation. However, the Bible tells us that Christ's death and resurrection is able to give us the certainty and the security of heaven and salvation.

Genesis 11 records that in the past man has attempted a form of Baha'ism in a place called 'Babel'. The book of Revelation tells us that man will try it again in Babylon. Several times in history men have tried to unite races giving them one language, one faith, and every time it has failed. Man's attempts have failed because he has sought to achieve it in a way that God had not ordained.

Unity cannot be achieved by pretending problems do not exist or, by ignoring realities that cause division. Lasting unity can only be achieved through truth, and truth divides. That is why there is a separation between the saved and the lost today. That is why one day soon the Lord Jesus Christ, who is the truth, will come again and separate the sheep from the goats and send the goats to punishment and send the sheep to their inheritance. The truth uncovers sin but hallelujah, He who is the truth died for sin and can save us from sin! We must admit our sin and believe the truth of God's provision for sin, which is in the Saviour alone.

Reader, have you done this? The Baha'i Faith claims to bring all nations together. Ephesians 2:14 says,

> For He is our peace, who hath made both one, and hath broken down the middle wall of partition between us.

Christ has done what the Baha'i Faith could not do. We read from Micah 4 of a future day on this earth when there will be a temple in Jerusalem and all of the nations of the earth will come to worship. Each nationality will not worship their indigenous god or an unknown god who has no name but, Jehovah, the God of Jacob, will be worshipped!

Revelation says that worshippers will come from every people, tribe, tongue and nation. God will achieve what Baha'ism has failed to do. He will finally and perfectly unite humanity together in truth. He will unite them together in Christ.

I would exhort you: do not settle for a poor substitute! Take the Saviour that God has provided and be a part of God's masterpiece of uniting grace: the Church of Jesus Christ universal.

Footnotes

1   From a BBC TV documentary on the Baha'i Faith, Everyman, 1985.
2   Added by author for purposes of clarity.
3   From the TV documentary Beyond Belief, made by Northland Films for Ulster Television.
4   Added by author for purposes of clarity.
5   Ibid.

Chapter 10
Islam

Even though the Islamic faith has a familiar presence in most Western countries, many people are uncertain of Islamic beliefs.

The fact that Islam is an evangelistic religion seeking to proselytise others does not appear to be widely understood despite Secretary General of the Islamic Council of Europe, Salem Azzam saying that,

> The first objective of the Islamic council is to assist, support and supplement the activities... of da'wah.

Da'wah is the Islamic 'mission' to convert the world to the Islamic faith.

Today, in the United Kingdom, there is much evidence of such sustained evangelism. Buildings that were once used in Christian worship are now Muslim mosques dedicated to the worship of 'Allah'. Regents Park Mosque in London is now one of the largest mosques in Europe. It is estimated there are now 2 million Muslims in the United Kingdom and probably just over 200 mosques. In Britain, on a daily basis, there are approximately 22 million copies of Muslim newspapers published. Two million Muslims, 200 mosques and 22 million copies of newspaper, in anyone's estimation, is evidence of a vibrant religion. One of the reasons why there is this growth of the Muslim faith is that we now live in a pluralistic or multicultural society.

The increased influence that religions, other than Christianity, have brought to bear on some of the institutions of our nation here in the United Kingdom is observable.

Recently the first Muslim Baroness to enter the House of Lords, Baroness Uddin, was permitted in her initiation to swear oath in the name of Allah.

A new study undertaken by 'Yahya' Birt, formerly Jonathan Birt, the son of Lord Birt the former Director-General of the BBC, is interesting as it presents a breakdown of the latest census figures to show that there are now 14,200 indigenous British people who have converted to Islam. The Muslim Council of Britain has co-opted Joe Ahmed Dobson, another Muslim convert and son of Frank Dobson the former government Health Secretary, to the chair of its regeneration committee. Many citizens in Western countries think immigration alone is the reason for the increasing insurgence of Islam in the West today and therefore they are surprised to learn that so many nationals are being converted.

There are approximately 1.2 billion Muslims worldwide. The significance of that figure can be understood when compared to approximately 1.9 billion Christians in the world: 'Christian' is used here in the broadest possible sense.

Though the Muslim faith purports to be one united religion there are certain sects within it, among them the Sunnis, the Shi'ites, and the Sufis. Incidentally, the Koran condemns such divisions.

The Muslim faith, in general, is moving in massive strides in our world, so much so that it has been predicted that by the year 2025 a third of the world's population will be Muslim. By 2010 Islam will be the second-largest religion in the USA, and it is currently the second-largest religion in Europe. It is claimed that 1000 Muslim missionaries are trained every year and then sent out to evangelise the world for Allah. Indeed, it is the fastest growing religion in the world today.

Muslims are taking their unbiblical message across nations and continents at a staggering rate. Christians who have the truth found in the Bible need to ask themselves the question as to how their mission of world evangelism compares with Islam's.

In a world that has become more and more subjective and abstract in its beliefs, Islam, with its religious clarity, has an increasing universal appeal. Disillusionment with the Christian Church can make conversion to Islam attractive. Islam's simple creedal statement and easy to understand doctrines make it accessible to people. Its appeal is increased because it is not an ethnic religion: no one is born a Muslim. There are no racial barriers; anyone can join what is called the 'Ummah', the community of the faithful. All these factors contribute to Islam's spread around the world.

Islam is also spreading because of a backlash against Western secularism. Some Muslims perceive that certain Arab nations are in danger of becoming too 'Westernised' because of the influence of oil trade with the West. Some in the Muslim world perceive the West as immoral and decadent and therefore the fear is that Western influence may be detrimental to Islamic society, culture and religion. This reaction against secularisation has fuelled a resurgence in fundamentalist Islam.

Globally there is a worrying growth of extreme fundamentalist Islam. The attack on the Twin Towers in New York, and multiple international terror atrocities, including suicide bombs in London and other international cities all heighten our awareness of an extremely militant strain of Islam. Today in the Middle East there are more Islamic regimes, than there have ever been; most desiring to reintroduce Shari'a law, which is simply Islamic law in its most extreme form. Among other edicts Islamic law demands that a person caught in adultery should be executed and a thief should have his hand cut off. Many more fundamentalist Muslims believe Shari'a law should be universally imposed upon all nations of the world.

One major expression of fundamentalist Islamic faith today is the aggression directed against the re-emergence of the modern state of Israel. The Holy Scriptures teach clearly that Israel was God's chosen ancient people and that Abraham's son Isaac was the son of promise. However the Islamic faith claims that it was Abraham's son Ishmael who went up Mount Moriah with Abraham to be sacrificed. Muslims believe the promise of the Holy Land was given to Ishmael and not Isaac therefore, they maintain, Palestinian Muslims and, not the Jews are the rightful inheritors of the land.

What we seek to do in this book is to analyse and critique different faiths in the light of what the Bible has to say. As previously stated in this book Christians must welcome and care for all who come to their shores, no matter what their faith, race or culture. We must defend their right to worship their god in their own way.

The great tragedy however is the fact that many Muslim regimes do not afford the same religious liberties to Christians. Today many Christians in Muslim lands are martyred and persecuted because they will not deny their faith and embrace Islam. Often Christian preaching is outlawed and Christian missionaries are expelled on a regular basis from these countries. Sadly, not many political voices in the West are defending the rights of persecuted Christians. Meanwhile, some Muslims are intent on using the liberty in other lands to spread their message by Jihad; the sword, if necessary.

The Origins Of Islam

Mohammed, the founder of Islam, was born 570AD and lived for a time in Mecca, which eventually became the geographical centre of Islam.

It was Mohammed's regular practice to travel into the wilderness to visit a certain cave. On one of these visits Mohammed, during a time of contemplation and meditation, claimed that the angel Gabriel appeared to him. This was the first of many encounters that Mohammed was said to have had with Gabriel. Mohammed claimed that the angel continued to reappear to him for the next 23 years.

Supposedly Gabriel gave this command to Mohammed,

> Recite in the name of the Lord who has created,
> Created man from clots of blood,
> Recite, seeing that the Lord is the most generous,
> Who has taught by the pen,
> Taught man what he did not know.

The Arabic word for 'recite' is the word 'Qur'an', often spelt in English 'Koran' which, of course, is the name for 'the noble book'; 'the holy book', of Islam.

Mohammed was said to write down what God was reciting, word for word. Muslims believe that the Koran was written down by God on tablets in heaven and then was recited to Mohammed. Though he wrote it all down, Islam maintains that human interpretation was not incorporated. Therefore Mohammed was given these revelations of God that were never given before to men. Here we see in the origins of Islam the **theological** trait of a cult or false religion: the claim to **new revelation** never before known.

Within a century of Mohammed allegedly receiving these revelations, Islam had conquered an area greater than the Roman Empire in its height!

The Doctrines Of Islam

There appears to be some confusion as to the number of doctrines in Islam. This book knows of six.

The first doctrine is the belief that there is **'one God' and his name is Allah**. There is no Triune Godhead, Father, Son and Holy Spirit rather one god called Allah who is all seeing, all knowing and all powerful.

The second doctrine concerns **'angels'.** Angels are particularly important to the Muslim faith. It was the angel Gabriel who recited the Koran to Mohammed.

There is also a fallen angel in the Muslim theology called 'Shaitan'; similar to Satan.

The third doctrine relates to **'scripture'**. The Koran is not the only holy book in Islam; Islam believes in four inspired writings. The first is the Torah; the first five books of the Old Testament; Genesis to Deuteronomy. The second is the Zabur; the Psalms of David. The third is the Injil, which is basically an account of the life and works of Jesus. The fourth book is the Koran; Allah's final word.

The fourth doctrine is about **'Mohammed'**. The Koran lists 28 prophets of Allah, including Adam, Noah, Abraham, and even Jesus Christ. Mohammed is the last of the prophets and is understood as the greatest.

The fifth doctrine deals with the **'end times'.** This is the belief that the dead will be resurrected and then judged by Allah. Those who are righteous will be sent to heaven, which is described as a place of sensual pleasure. Many young suicide bombers lay down their lives having been promised 70 supernatural perpetual virgins who will satisfy their sensual desires for eternity. The unrighteous are those who oppose Allah and Mohammed and they will go to hell to be tortured forever.

The sixth doctrine concerns **'predetermination'**. Muslims believe Allah has predetermined everything by unchangeable decrees; a kind of fatalism

The word 'Islam' means 'submission to the will of God'. The word 'Muslim' is derived from it and means 'one who submits to the revealed will of God'. A holy person is one who follows God in His revealed way and who submits to God's will. In Islam, you submit to God's will through the practice of the 'five pillars of Islam'. If these pillars are fulfilled, and an individual remains in the Muslim faith then 'Jannah'; heaven, is a possibility, although never assured.

Muslim salvation therefore, is a salvation of works.

What are these 'five pillars'; these religious practices that are an attempt to earn salvation?

The first pillar is the **'declaration of the faith'; Shahada.** It is the verbal confession to be recited every day that declares,

> There is no true God except Allah, and Mohammed is the Messenger
> of Allah.

The second pillar is **'prayer'; Salat** The Muslim prayer involves confession of sins, which begins first of all with the purification of the body. Muslims ritually wash themselves. There are strict religious rituals laid down on how to purify the place, where one prays and on how to perform the ritual washing of the body. Even the precise physical movements and the exact words of the prayers are prescribed. The final act of prayer is to bow down with the forehead touching the ground symbolising submission to Allah. Such prayer is performed five times a day. Eventually, it is believed, there will be purification of the soul.

The third pillar is **'fasting'; Saum** which is predominantly practiced in the month of Ramadan. During Ramadan the Muslim is required not to drink, eat or engage in sexual relations during the daylight hours.

The fourth pillar is **'alms'; Zakat** which is charity to the poor. Mohammed was an orphan and valued charity greatly; therefore almsgiving holds a prominent place in Islam.

The fifth pillar is **'pilgrimage'; Hajj** to Mecca. Mecca is an astounding sight to witness. In the centre of the multitude of pilgrims there is a distinctive black cube called the 'Ka'aba' which was, reputedly the temple of idols where Mohammed discovered Allah to be the chief god of the idols.

Each Muslim is encouraged to make the pilgrimage to Mecca at least once in life provided they are physically able and can financially afford it. This pilgrimage is to be taken on the first half of the last month of the lunar year.

Many in our relativistic age conclude that Muslims worship the same God of the Christians and Jews. 'Allah' they claim is simply an Arabic name for God. On closer inspection, that is most definitely not the case. The Muslim god is not the Christian God or the Jewish God. If a £10 note is compared with a counterfeit note, how is the genuine article discerned? One does not seek to identify the similarities; obviously they would not provide the necessary information. One concentrates on the differences. Two genuine notes will have no differences. When we look at the differences between the Bible and Islam we discover quickly the discrepancies.

What Is Missing From Islam?

What is the difference between Islam and the biblical truth of Christianity?

The first and most obvious difference is that **the God of the Bible** is missing from Islam.

The black box, the Ka'aba, in the middle of the stadium in Mecca was originally found by Mohammed to be full of idols. Upon finding them, Mohammed claims that by God's leading he rejected all the other idols and chose the chief god Allah as the true deity. However, what most Muslims do not know is that the name of 'Allah' existed before Mohammed founded the Muslim faith. This is very controversial, but nevertheless is vital in our understanding of Islam's roots. The name 'Allah' is found originally in polytheistic paganism, yet the first doctrine in Islam is that there is one God and only one.

According to *The Encyclopaedia of Religion*,

> Allah is a pre-Islamic name corresponding to the Babylonian god Bel.[1]

Much ancient worship included the worship of the sun god, the moon god, and the stars. Baal worship, condemned in the Old Testament, was a similar form of worship. Scholars have now pointed out that in Arabia the sun god was female, and the moon god was male. This male, moon god was called by a variety of names but we know that one of them was 'Allah'.

Allah was married to the sun god and they had three daughters. This family of gods were viewed as 'high deities'.

The Encyclopaedia of World Mythology and Legends states of ancient people that,

> Along with Allah…they worshipped a host of lesser gods and the daughters of Allah.[2]

Archaeologists have uncovered numerous statues and hieroglyphic inscriptions in which a crescent moon is seated on the top of the head of a deity symbolising that they are the moon gods. Interestingly the crescent moon is a symbol of Islam today. It can be observed on top of mosques and even on some national flags.[3]

The God of the Bible is different from Allah because He is a God of love. The Koran betrays a tragic absence of a loving God. Allah, as he is revealed cannot love the sinner. In Islam the sinner and the ungodly are condemned. The Koran prescribes a religion of law rather than grace. Although Allah is called 'the forgiving, the merciful, the all-compassionate', you will not find one instance in the Koran where he exercises that power to have compassion over, for instance, one who is caught stealing, or one who is caught in the act of adultery.

In contrast in John 8 it is recorded that the Lord Jesus Christ had compassion on a woman caught in the very act of adultery and it was the enemies of Christ and God, the legalistic Pharisees, who wanted to stone her.

Our Lord Jesus Christ is a Saviour who demonstrated the love of God in that while we were still sinners He died for us; Romans 5:8. Romans 5:6 declares that,

> …Christ died for the ungodly.

The New Testament gospel is one of grace and unmerited favour; any trace of which cannot be found in Islam. In fact, it is not to be found in any other faith other than biblical Christianity.

We know from John 3:16-17,

> For God so loved the world, that he gave his only begotten Son, that whosoever believeth in him should not perish, but have everlasting life. God sent not his Son into the world to condemn the world; but that the world through him might be saved.

The love of God's heart is revealed in the sending of His Son to be our Saviour.

First John 4:8 declares,

> . . . God is love.

Islam does not appear to communicate the same compassionate and gracious spirit that is evidently found in the love of Christ. Is this the reason why Islam is regarded by some as a religion of the sword?

Secondly **the Christ of the Bible** is missing from Islam.

Muslims do not believe in the deity of our Lord Jesus Christ. They do not believe Christ is the incarnate Son of God as John 1:1, 14 states,

> In the beginning was the Word, and the Word was with God, and the Word was God. . . . And the Word was made flesh, and dwelt among us, (and we beheld his glory, the glory as of the only begotten of the Father) full of grace and truth.

God's Word says that Jesus Christ is God manifest in flesh. The Pharisees and religious Scribes attempted to stone Christ because He, being a man, was making Himself God; John 10:33. Islam will go as far as to say that Christ was a prophet, even sinless, but they will not affirm that He is the Son of God and the Saviour of the world. Muslims believe that Christians blaspheme in their ascribing of deity to Christ. This to Muslims is the unpardonable sin. Yet, almost every page of the New Testament testifies to the fact that Jesus Christ is, God's Son and God the Son; God manifest in flesh and the Word of God incarnate.

Muslims do, however, display a measure of respect for Christians. Even though today there is much contention between Muslims and Jews in particular, Mohammed saw both Jews and Christians as 'people of the book'; the Bible. However the Koran in Surah 4:171-172 makes clear the Muslim view of Christ when it states,

> People of the book, Go not beyond the bounds of your religion. . . The Messiah, Jesus son of Mary, was only the Messenger of God, and His word that He committed to Mary, and a Spirit from Allah. So believe in Allah and His Messengers, and say not, 'Three'. God is only One God!

Not only does the Koran deny the Triune Godhead, but it seems in places to deny that the Christ died on the cross. Surah 4:156-158 states only that, it was made to appear as if He died on the cross. Consequently Muslim belief regarding the cross is diverse: some Muslims believe that God caught Christ up before He went to the cross or that God caught Him up from the cross; other Muslims think that someone else, possibly Judas Iscariot, was crucified in the place of Christ, even by mistake or whilst other Muslims think that although Christ was on the cross, He did not in fact die.

The Holy Scriptures however are clear.

In 1 Corinthians 15:3-6 the Apostle Paul writes,

> I delivered unto you first of all that which I also received, how that Christ died for our sins according to the Scriptures; And that He was buried, and that He rose again the third day according to the Scriptures: And that He was seen of Cephas, then of the twelve: After that, He was seen of above five hundred brethren at once; of whom the greater part remain unto this present, but some are fallen asleep.

Verse 17 of the same chapter Paul reasons,

> And if Christ be not raised, your faith is vain; ye are yet in your sins.

This is the message that God revealed to men, and that was preached by the early Church. Praise God, it is a historical fact that Christ did die and rose again, and therefore when we believe in Him we are saved.

Mohammed believed that Jesus Christ foretold Mohammed's coming. Muslims claim that when Christ spoke of the coming of the Paraclete in John's Gospel that He was actually predicting the coming of Mohammed and not the Holy Spirit. Some Muslim traditions do believe that Christ will return but upon returning will marry, have children, and break the symbol of the cross acknowledging Islam to the world as the true faith.

The third truth that is missing from Islam is the **Grace of the Bible.** For a Muslim, sin is lack of obedience to Allah's law. A Muslim understands himself to be sinful only by an act, or by the lack of an act, but he does not see himself as a fallen creature: as a sinner by nature as the Bible teaches in Romans 3:23,

> . . . all have sinned and fallen short of the glory of God.

The Muslim understanding of sin, taken to its logical conclusion, means that if men do not have a sin nature, then, they do not need a Saviour. Redemption from an external source is not needed because according to the Islamic faith following the five pillars of Islam and believing the doctrines of the faith can achieve salvation. Salvation is believed to be self earned by a legalistic system of obedience. Then, one day Allah will hopefully judge that the Muslims good deeds have out-weighed their bad and they can be admitted into 'Jannah'; heaven.

Who of us can outweigh the bad in our lives by the good? Thankfully the Bible teaches us that God does not require us to earn our salvation; rather the gospel is of grace, it is unearned. Christ has delivered us from our sin through His death and resurrection. We are to repent and believe the gospel.

Ephesians 2:8-9,

> For by grace are ye saved through faith; and that not of yourselves: it
> is the gift of God: Not of works, lest any man should boast.

On the cross man's sin, by imputation, was laid on Christ and by personal faith in Him, God's righteousness can be exchanged for our sin. God imputes His righteousness to us by grace through the act of faith. This is the gospel! It is missing from Islam.

The Bible clearly teaches that Christ is the Son of God. He is the Saviour of the world who died, rose again and will return to judge the world.

Is that the Christ you believe in? The Christ who is not just a prophet, not only a good teacher, or moral man, but One who is also the Saviour of the world and the Son of God.

The Lord Jesus Christ in John 14:6 clearly stated,

> I am the way, the truth, and the life: no man cometh unto the Father,
> but by me.

The only way that God accepts a sinner is when a sinner pleads by faith the merits of His own Son.

You need to identify with the work that Christ accomplished on the cross, you need to identify yourself as a sinner, and confess - 'Lord, I am guilty of everything that You have charged me with. The Lord Jesus was not guilty of it, yet He suffered for it. I thank You for that, and I trust that work as sufficient to save me, and I ask that You will give me Your righteousness through His death. Save me now!'

Do you have a low view of yourself and a high view of the Lord Jesus Christ and His grace? If you do not you cannot be saved; there is no other way!

Footnotes

1 The Encyclopaedia of Religion, 1979, I:117.
2 The Encyclopaedia of World Mythology and Legend, I:61.
3 For more information on the origins of Islam see, Robert Morey, Islamic Invasion (Harvest House, 1992).

Chapter 11
Roman Catholicism

Many evangelical treatments of cults and religions omit an assessment of Roman Catholicism. There are a number of reasons for this.

Firstly, there is the belief that the Roman Catholic Church is another Christian Church and therefore it could not be considered another religious belief.

Secondly, there is an increasing ecumenical spirit prevailing, particularly in the Western Church that emphasises unity among religions and all Christian sects. Ecumenism encourages fellowship on the grounds of common beliefs rather than allowing differences to divide.

Thirdly, there is the understandable fear that in speaking out against Roman Catholicism, Roman Catholics may be ostracised from our efforts in evangelism. There are those sincere people who do not want to be critical of another person's faith, in case they disturb a potential mission field. Indeed, such an evangelical objection was raised regarding this particular study. The concerned man felt that this chapter was in danger of offending the Roman Catholic people whom he was trying to win with the gospel.

In reply to this fear it must be stated that this chapter does not set out to offend unnecessarily anyone or to put an unnecessary hurdle in the way of an individual trusting Christ by irresponsibly critiquing Roman Catholicism. However, if Christ is the truth, and the truth is what sets men free, it is imperative that evangelism must be honest. Evangelism must grapple transparently with the issues at hand, stating clearly and tenderly what the Bible teaches and what it does not. If this is accomplished faithfully and it is carried out in the love and compassion of Christ, then the only offence and stumbling-block possible, is the truth itself.

Roman Catholicism And Church History

'Catholic' means 'universal', and there are those who argue that Christian history shows that the Roman Catholic Church is none other than the original New Testament Church, in its modern form. It is alleged that Roman Catholic traditions and doctrines have been passed down from the Apostles to the modern day Church.

Is the Roman Catholic Church the natural descendent of original New Testament Christianity?

A brief summary of Church history will suffice to answer this question.

The Apostolic Church existed from the early 30s AD to 100AD. It was between the 40s to the mid-90s of this period that the New Testament was written.

The Apostolic Church period was a time characterised particularly by the persecution meted out by the Roman Emperors, Nero and Domitian. Several of the New Testament Epistles were written in reaction to such persecution. It was also a time of expansion of the early Church; particularly the missionary journeys of Paul and Barnabas around the known European world.

This Apostolic Church period ends about the year 100AD with the death of the Apostle John; the writer of the Gospel of John, 1, 2 and 3 John, and the book of Revelation.

After 100AD came a time that could be classed as the Persecuted Church: the year 100 through to 313AD. This period was characterised again by Roman persecution but this time it was a more planned and orchestrated onslaught.

For these first three centuries of the Church, Christians generally regarded the Bible as their only standard of rule, belief and practice.

In 311AD however, Emperor Galerius issued the 'Edict of Toleration', signalling a change in how Rome treated the Church. This Edict of Toleration proclaimed that Christians should not only be tolerated but also, that they should be allowed to worship in the Roman Empire. In 313AD the Emperor Constantine issued the 'Edict of Milan' which granted Christians not only toleration, but also total freedom.

The 'Edict of Milan' is important because it paved the way for the unification of the Church and State. In 324AD when Emperor Constantine made Christianity the official religion of the Roman Empire, thousands of pagans superficially 'converted' to Christianity, simply to benefit from the State. These 'converts' brought with them much of their pagan traditions. Many pagan gods, beliefs, and practices were assimilated into the new 'Christianity'. It is from this period that priests, unbiblical rituals, image worship etc can be observed in the Church.

Many of these pagan trends that were 'Christianised' can be traced back to Ancient Babylon, even to the Tower of Babel. The book of Revelation, particularly in chapter 17, teaches that these same characteristics of pagan Babylon will be found in the religious system of the End Time period.

To investigate further the similarities between Roman Catholicism and the worship of Ancient Babylon read 'The Two Babylons' by Alexander Hislop. Hislop's book shows that Babylonish worship is still found in Roman Catholicism, and the book predicts that such worship will, in the future, be found in the ecumenical Church that will emerge at the End Times.

From about 313 to 590AD the State Church was well established. Many of the views, recognisable today as 'Roman Catholic', were formed; perhaps not dogmatically but at least in embryo.

The organised Church changed from, what until then had been the 'Catholic Church' with each Bishop equal to one another, to become the 'Roman Catholic Church', with the Bishop of the Church of Rome as first among equals.

The Roman Catholic Church claim that when the Apostles Peter and Paul founded the Church in Rome Peter, having been appointed by Christ as His representative on earth, became the first Bishop of Rome. The 'Apostolic Succession', adopted by the Roman Catholic Church means that all the succeeding Bishops of Rome inherit this vicarship of Christ.

In 445AD the Roman Emperor officially recognised the primacy of the Roman Bishops and by 590AD the western wing of the organised Church accepted the claim that the Bishops of Rome inherit the vicarship of Christ. Leo I, 440-461AD, was the first Roman Bishop to assume the title Pope and he claimed judicial authority for the Roman Church over the entire Church.

The period that followed were the dark days of Christianity because the Mediaeval Church from 590 to 1517AD was, to a large extent, semi-pagan in its belief.

However, between 1517AD and 1648AD a rediscovery of some of the teachings of the Bible transformed this semi-pagan Church into the Reformation Church. The Word of God was once again being studied and consequently some in the Church began to protest against the false beliefs of the semi-pagan Mediaeval Church. Such protesters were labelled as 'Protestants'. Many of the original Protestants were Christians who stood up for the doctrines of the Bible. This was effectively the beginning of the Reformation.

Tradition And The Roman Catholic Church

The Second Vatican Council, 1962-65, attempted to bring about certain reforms to promote unity in Christendom. Effectively, however, Roman Catholic doctrine stayed the same, particularly in relation to how it viewed tradition.

Vatican II Chapter 2 paragraph 9 reads,

> Consequently it is not from sacred Scripture alone that the Church draws her certainty about everything which has been revealed. Therefore both sacred tradition and sacred Scripture are to be accepted and venerated with the same sense of devotion and reverence. . . . It is clear therefore that sacred Scripture and the teaching authority of the Church, in accord to God's most wise design, are so linked and joined together that one cannot stand without the other.

Another quotation from the *Catechism of the Catholic Church*, paragraph 81 states,

> Tradition transmits in its entirety the Word of God which has been entrusted to the Apostles by Christ the Lord and the Holy Spirit. It transmits it to the successors of the Apostles.

The Roman Catholic Church therefore, does not see the Bible as the only channel of God's Word. Peter and then his successors, the Bishops of Rome, are also considered mediums. Vatican II, commenting on the relation between the Scriptures and tradition, states,

> One cannot stand without the other.

Tradition in Roman Catholicism is elevated to the place of revelation. That makes tradition a **new revelation:** additional to the Bible. The claim to **new revelation** is a **theological** characteristic of a cult and false religion; inevitably it leads to the claim that salvation is **exclusively** found in the cult or religion and consequently **salvation is forfeited** upon leaving the group. All these theological trends are present in Roman Catholicism.

Roman Catholics misunderstand the role of tradition in the Bible. Tradition *is*, on occasions, spoken of positively in the Bible.

In 2 Thessalonians 3:6 Paul says,

> Now we command you, brethren, in the name of our Lord Jesus Christ, that ye withdraw yourselves from every brother that walketh disorderly, and not after the tradition which he received of us.

Again in 2 Thessalonians 2:15 and 1 Corinthians 11:2, tradition is spoken of in positive terms.

Whilst it is evident that the Bible does speak positively about some traditions in the early Church, nowhere does it sanction the Roman Catholic Church's teaching that the traditions of men and traditions of Scripture are equal.

Can a tradition still be God's revealed will if it blatantly contradicts what is taught in God's revealed Word?

In Mark 7:8-9 the Lord Jesus speaks strongly to the Pharisees on the subject of tradition. He says,

> Laying aside the commandment of God, ye hold the tradition of men, as the washing of pots and cups: and many other such like things ye do. And he said unto them, Full well ye reject the commandment of God, that ye may keep your own tradition.

Christ spoke similar words, as recorded in Matthew 15. The Apostle's teaching was the same in Colossians 2:8 where Paul says,

> Beware lest any man spoil you through philosophy and vain deceit, after the tradition of men, after the rudiments of the world, and not after Christ.

The simple teaching of the Bible is that if traditions contradict Scripture then they cannot be of God. God's Word cannot contradict itself. God has given us His Word and as Jude 3 says we are to,

> Earnestly contend for the faith which was once delivered unto the saints.

God's Word has been given, and we are called in 1 John to distinguish between the spirit of truth and the spirit of error, which is only possible when the Holy Scriptures are our absolute authority in doctrine and practice.

The Papacy

The Creed of Pope Pius IV, section 10, states what a true Roman Catholic ought to acknowledge regarding the Papacy. It reads,

> I acknowledge the Holy Catholic Apostolic Roman Church for the Mother and Mistress of all Churches, and I promise and swear true obedience to the Bishop of Rome...Successor to St Peter, Prince of the Apostles and Vicar of Jesus Christ.

The Roman Catholic Church claims that this teaching is based on several texts of Scripture. Probably the most notable of these is Matthew 16, where we read in verse 15 that the Lord Jesus asked Peter,

> Whom do men say that I am?

In verse 16 Peter confesses,

> Thou art the Christ, the Son of the Living God.

In verse 18, after the Lord says that flesh and blood did not reveal this to him but his Father in heaven, the Lord says to Peter,

> Upon this rock I will build my Church; and the gates of hell shall not prevail against it.

Roman Catholicism claims that because Peter's name means 'Rock'; 'Petros', the Church was built upon him and, subsequently on every successive Bishop of Rome. However, from the Reformation, Protestant theologians and scholars have appreciated in this verse that there is a different word used for 'Peter' and for 'rock'.

The word 'Peter' is the Greek word 'Petros', literally meaning 'a stone' or 'a rock that is detached from the earth' whereas the word used for the 'rock', on which Christ would build His Church, is the word 'Petra,' which means 'an immovable rock'.

Thus, after Peter confessed of Christ, 'Thou art the Christ, the Son of the Living God,' Christ declares to Peter, 'Thou art Petros,' a stone, 'and upon this Petra,' this immovable rock, 'I will build my Church and the gates of hell shall not prevail against it.'

There is an obvious play on words in the Greek language. If the Lord wanted to state clearly that He was going to build His Church upon Peter; 'Petros', surely He could have said, 'Thou art Peter and upon thee I will build my Church.'

Roman Catholicism also draws attention to verse 19 where the Lord tells Peter,

> I will give unto thee the keys of the kingdom of heaven: and whatsoever thou shalt bind on earth shall be bound in heaven: and whatsoever thou shalt loose on earth shall be loosed in heaven.

From this Roman Catholicism concludes that Peter, as the Bishop of Rome, has the keys to the Church, and therefore his successors to the See of Rome also enjoy this privilege.

However, it is recorded in the Acts 2 that Peter fulfilled this verse being the first to unlock the door of the Church to the Jews on the Day of Pentecost. The book of Acts then goes on to record in chapter 10 that it was Peter who unlocked the door of the Church to the Gentiles, again, through the preaching of the gospel.

Matthew 16:19 does not teach that Peter was the first Pope with the authority to take people to heaven or to send them to hell. Neither does it teach that Peter controlled the Church, as its first Pontiff. Rather, this verse foretold that through the preaching of the gospel, Peter opened the Kingdom of God to the Jews, Acts 2 and to the Gentiles, Acts 10.

Revelation 3:7 teaches that only the Lord Jesus is able to open and to shut; only He has those eternal keys of glory. Later on in Matthew 18:18 the same injunction was given to all the Apostles,

> Verily I say unto you, Whatsoever ye shall bind on earth shall be bound in heaven: and whatsoever ye shall loose on earth shall be loosed in heaven.

There are various texts that refute the claim that Peter was the first Pope.

Firstly, in Matthew 23:10-11 the Lord Jesus said,

> Neither be ye called masters: for one is your Master, even Christ. But he that is greatest among you shall be your servant.

This is reinforced when the Lord Jesus, in the same vein, said in Mark 10:44-45,

> Whosoever of you will be the chiefest, shall be servant of all. For even the Son of man came not to be ministered unto, but to minister, and to give his life a ransom for many.

The Lord's words describing the humility expected of His servants do not seem to reflect the characteristics of the hierarchical system of the Pontificate.

Secondly, the Apostle Peter wrote in 1 Peter 5:1,

> The elders which are among you I exhort, who am also an Elder, and a witness of the sufferings of Christ, and also a partaker of the glory that shall be revealed.

Peter included himself among the Elders and certainly he did not elevate himself as the Bishop of Rome.

Thirdly, we see in Acts 8:14 that Luke records,

> Now when the Apostles which were at Jerusalem heard that Samaria had received the word of God, they sent unto them Peter and John.

Today, we cannot conceive of the Pope being sent by his Cardinals or Bishops, yet Peter and John subjected themselves to others in the early Church.

Fourthly, the account of the Council of Jerusalem, given in Acts 15, records that Peter was present, yet it was primarily the Apostle James' counsel that was heeded. Would that not seem strange if Peter was the head of the Church?

Fifthly, in 2 Corinthians 11:5 Paul claims concerning himself,

> For I suppose I was not a whit behind the very chiefest Apostles.

Paul claims to be on the same level footing with all the other Apostles: including the Apostle Peter.

Sixthly, Paul records in Galatians 2:9,

> When James, Cephas, and John, who seemed to be pillars, perceived the grace that was given unto me, they gave to me and Barnabas...

Note that Paul groups James, Cephas; Peter, and John together as pillars of the Church. For Paul there was not one apostolic head, but the Apostles were each pillars of the Church.

Seventhly, in Galatians 2:11 Paul recounts that,

> When Peter was come to Antioch, I withstood him to the face, because he was to be blamed.

In this Galatian controversy Paul reprimanded Peter to his face! Obviously Paul found Peter to be at fault on this occasion.

It would seem inconceivable that this should happen if Peter, as the first Pope, was infallible in pronoucements relating to Church dogma.

Eighthly, Paul lists in Ephesians 4:11 gifts given to the Church. He says God,

> Gave some, apostles; and some, prophets; and some, evangelists; and some, pastors and teachers.

First in line are the Apostles, not the Bishop of Rome, or a Pope, but the Apostles.

It is worthy of note that the Pontificate and hierarchy of the Roman Catholic system corresponds to one of the **structural** characteristics we have observed in a cult or false religion: a strong **authoritarian leadership**.

The Mass

The Mass is much more than simple symbolism; it is the centre of Roman Catholic worship. It is seen as a real sacrifice for the sins of the living and the dead; the same sacrifice as Christ's sacrifice on the cross. As the Priest stands before the emblems and says, 'This is Christ's blood and body,' he is actually, it is claimed, administering a miraculous power that changes the emblems into the literal body and blood of Jesus Christ. This process is called transubstantiation.

When the Scriptures are consulted it is clear that Roman Catholicism's doctrine of transubstantiation is an invention of man. In Hebrews 10:11-12, where the role of the sacrifice in Old and New Testaments is compared we read that,

> Every priest standeth daily ministering and offering oftentimes the same sacrifices, which can never take away sins: But this man, after he had offered one sacrifice for sins for ever, sat down on the right hand of God.

The Bible is clear that Christ accomplished one sacrifice for sins forever and then sat down: the work having been finished. Hebrews 10:13-14 clarifies further,

> From henceforth expecting till his enemies be made his footstool. For by one offering he hath perfected for ever them that are sanctified.

Then again in Hebrews 10:18,

> Now where remission (forgiveness)[1] of sin is, there is no more offering for sin.

Hebrews 7:24-25, referring to Christ's resurrection life, teaches that Christ is the only one who can claim to bring men to God. Christ can have no successors in this regard, for,

> This man, because he continueth ever has an unchangeable (lit. non-transferable)[2] priesthood. Wherefore he is able also to save them to the uttermost that come unto God by him, seeing he ever liveth to make intercession for them.

When Jesus says, 'This is my body, this is my blood' He qualifies this with John 6:63,

It is the spirit that quickeneth; the flesh profiteth nothing: the words that I speak unto you, they are spirit, and they are life.

Christ Himself explains that He was using figurative language when He said, 'This is my body, this is my blood.' Christ was physically sitting beside His disciples as He spoke these words, which proves that His literal body could not reasonably be present in the bread and wine. These, as Christ Himself said, were spiritual words; in the same sense that Christ was not speaking literally when He said, 'I am the door' and 'I am the bread of life'. The bread and wine signified what Christ would do at Calvary.

Probably the most helpful verse on this subject is John 19:30, where the Lord Jesus cried from the cross 'Tetelestai'; 'It is finished!' Christ completed His redemptive sacrifice at the cross; therefore there is no need for its repetition or re-enactment.

Roman Catholicism teaches that Christ's sacrifice needs to be perpetually repeated in the Mass. The following is an interview with Father Richard Chilson, who is the author of eight books on the Roman Catholic faith, including *Catholic Christianity* and *An Introduction to the Faith of Catholics*. When questioned on why the Roman Catholic Church seeks to continue the sacrifice of Jesus at the mass he replied,

> The Eucharist for Catholics is ultimately a mystical understanding … the Eucharist, by making present that sacrifice throughout history, helps us to open our eyes to what is really going on continually - that God is continually, through Jesus Christ, reconciling the universe to Himself. It allows us to personally come into that moment, and be reconciled with God again and again and again. For a Catholic it continues before the sacrifice of Calvary, the sacrifice of Calvary does not begin at that point, it begins really at the foundation of the world - it goes forward in history and it goes backward in history as well.

Father Richard Chilson was asked why the Roman Catholic Church focus on the continuance of Christ's sacrifice, when other 'Christians' celebrate that Christ's sacrifice is finished. After a very long pause, he replied,

> I don't know if I can answer that. I'm sorry, I know that's a real issue
> between Protestants and Catholics, but I don't know if I can answer it
> in any better way than I've already kind of stumbled on.[3]

The reason why a biblical answer cannot be given as an explanation for the Mass is because the Mass is not found in the Bible. The doctrine of the Mass contradicts Scriptural teaching. John 19:30 teaches that Christ's sacrifice for sins is finished, whereas the Mass teaches that the sacrifice must be perpetuated if people are to be saved.

Mary And The Veneration of Saints

In 1854 Pope Pius IX pronounced the doctrine of the Immaculate Conception. Previously the Roman Catholic Church had no such doctrine.

Its introduction confused some within the Church: Romans 6:23 teaches the wages of sin is death and if Mary was not a sinner, did she or did she not die and if she died, did she decay? An explanation was needed.

In 1950 Pope Pius XII pronounced the doctrine of the Assumption of Mary. This taught that Mary was assumed into heaven at death.

Liguri, a Doctor of the Church, taught that Mary *did* in fact die, though she did not decay. He also asserted that she was taken up, by the Lord, into heaven. This, is intrinsic doctrine that must be accepted. Roman Catholic doctrine pronounces an anathema upon all those who do not accept this Marian teaching.

Many misunderstand the doctrine of the Immaculate Conception, thinking it is the belief in the virgin birth. The doctrine of the Immaculate Conception has nothing to do with the virgin birth. The Immaculate Conception teaches that *Mary* was conceived without sin, therefore she cannot be considered as a sinner. This is a complete fallacy.

Luke 1:46-47 records that after the Lord Jesus was born Mary, in the Magnificat, rejoiced in God as her Saviour. Mary testifies that she needed a Saviour; she even brought a sin offering to the temple.

Only sinners need a Saviour and a sin offering.

In 1917 in Fatima, it was claimed that Mary appeared and, uncharacteristically, promoted herself, saying to her devotees,

> God wishes to establish in the world devotion to my immaculate heart. My immaculate heart will be your refuge and the way to lead you to God.

Today, there are those who claim to have heard and seen Mary in modern apparitions, visions and sightings.

The Roman Catholic Church teaches that the Triune Godhead has crowned Mary Queen of Heaven. Yet in the Bible, Jeremiah 7 condemns the worship of a pagan Queen of Heaven in Israel's day.

Mary's importance in Roman Catholic doctrine as a mediator to Christ and God was illustrated recently, in an advert from the *Catholic Standard and Times*. It read,

> He hasn't said no to her in 2000 years, what would you have her ask Him?

In effect, Roman Catholicism has elevated Mary to a position of deity: a co-redemptrix in our salvation, and a co-mediator to bring us to God. She is seen as the mediator and dispenser of all grace. Christ, Roman Catholicism teaches, cannot disobey His mother.

Tragically Roman Catholic tradition has confused Mary's position with that of Christ Himself. One Roman Catholic said,

> I feel, whenever I have a problem and I'm praying, I feel that if I talk to Mary she would have more sympathy with me, and she can understand my motives if I feel I've done something wrong better than Jesus could or God. She's kind of like the mediator for me.[4]

The Bible however, teaches that Christ alone, has paved the way of salvation for us and it is to Him we must come by faith.

Hebrews 4:16 instructs us to come straight into the presence of God through Christ's own blood.

First Timothy 2:5 says,

> There is one God, and one mediator between God and men, the man Christ Jesus.

While Mary was blessed to bear Christ into the world, Mary does not figure at all in God's revealed method of approach to His throne.

In addition to Mary worship Roman Catholicism practises the veneration of Saints, angels, images and various 'holy' objects.

The second Commandment teaches in Exodus 20:4-5,

> Thou shalt not make unto thee any graven image, or any likeness of any thing that is in heaven above, or that is in the earth beneath, or that is in the water under the earth. Thou shalt not bow down thyself to them, nor serve them: for I the LORD thy God am a jealous God, visiting the iniquity of the fathers upon the children unto the third and fourth generation of them that hate me.

This second Commandment that prohibits bowing down to images is not included in the Roman Catholic Ten Commandments. It does not comply with Roman Catholic tradition and so it is rejected. The tenth Commandment of Exodus 20:17 has been separated into two thus giving Roman Catholicism the designated number: ten.

The Gospel According To Rome

Roman Catholics believe that men are born in sin and therefore there is a 'sin problem' from which men need deliverance. Baptism provides for the Roman Catholic this deliverance, which is why it is so important that Roman Catholic babies are baptised just after they are born. According to Roman Catholic dogma, baptism cleanses and removes original sin. It is understood to infuse grace into the life of a child. Thus, baptism is claimed to be initial justification.

Incidentally, there are approximately six million babies and two million adults baptised each year in the Roman Catholic Church.

Even after baptism, Roman Catholicism maintains that a person is still considered a sinner. The Roman Catholic Church teaches that as a person continues to sin more grace is needed to preserve that grace first imparted at baptism.

Christ, according to Roman Catholicism, initiated seven sacraments to preserve and increase this grace. These sacraments are **baptism**; reconciliation, which is **penance**, a trying to atone for sins in confession to a priest; **holy eucharist** or the Mass; **confirmation**; **marriage**; **holy orders**; and the anointing of the sick or the **last rites**.

All of these sacraments practiced throughout life will, according to Roman Catholics, keep them in a state of grace and effectively, increase grace. If however, they continue to sin they will require re-justification.

Even if a Roman Catholic keeps all the sacraments yet fails in only one way they are taught that they will need re-justification to replace that forfeited grace. If a Roman Catholic commits a Mortal Sin, which is one of the more serious sins, grace they believe, can be killed. If a person dies having committed a Mortal Sin, Roman Catholics believe they go straight to hell. The lesser Venial Sins are seen to weaken the life of grace.

According to Roman Catholicism, after committing Mortal or Venial Sins, the soul needs re-justification, which comes through penance or through confession to a Priest. If penance is accomplished then it is believed possible to atone for sins.

The big problem with such a system is that it is impossible to get people to stop sinning!

According to Roman Catholicism all these sins, both Mortal and Venial, accrue to us a temporal punishment after death that will come in the form of Purgatory. Roman Catholic salvation depends essentially on the condition of the soul at the moment of death. Even if a life of obedience to the teaching of the Roman Catholic Church has been achieved from birth, it is the state of the soul at death that will determine one's eternal destiny.

Purgatory implies that Christ's death on the cross was not sufficient to take us to heaven; to save us completely. The Roman Catholic Church teaches that we can actually help atone and help pay for our own sins.

Roman Catholic doctrine perverts the very word 'grace'. In the Roman Catholic system grace can be earned. Yet the very definition of 'grace' is 'unmerited favour'! It is a gift that cannot be earned. It is a free gift to mankind because of what the cross cost Christ. Yet, Roman Catholicism puts a price on salvation that every sinner must pay if they are to be saved.

Scripture, however, teaches,

> For by grace are ye saved through faith; and that not of yourselves: it is the gift of God: Not of works, lest any man should boast. Ephesians 2:8-9.

Therefore we conclude that a man is justified by faith without the deeds of the law. Romans 3:28.

Therefore being justified by faith we have peace with God through our Lord Jesus Christ. Romans 5:1.

I do not frustrate the grace of God: for if righteousness come by the law then Christ is dead in vain. Galatians 2:21.

The Scriptures declare the sentiment of the old gospel hymn, 'It is enough that Jesus died, and that He died for me.'

Ecumenism

Ecumenism is the attempt to unify Christian denominations and sects, and even, other religious systems, into one ecclesiastical body.

Roman Catholicism has undergone an image change since Vatican II in 1965. Public relations with other non-Christian religions and separated Christian brethren do seem to have mellowed. Roman Catholicism now encourages dialogue with other faiths.

Below is an extract from a video documentary entitled *Catholicism: Crisis of Faith* produced 1991 that outlines exactly where the Roman Catholic Church stands on the issue of ecumenism.

Catholic publishers...have produced numerous books designed to enrich Catholic spirituality with Eastern religion: *A Taste Of Water: Christianity Through Taoist Buddhist Eyes* was co-authored by a Priest and a Nun. *Love Meets Wisdom: A Christian Experience of Buddhism,* written by a Jesuit Priest; and *Buddhist Emptiness and Christian Trinity,* which shows how Buddhist-Christian dialogue has gone beyond mutual understanding to mutual transformation. Pope John Paul II personally took the initiative to unite the leaders of the world's religions for a prayer summit at Assisi, Italy in 1986. They came from around the world: Catholics, Protestants, Orthodox and Jews. Muslims from nine nations sang from the Koran. American medicine men called on the Great Spirit. Buddhism's Dali Lama, traditionally regarded as a living deity, chanted rhythmically. Animists from Africa, Hindus, Zoroastrians – 'We will stand side-by-side asking God to give us peace.' With that papal invitation, 160 leaders from the religions of the world gathered to petition God. While toleration for the cultures of others is commendable, this summit treated all religions as equally valid, an endorsement without precedent in the history of Christianity.

Like his predecessor, the present Pope Benedict XVI, once elected was reported by Reuter's News Agency as asking the Christian Church worldwide to unite. The report read,

> The new Pope Benedict praised dialogue with Muslims for the first time and issued another call for Christian unity, renewing a theme he has made a hallmark of the early days of his papacy.

Significantly however, Roman Catholicism has not changed in its doctrine, even after Vatican II. She confesses still of herself that she is always the same and so remains the one true Church.

An article in the *The Times* newspaper on July 11th, 2007 p.8 reinforced this stance. The article carried the headline: *'If it isn't Roman Catholic then it's not a proper Church, Pope tells Christians.'* Journalists Richard Owen and Ruth Gledhill detailed how the Vatican, in a document issued with the full authority of the Pope, has described Protestant and Orthodox faiths as, 'not proper Churches' with Roman Catholicism as 'the one true Church of Christ.'

This document maintained that the Orthodox Church had suffered from a 'wound' because it did not recognise the primacy of the Pope. This wound apparently, was 'still more profound' in Protestant denominations. *The Times* article also reported that Anglican leaders have reacted with dismay at these statements, accusing the Roman Catholic Church of paradoxical behaviour and stating that the new 16 page document constituted a major obstacle to ecumenism.

Paul, however in 2 Corinthians 6:14-18, does not endorse ecumenism when he exhorts Christians to

> Be ye not unequally yoked together with unbelievers: for what fellowship hath righteousness with unrighteousness? And what communion hath light with darkness? And what concord hath Christ with Belial? Or what part hath he that believeth with an infidel? And what agreement hath the temple of God with idols? For ye are the temple of the living God; as God hath said, I will dwell in them, and walk in them; and I will be their God, and they shall be my people. Wherefore come out from among them, and be ye separate, saith the Lord, and touch not the unclean thing; and I will receive you. And will be a Father unto you, and ye shall be my sons and daughters, saith the Lord Almighty.

Roman Catholicism is an apostate version of Christianity. It is a manmade religion that, by their own tradition, has made void the commandments of God. Paul warns all Christians in Gal 1:8-9,

> But though we, or an angel from heaven, preach any other gospel unto you than that which we have preached unto you, let him be accursed. As we said before, so say I now again, If any man preach any other gospel unto you than that ye have received, let him be accursed.

The Reformer's cry ought to be our cry today, 'Sola Scriptura', Scripture alone, 'Sola Fide', faith alone, and 'Only through Christ alone' can we come to God. The eternal salvation of billions depends upon these truths.

May I ask, have you experienced the salvation described in the Bible? This is not the salvation of Roman Catholicism or the salvation of liberal or nominal Protestantism, but the salvation of the Bible. The Bible testifies that this was the reason it was written and given to men: that they could be sure of personal salvation.

First John 5:13 says,

> These things have I written unto you that believe on the name of the Son of God; that ye may know that ye have eternal life, and that ye may believe on the name of the Son of God.

You can know that you are saved for certain because the Lord Jesus died, paid the penalty for your sin, was buried in the grave having completed the work of atonement, rose again on the third day, ascended to heaven and is able to save all who repent and believe in Him. He offers the free gift of grace to all who will receive it by faith, and faith alone.

Footnotes

1   Added by author for purposes of clarity.
2   Ibid.
3   From the video documentary Catholicism: Crisis of Faith, Lumen Productions, 1991.
4   Ibid.

Chapter 12
Cooneyites

Officially the Cooneyites do not have a name. Those outside the group have given any names that may designate them.

These names include:

'Cooneyites' after one of their leading teachers, Edward Cooney.

'Two-by-Twos' based on Mark 6:7 and Luke 10:1, where it is recorded,

> And he...began to send them forth by **two and two**; and gave them power over unclean spirits.

Today the Two-by-Twos is a larger group than the Cooneyites. It is estimated that there are between a quarter to three quarters of a million Two-by-Twos worldwide.

In the course of their history the 'Two-by-Twos' and 'The Cooneyites' became two separate groups. Despite this split the two groups held many of the same beliefs and practices.

'**Go-Preachers**'. This is a name based on Matthew 10:7, where the Lord Jesus Christ instructed His disciples,

> And as ye **go, preach**, saying, The Kingdom of heaven is at hand.

'**Dippers**' which is attributed to the Cooneyites because of their practice of water baptism by immersion.

'**The Nameless House Church**', because Cooneyites do not congregate in buildings designated for worship but rather they meet in homes. This is because Cooneyites believe that to meet in a designated Church building is unbiblical. Following on from this, Cooneyites believe that those who worship in a building prove that they do not belong to the true Christian Church. Cooneyites use proof texts like Acts 7 and 17, which states that God dwells not in temples made with human hands.

'**Pilgrims**' or '**Tramp Preachers**', because although Cooneyites worship in homes, they do not allow their preachers and evangelists to have houses of their own.

'**The Jesus-Way**' is ascribed, because the gospel the Cooneyites preach is not one of grace but one of works.

'**Irvinites**', after their founder William Irvine.

The Cooneyites however, maintain that they are the 'nameless ones', abhorring denominational tags.

Though the Cooneyites claim to have taken no name, they have themselves used names in the past. On occasions the law of the land, in certain jurisdictions where they resided, has forced them to register with the government as a named religious group.

In the United Kingdom in 1914, when the First World War broke out, all religious organisations were forced to register. The Cooneyites registered under the name 'The Testimony of Jesus'. Then in the USA in 1942, during the Second World War, the Cooneyites registered under the name 'Christian Conventions'. Around the same time in Australia and New Zealand the Cooneyites called themselves 'The Christian Assemblies'.

Like other cults underneath the umbrella of 'Christendom', the Cooneyites believe that they are the true and sole descendants of New Testament Christianity. They claim **exclusivity**; a **theological** trait of all cults. In their preaching this can be detected in their strong condemnation of all other expressions of Christianity. Cooneyites maintain that their itinerant Tramp Preachers are the only true servants of the Lord today. Cults are renowned for insisting that salvation can only be obtained within their ranks and through their preachers.

Between 1905 and 1907 the belief that their itinerant Tramp Preachers were the only true servants of the Lord developed into the 'The Living Witness Doctrine'. This doctrine taught that the lost could only be saved through the preaching of Cooneyite pilgrims.

This 'Living Witness Doctrine' however, was the cause of subsequent division within the group.

The Cooneyites have no formulated statement of faith thus making it difficult to analyse their beliefs. Nevertheless, some obvious beliefs can be ascertained from their origins and their various practices and teaching.

Origins

The Cooneyites are unique in being the only cult with its origins in Northern Ireland. The founder of the group, William Irvine, professed Christian conversion in 1893 in the town of Motherwell. In 1895 he joined the Faith Mission to serve the Lord as a Pilgrim. In 1896 he was sent to Ireland to County Antrim and later on he went to County Clare in the South of the island.

Accounts of his ministry would lead us to believe that William Irvine was a very strong believer and an accomplished preacher of the gospel. The records show that he had considerable success in his evangelistic missions with the Faith Mission.

In good faith several denominations helped William Irvine by lending their premises or by attending his missions. However, William Irvine felt that these Churches were somewhat deficient in the ability to disciple new converts so, after his missions it was his practice to disciple converts himself, outside the Church.

Without realising it, William Irvine was establishing himself as a special leader with a group of followers around him. It was not long before, in his preaching, William Irvine began to denounce all Christian Churches as deficient in truth. This behaviour became so serious that by 1901 the Faith Mission severed its ties with William Irvine and he, subsequently, severed his own ties with all Churches.

Another leader of the Cooneyites was Edward Cooney.

In 1884 Edward Cooney professed faith in Christ and it is said that from that moment he won many other souls to Christ. Edward Cooney appeared to be greatly used in gospel ministry. In 1887 Edward Cooney met William Irvine and they became co-workers. In 1901 Edward Cooney withdrew himself from his father's growing business in Enniskillen, Northern Ireland and became a full-time worker along with William Irvine.

Both men were particularly scathing in their attacks on the Churches of the day. Frequently, Edward Cooney directed his hearers to have nothing to do with contemporary Christianity. This proclamation of the defectiveness of the Churches is the precursor to the claim of **exclusivity**; the announcement that their movement is the true Church in the world today and the only modern succession of the Apostolic Church.

The Movement's growth was rapid and by 1904 there were over 150 Go-Preachers. These were full-time evangelists and workers. A great number gathered at the

Cooneyite First Annual Convention, which was held in Crocknacrieve. From its inception the Movement spread throughout Great Britain and then into the USA and Canada, as Cooneyites emigrated.

Divisions

Tensions began to arise within the group as a result of various controversial teachings.

At one period in William Irvine's ministry he believed that he was one of the two witnesses prophesied in Revelation 11. These witnesses were destined to be killed, and then three and a half days later were to rise again.

It appears to have been in response to this claim that the majority of the Cooneyite Movement wanted to discipline William Irvine. Resisting such discipline, he withdrew from the group. Still maintaining the claim to be one of the apocalyptic witnesses, the deluded William Irvine moved to live in the city of Jerusalem in 1920.

William Irvine died in 1947 and three and a half days later he was still dead, proving, that his claims to be one of the two witnesses of Revelation was false.

It should be said that some of William Irvine's more extreme views developed after he had broken off from the main Cooneyite Movement; however it was William Irvine who set the sails of the Cooneyite Movement both in doctrine and in practice.

Divisions among the 'nameless ones' were deepened when Edward Cooney decided he did not agree with the 'Living Witness Doctrine' and in 1928 he was excommunicated for his unwillingness to embrace this doctrine. At this point the Movement split into two groups: the 'Two-by-Twos' and 'the Cooneyites'. The greater number were the Two-by-Twos and a small minority group in Northern Ireland, the Cooneyites, followed Edward Cooney describing themselves as the remnant or the outcasts. Today this second group can also be found in Scotland, Norway, Australia and in the USA.

However, it was not long before Edward Cooney's teaching began to cause dissension among the remnant in Northern Ireland. These outcasts could not subscribe to Edward Cooney's teaching that lost souls could have a second chance of salvation after death. Consequently Edward Cooney sailed to Australia, where in 1960 he died.

The Teachings Of The Cooneyites

One of the Cooneyite central claims is that they are the natural descendants of the New Testament Church but through all the years of Church history there is not a trace of any group similar to the Cooneyites, until the 1800s.

What do the Cooneyites teach and how do Cooneyite teachings compare with the doctrines of the Bible?

Cooneyites claim that the teachings espoused by William Irvine were largely based upon the words spoken by the Lord Jesus to his first disciples. These words are recorded in Matthew 10:9-10.

> Provide neither gold, nor silver, nor brass in your purses, nor bag for your journey, neither two coats, neither shoes, nor yet staves: for the workman is worthy of his meat.

William Irvine took these two verses out of context yet upon them established a movement of workers who went out in the same manner: preaching two-by-two. Such workers preached that sinners ought to take the Lord Jesus Christ as their example, and consequently the 'Two-by-Twos' gospel became known as 'The Jesus-Way'. These 'Tramp Preachers' lived in poverty, having only one change of clothes. They took no money with them; they lived in other people's homes and they desired to obey, literally, this injunction that the Lord Jesus gave to the twelve in Matthew 10, and the seventy disciples recorded in Luke 10.

An uninformed reader of the Scriptures may believe such unswerving obedience to the original commands of Christ is authentic and commendable but, once again, it is an example of how cults can misunderstand the Holy Scriptures.

Matthew 10:5 states,

> These twelve Jesus sent forth, and commanded them, saying, Go not into the way of the Gentiles, and into any city of the Samaritans enter ye not: But go rather to the lost sheep of the house of Israel.

In the same context as the charge to go 'two-by-two' Jesus commands His disciples not to preach the message to the Gentiles but to the lost sheep of the house of Israel. The Two-by-Twos and the Cooneyites however, go to the Gentiles and preach the gospel. To be consistent in their obedience to Matthew 10 the Cooneyites should be preaching in Israel and not in Gentile Northern Ireland!

Also of significance is the specific message that the Lord Jesus gave the disciples to preach, which is recorded in Matthew 10:7,

> …The Kingdom of heaven is at hand.

This message was that the Kingdom of God was near to the Jews in the person of the Lord Jesus Christ: their promised Messiah. The Kingdom of heaven was 'at hand' by the Lord Jesus being in their midst. As we read through Matthew's Gospel we find, at that time, through unbelief, the Jews forfeited the Kingdom because they would not accept the Lord Jesus Christ as their King. As a result of this rejection of Messiah, the gospel is now to be preached to the whole world and that necessitated a new universal message of grace to all nations and a new worldwide commission; Matthew 28:19-20.

Today the message, which is to be preached to the whole world, is not the same message that was preached to the Jews in Jesus' day. Then, the Jews were being called by Messiah to accept Him as the Promise One.

Another crucial point that the Cooneyites have misunderstood is that this commission and the practical injunctions in Matthew 10:9-10 were temporary and preparatory.

In Luke 22:35-36, Christ, at a later stage in his ministry upon the earth, is recorded as giving an opposite command to the same disciples, which effectively undoes the previous command recorded in Matthew 10.

Luke 22:35-36 reads,

> And he said unto them, When I sent you without purse, and wallet, and shoes, lacked ye any thing? And they said, Nothing. Then said he unto them, But now, he that hath a purse, let him take it, and likewise his wallet: and he that hath no sword, let him sell his garment, and buy one.

It is clear from the history book of the Church; the Acts of the Apostles, that the Church did not practise these injunctions given in Matthew 10. In fact, apostolic behaviour to the contrary is recorded. When Peter was at Joppa he was there alone. When Cornelius, in Acts 10, sent for Peter, Peter went alone. Philip the evangelist was alone when he went to preach to the Samaritans. The twelve disciples of the Lord Jesus in Matthew 10 were told specifically not to go to the Samaritans, but Philip went, and he went alone! Then the Spirit miraculously caught Philip away into the desert to speak to the Ethiopian Eunuch. Philip spoke to the Ethiopian Eunuch alone and when he returned to Azotus he preached the gospel in many towns and villages, and he did it all alone!

We also see this practice of preaching alone in the life of Paul. When Paul preached in Damascus he preached alone, later when he was sent to Tarsus in Acts 9, he preached alone. Acts is full of different accounts of men going alone to preach the gospel. There are occasions when they went in twos, but they also went in threes, fours, they even went in sevens and eights!

In our Lord's last commission recorded in Matthew 28:19-20 He said,

> Go ye into all the world and preach the gospel to every creature, baptizing them in the name of the Father, and of the Son, and of the Holy Spirit: Teaching them to observe all things whatsoever I have commanded you: and, lo, I am with you alway, even unto the end of the world. Amen.

Matthew 10's practical injunctions are not found here in Christ's final evangelistic commission. Therefore, these Cooneyite deductions from Scripture transgress the basic and fundamental rules of sound Bible interpretation.

Another distinctive Cooneyite teaching is the 'Living Witness Doctrine'. This was the teaching that it was only through their preachers that people could be converted. Cooneyites maintain that God's Word is a dead book that does not come alive until one of their preachers, and only their preachers, takes it up and preaches from it. However, God's Word clearly testifies to the opposite. Paul writing to a Church that had splintered into factions says in 1 Corinthians 3:5-7,

> Who then is Paul, and who is Apollos, but ministers by whom ye believed, even as the Lord gave to every man? I have planted, Apollos watered; but God gave the increase. So then neither is he that planteth any thing, neither he that watereth; but God that giveth the increase.

Of course ministers of the gospel must be holy, and must be 'worthy of the calling wherewith they are called'; Ephesians 4:1. Nevertheless the power is not in the minister but in the Word of God.

James 1:18 says,

> Of God's own will begat he us with the word of truth....

Christians are begotten, born-again through the Word of God.

Hebrews 4:12 says,

> For the Word of God is quick (living)[1], and powerful, and sharper than any twoedged sword, piercing even to the dividing asunder of soul and spirit, and of the joints and marrow, and is a discerner of the thoughts and intents of the heart.

The word 'quick' means 'living'; so the Bible is a living book! It is the Eternal Living Word. It cannot be dead!

Many Christians have come to faith in Jesus Christ without a preacher present. Charles Wesley came to knowledge of salvation through reading Martin Luther's commentary on Galatians 2:20. John Wesley, his brother, came to Christ through reading the preface of Martin Luther's commentary on the book of Romans. The Gideons International testifies to the fact that today people in hotel rooms, or in taxis, or on holiday are saved through reading God's Word.

First Peter 1:23 clearly states that we are born again of the incorruptible seed of the Word of God.

It is evident also from Cooneyite preaching that there is confusion, or at least a lack of clarity, regarding whether or not the Lord Jesus Christ is God. Some Cooneyites will affirm that Jesus is the Son of God, but He is not God the Son.

The Bible, as stated in previous chapters, makes the deity of our Lord Jesus Christ abundantly clear.

John 1:1,

> In the beginning was the Word, and the Word was with God, and the Word was God.

The Cooneyites misunderstand the meaning of this verse in claiming that the Word here is preaching. John 1:14 continues on to say that the Word became flesh and dwelt among us. Therefore the Word is the incarnate Christ.

The book of Hebrews shows how the Lord Jesus has a greater name than angels: the Lord Jesus is greater than the prophets, and the Lord Jesus is greater than Moses and Aaron. In fact Hebrews 1:8 testifies that Jesus Christ is God when it records God the Father saying to the Son,

> ...Thy throne, O God, is for ever and ever....

Cooneyites believe in grace, but discernible in their teaching is the proclamation of a salvation of works rather than grace. This contradicts the Bible, which states that salvation is by grace alone.

There is a whole book in the Bible written on that very subject: Galatians. The Galatian controversy concerned false teachers called Judiasers who claimed that whilst the death of Christ was vital to salvation, a Christian must add to it by circumcision and compliance to the rites of the Law of Moses. Paul declared that such a gospel is not the gospel at all: unless the gospel preached is by grace alone through Christ's sacrifice it is not the biblical gospel. That word 'alone' is vitally important because grace cannot be added to by human virtue or righteousness.

There can be no certainty in the Cooneyite version of salvation because it is works based. Those who have heard their message and those who have been converted out of their numbers to the true gospel testify, that there is little or no attention paid to the shed blood and the finished work of our Lord Jesus Christ on the cross. In fact, to the contrary, Cooneyites claim that man must continue the work that Christ began on the earth.

Cooneyites misinterpret what Luke said in Acts 1:1. This is where Luke referred to writing his Gospel as a means to record all that Jesus began to do and teach. Luke simply meant that he was compiling a record of the life and ministry of Christ. Cooneyites teach that what Jesus began we must continue. Luke in Acts 1:1, however, was not writing about the efficacy of Christ's sacrifice, or of propitiation, or of the redemption that Christ has purchased. When Scripture does address these matters it is abundantly clear. From Christ's own lips is the assurance of the complete nature of His redemptive work. It is recorded in John 19:30 that hanging on the cross Jesus said,

> …It is finished…!

The book of Hebrews was written to show that one sacrifice for sins, forever, has been made and Christ has now sat down having finished the work. In John 17:4 before His death, knowing the work He would accomplish, Jesus said,

> …I have finished the work that Thou gavest me to do.

Like every other cult, the way of salvation for Cooneyites can only be achieved through an outward conformity to a particular lifestyle, rather than an inward experience of the new birth through the grace of God in Christ. Even if the lifestyle Cooneyites seek to emulate is Jesus'; it is not enough - why? This is simply because no sinner can live up to the standard of His lifestyle.

Inevitably teaching that is absent of grace will encourage extreme legalism, as many ex-Cooneyite members have testified.

The biblical gospel is simply that of the finished work of redemption that our Lord Jesus accomplished on the cross. Paul testifies in 1 Corinthians 15:1-5 that the message He gave to the Corinthians was that which was given to Him by God:

> … Christ died for our sins according to the Scriptures…and rose again the third day according to the Scriptures.

The Lord Jesus Christ shed His precious blood in order that in Him, and in Him alone, we might have redemption.

Ephesians 1:7 says we can have,

> … redemption through his blood, even the forgiveness of sins. …

The Bible is clear on how we benefit from this gospel message.

Romans 5:1 tells us that,

> Therefore being justified by faith, we have peace with God through our Lord Jesus Christ.

Ephesians 2:8-9 distinctly states,

> For by grace (God's unmerited gift of favour)[2] are ye saved through faith; and that not of yourselves. …

Faith embraces grace; it is faith and faith alone in Christ that will save our eternal soul. We are justified by an act of God.

Paul says in Romans 8:33,

> It is God that justifieth.

God justifies the guilty sinner who believes in Jesus. Righteousness is not within our ability, in fact, Isaiah says that our righteousness are as filthy rags in the sight of God; Isaiah 64:6. If we are ever to be in the presence of God we need to have the very righteousness of God, and the righteousness of God is found in Christ alone. The Bible teaches that God justifies men because on the cross Christ was punished for our sins and through faith in Him God's righteousness in Christ is given to us.

Romans 4:16 states,

> Therefore it is of faith that it might be by grace.

God's righteousness is imputed to us by faith. Paul in Galatians 2:21 reasons,

> I do not frustrate the grace of God: for if righteousness come by the law, then Christ is dead in vain.

and then in Romans 11:6 he states

> And if by grace, then is it no more of works: otherwise grace is no more grace. But if it be of works, then it is no more grace: otherwise work is no more work.

Salvation is either by grace or by work, and praise God it is by grace - amazing grace!

In John 6:28, the legalistic religionists of the day asked Jesus,

> What shall we do that we might work the works of God?

Jesus answered them in John 6:29,

> This is the work of God, that ye believe on Him whom He hath sent.

Jesus did say, 'I am the way', John 14:6, but this way was not found in His example. *He* is the way. Incidentally when Jesus spoke these words in John 14 He was on His way to the cross. He was going to heaven to prepare a place for us and He did not say, 'My example is the way', or 'My teaching is the way', but He stated that 'I am the way', and to be with God you must be in Him. Being in Christ is possible only through the work of the cross and the power of His resurrection. Christ alone is the way, and He has prepared heaven for His own by the way of the cross.

Many who have encountered Cooneyites on a personal level attest to their great morality, charity and general kindness. Cooneyites are to be commended for their neighbourliness and friendliness but it must be said that however upstanding a person's life may be, that cannot alter the unchangeable eternal truths established in the Word of God.

The Cooneyites like many others involved in cults and religions, are extremely nice people but their gospel preaches another Christ and that is the tragedy.

Paul states in Galatians that anyone who preaches another Jesus, though he be an angel from heaven, let him be anathema, Galatians 1:8-9. The Cooneyite movement bears the marks of a cult, in particular, an **authoritarian leadership** and an **exclusive** self-centredness in the claim that they alone are God's people.

Walter Martin, author of *The Kingdom of the Cults*, perceptively commented that a cult is,

> A group of people gathered around someone's misinterpretation of the Bible.

Let everyone who bears the name Christian take care that they do not fall into the danger of elevating the traditions of men above the Word of God. Let us always beware of men's misinterpretations.

Paul exhorts us in 2 Timothy 2:15-16 to,

> Study to shew thyself approved unto God, a workman that needeth not to be ashamed, rightly dividing the word of truth. But shun profane and vain babblings: for they will increase unto more ungodliness.

The New Testament teaches that as the end of the age approaches false teachers will increase more and more. Every Christian should seek an increased knowledge and understanding of the Holy Scriptures. Every Christian should worship in a Church where the Scriptures are faithfully expounded. Read the Word of God yourself and emulate the Bereans who, after hearing even the preaching of Paul and Silas,

> ... searched the scriptures daily, whether those things were so; Acts 17:11.

Footnotes

1 Added by author for purposes of clarity.
2 Ibid.

Chapter 13
Hinduism

Hinduism must be the most complex of all the cults and religions considered in this book. Bruce J. Nicholls comments,

> Of all the world's great religions, Hinduism is the most difficult to define. It did not have any one founder.... It has many Scriptures which are authoritative but none that is exclusively so. Hinduism is more like a tree that has grown gradually than like a building that has been erected by some great architect at some definite point in time.[1]

Origins

Hinduism is a religion that has evolved through various stages of Indian history. We first hear of it when the Aryan people conquered the inhabitants of the Indus Valley and, brought their religious practices with them. Accordingly we find the primitive

Hindu faith in embryo among these ancient people. This religion was very simple; a religion of hymns and prayers known as the 'Vedas'.

'Vedas' simply means 'wisdom' or 'knowledge' and it was believed that this knowledge could bring men to God. Incorporated in the Vedas was a belief in many varied gods and goddesses. Over the years this ancient religion would evolve through Indian history to become today's 'Hinduism': the dominant religion of the continent. Hinduism therefore, owns no religious founder: making it unique among world faiths.

The name 'Hinduism' was given to this religion as a result of invading Muslim Persians of the 13th Century wanting to differentiate between their religion and the religion of the people of the Indus Valley.

Hindu origins and Indian history are essentially intertwined. Historians have narrowed Hindu development down to four basic periods in Indian history. The fourth period, around 200BC through to 200AD, was essentially when Hinduism, as we recognise it today, developed.

Estimates vary regarding how many Hindus there are in the world today. Some scholars believe that there are a staggering 700 million Hindus; most of them found in India. Considering that Hinduism is one of the oldest religions in existence, perhaps dating back 4000-5000 years, the number of devotees should not be surprising.

Hinduism has been described as being more of a way of life than a theological idea or philosophy. In fact, a former Indian President, Radha-krish-nan, said,

> Hinduism is more a culture than a creed.

As a result of its cultural nature, Hinduism can embrace a wide variety of other religious beliefs. Indeed, it actively seeks to accept other faiths leaving none outside. Hinduism often adapts the doctrines of other religions to fit into its own system and worldview. This is significant, as presently in Western society there appears to be a great acceptance of some Hinduistic philosophies and ideas. The present day impact of Hinduism on society should not be underestimated.

The Impact Of Hinduism On The West

The inroads that Hinduism has made in Western society can be traced back to the year 1893 when, in the city of Chicago in the USA, there was a World Parliament of Religions. One of the individuals who attended that Parliament was a man by the name of 'Vive-kan-anda'. Vive-kan-anda so impressed the varied gathering of religious devotees with his own spirituality and view of Hinduism as a great universal faith that, afterwards many were beginning to question the wisdom of continuing to send missionaries to the Indian continent!

From that Parliament of Religion in the nineteenth century, the influence of Hinduism in the West grew greatly and more so of late in our own generation. Os Guinness has observed this explosion of Eastern thought in the West and commented,

> The East is still the East, but the West is no longer the West. Western answers no longer seem to fit the questions. With Christian culture disintegrating and humanism failing to provide an alternative, many are searching the ancient East.[2]

The influence of Eastern spirituality is witnessed also in the many 'new age' trends that are derivatives of Hindu belief. Among these are groups such as the 'Hare Krishna', 'Osho' and 'The Divine Light Mission'. Popular practices such as Transcendental Meditation, yoga and meditation of various kinds are derived also from Hinduism. The modern 'New Age Movement' has been responsible for repackaging these Eastern beliefs for the purpose of 'selling' them to the Western world.

Although this impact of Hinduism on Western society really began in 1893, the counterculture of the 1960s played a key role in bringing it to such prominence today. This counterculture was essentially a reaction against the traditional Western values of technology, economics, materialism, reason and rationalism. The 'hippy' generation saw in the East an uncomplicated lifestyle and this radically different framework of belief attracted them.

The Hindu word 'guru' meaning 'enlightened master' or 'spiritual teacher', is now a household term, yet forty years ago most people would have been ignorant of its meaning. One prominent guru of the 1960s was the Maharishi Mahesh Yogi and, through developing Transcendental Meditation, he was responsible for popularising Hinduism. During the 1960s his association with celebrities such as the Beatles, the Beach Boys, the Rolling Stones and Mia Farrow helped to popularise this practice and as a result Transcendental Meditation received a worldwide press. This publicity was an intrinsic factor in the popularisation of Eastern philosophy and practice in the West. In fact one writer says that,

> Transcendental Meditation did for Eastern mysticism what MacDonald's did for the hamburger.[3]

Yogic Flying is associated with Transcendental Meditation. Many Christians believe that it is a supernatural phenomenon, even demonic in origin. They believe that the subtlety of Satan can certainly be seen in the way Transcendental Meditation made Eastern mysticism and effectively Hinduism, more accessible to Westerners.

Americans further accepted Transcendental Meditation when its instructors made the claim that one could practise this meditation technique without violating one's own personal faith or belief. The claim was, and still is, 'You can use yoga, Transcendental Meditation and the like to help holistically in body, mind, and even spirit: it does not have to compromise or conflict with your Christianity.' However, a spiritual health warning must come with forms of Eastern meditation, as its chief goal is to empty the mind consequently leaving a person vulnerable to demonic activity.

Biblical meditation, which is simply a conscious and reasonable contemplation of Holy Scripture, ought to be the only form of meditation practiced by the Christian.

The Maharishi Mahesh Yogi became so popular in the USA that the Maharishi International University was established in Ohio. It was founded by the Maharishi Mahesh Yogi in 1971 and continues to flourish today. Young Americans go there to study the theories of Transcendental Meditation and similar beliefs. Annually there are around 100,000 young Americans who journey from the West to the coasts of India in search of spiritual enlightenment.

Why is it so appealing to the young? The answer is that Hinduism and Eastern mysticism merge well with the New Ageism of our modern generation.

Hindu Scriptures And Beliefs

There is no single Hindu document that enshrines Hindu doctrine and belief. This is significant as it explains the great variation in the Hindu understanding of God.

There is no equivalent to the 'Bible' among Hindu writings but there are several 'Vedic Scriptures', filled with 'Vedas': wisdom. One volume of Hindu writings called the 'Bhag-a-vad Gita' has come to be regarded as the 'Bible' of Hinduism. Written around the first century AD, it is the best loved book of all. It has been made popular in our day by the Hare Krishnas who are often seen walking through towns, with shaven heads, wearing saffron robes, beating drums and singing 'Hare Krishna'.

The Hindu god is an impersonal force. Eerdmans' *Handbook To The World's Religions*, p.172, defines their understanding of God by saying,

> The individual Hindu may reverence one god, a few gods, or many gods, or none at all.

The quote continues,

> He may also believe in one god and in several gods as manifestations of that one god. He may express the ultimate in a personal way or in an impersonal way.

Hinduism is therefore a polytheistic religion: 'poly' meaning 'many' and 'theism' meaning 'a belief in god'. Proverbially Hindus believe in 33 million gods. Hindus are also pantheistic: 'pan' meaning 'earth' and 'theism' meaning 'a belief in god'. Therefore

Pantheism is the belief that God is intrinsically in all of nature. This explains the worship of nature and animal life seen in Hinduism.

Hinduism is also a 'monism'. Monism is the belief that the entire universe has one unitary principle that governs everything. This means that God is in everything and in everyone. This one force of God is believed to unify the whole universe regardless of religion or culture.

Though Hindus worship many gods there is a sense in which they also believe in one creator god. This creative force is called the 'Brahma'. All the other gods in Hinduism are expressions of that one creative force. Therefore, some Hindus claim to be monotheistic. Accordingly, Hindus can worship several gods and yet believe that they are worshipping only one god. Some Hindus worship the god Shiva, who is the destroyer god; others worship Vishnu, who is the preserver god. Brahma, Shiva and Vishnu form a kind of Hindu trinity. Vishnu's incarnations, which Hindus call 'avatars', are manifestations of their god in many varied forms. Krishna, as in Hare Krishna, is one of the manifestations or incarnations of the god Vishnu.

These manifestations of the Hindu gods, whether it is Brahma or Vishnu, are rarely in human form; rather they are in the form of animals or other wildlife. Vishnu is believed to draw near to man in ten different manifestations or 'avatars'. Among them are the fish, the tortoise, the boar, a half-man and half-lion creature and a dwarf. Krishna is a god in his own right; another Hindu god is Buddha, the 'enlightened one' and founder of Buddhism. The tenth manifestation of Vishnu has not yet appeared but it is expected.

The cow, the monkey and the snake are also revered as holy in Hinduism. Even rats are sacred. In fact some Indian village temples feed the rats at a cost of £2500 per annum. Apparently 15% of India's grain is also used to feed this vermin. The cobra, which is also worshipped, kills 20,000 of its devotees annually. The sacred cow gets most publicity. There are 159 million cows in India, which is 20% of the world's total population of cows. The cow is believed to be the Mother Goddess of life, so much so that some Indians will actually drink cow's urine to purify the soul.

Many Indian rivers are regarded as holy, in particular, the Ganges. It is believed that by bathing in the Ganges 'bad karma' is washed away. In fact, the greatest ever festival at the Ganges was held in the year 2000: it is called the 'Koum'. It was expected that 75 million pilgrims would appear. Channel 4 Television, in 2000, ran a series of programmes over that week called 'The Greatest Show on Earth'. It was claimed that the 'Koum' 2000 was the greatest gathering of humanity in the history of mankind.

The Hindu, like the Buddhist, believes in reincarnation. Salvation for the Hindu is to get out of the reincarnation cycle of continual birth, life, death and rebirth. It is an escape into a kind of oblivion, away from all earthly suffering. It is to be in a state of nirvana, a non-existence. This is understood as a submerging into the Brahma; the force of nature and creation.

During the second period of India's history the caste system developed. This system established four main castes in Hindu society. There were the Brahmans who were at the top; they were priests or scholars. Then there were the Shudra at the bottom; they were the slaves. There was no salvation for the Shudra. It is said that a Brahman, if he were dying of thirst, would not even take a drop of water from a Shudra lest he would be polluted. During all the years of societal evolution there eventually emerged 3,000 sub-castes. At the bottom of this social caste scale were 'the untouchables'. These people were not considered to be human. They were viewed as the dregs of society; only fit to live among the rubbish and the excrement of society. Females do not figure at all in the caste system. This is the reason why many baby girls were killed by their parents at birth.

The caste system has become a justification for the belief in karma and reincarnation. If you have bad karma you come back as a low caste. The problem is that some lower castes are not eligible for salvation. This creates a spiritual hopelessness and an abject poverty in society that seems irreversible.

If someone is eligible for salvation, because of his caste, then his spiritual goal is to practice 'the four paths of yoga'. The four paths of yoga are paths of knowledge and asceticism.

Sadhus as wondering holy men hope to win their salvation by relinquishing all pleasure and comfort. They take a vow of poverty, chastity and obedience. Some attempt incredible feats in their efforts to kill the self-nature within. Some have lain on beds of nails, stayed silent for years, grown their hair in seven feet long braids and others have stood on one leg like a stork for months on end. Some Sadhus have been known to hold out their arm for months and even years until it had atrophied.

Does the Bible Fit the Hindu Mould?

Do the Christian Scriptures fit into the Hindu system? There are those in Hinduism and Christendom who claim they do; even teaching that the Hindu god, the Brahma, finds a manifestation in Christ and Jehovah and that the Hindu 'trinity' can be likened to the Father, Son and Holy Spirit of Christianity.

This is not the case.

Firstly, the Bible reveals **One True and Living God**. In Romans Paul taught those Christians in Rome, surrounded by pagan polytheism, how the true and the living God has revealed Himself.

Romans 1:20 says,

> The invisible things of him from the creation of the world are clearly seen, being understood by the things that are made, even his eternal power and Godhead; so that they are without excuse.

Paul cites the fact that this one true God is the Creator of all people as the reason why we are without excuse before Him. In Romans 2:15 Paul declares that God has written the requirements of His Law on the hearts of every man. Accordingly, this one true God can be perceived in conscience and in creation. Later in Romans Paul talks about the revelation of the Gospel through Jesus Christ.

The Hindu has developed a wisdom that professes to be the way to God and they have become in the words of Paul, to be fools.

Romans 1:21-22 says,

> Because that, when they knew God, they glorified him not as God, neither were thankful; but became vain in their imaginations, and their foolish heart was darkened. Professing themselves to be wise, they became fools.

Hinduism and many other man-made religions have, as Romans 1:23 states,

> ... changed the glory of the uncorruptible God into an image made like to corruptible man, and to birds, and fourfooted beasts, and creeping things.

This characteristic is manifest in Hinduism perhaps more than in any other world religion. Here is a religion that worships animals as manifestations of their god.

The entire Bible reveals to mankind that there is only one true and living God. He is the Creator God of Genesis 1:1 who pre-existed everything. That rules out polytheism, pantheism, and monism. Before there was a world, before there was a universe, before there was another principality or power, there was God and God alone. He is always presented in Holy Scripture as distinct from His creation. Numbers 23:19 tells us that God is not a man. There are serious consequences when we reject the knowledge of the true Creator God, as revealed in creation, conscience and the Bible.

Romans 1:28 says,

> ...even as they did not like to retain God in their knowledge, God gave them over to a reprobate mind, to do those things which are not convenient....

Like the Romans in Paul's day, Hindus, among others in our day, have broken the first and the second commandment. Other gods have been put before and beside Jehovah and there has been a falling down in idolatrous worship of figures and forms of created beings. The Bible tells us that behind every idol, whatever that idol be, is a demon; 1 Corinthians 10:19-20. Therefore Hinduism, according to the Bible is a form of demon worship. In fact the Bhag-a-vad Gita, in chapter 10 records Krishna declaring,

> I am the prince of demons.

The Bible testifies that there is one God and one mediator between God and men; the man Christ Jesus. Jesus Christ is God's only begotten Son. Christ is not, as Hindus say, an enlightened holy man like a Sadhu but rather, Christ is God's very Word: the expression of His own person. Christ is God's way, the truth and life. Jesus Christ is the Son of God and God the Son.

Theologically Hinduism proves itself to be a false religion in claiming to supply **new revelations** of God other than the Lord Jesus Christ.

Hebrews 1:1-2 makes clear that God has only given one revelation of Himself:

> God, who at sundry times and in divers manners spake in time past unto the fathers by the prophets, Hath in these last days spoken unto us by his Son, whom he hath appointed heir of all things, by whom also he made the worlds....

This biblical truth is an absolute, which is in contrast to the relativistic nature of the Hindu belief, which changes under different circumstances.

Hinduistic relativism does not allow for this absolute truth. For Hindus all truth is relative. The gospel of Jesus Christ is distinct from Hinduism as it is a message of absolute truths.

John 1:17 says,

> For the law was given by Moses, but grace and truth came by Jesus Christ.

The Lord Jesus Christ is God's absolute truth. He is the Word of God manifest and the only manifestation of God's truth. In John 17:17 Christ said that God's Word was truth and Jesus Christ is declared in the Bible as God's Word: John 1:1.

Secondly, according to the Bible, **sin is not an illusion**, as Hinduism claims. Vivekan-anda at the Parliament of Religions in 1893 stated,

> It is a sin to call a person a sinner.

Hinduism teaches that God is in everyone and that man's greatest problem is not sin but ignorance of the fact that he is divine himself!

The Bible teaches that man's greatest problem is that he is far from being a god; indeed he is separated from God because of his sin.

All men, whatever their caste, have sinned and fallen short of God's glory: Romans 3:23.

In fact, in John 8:44 Jesus spoke to the Pharisees, the religious men of His day, and said,

> Ye are of your father, the devil; and the deeds of your father you will do.

Hinduism, like all false religions and confusing cults in the world, has no answer to the problem of sin. They might disguise sin by calling it 'bad karma' but the tragic fact remains that they have no answer for it.

Thirdly, salvation, according to the Bible, is available as **a free gift based upon a finished work**. That is why the Bible cannot assimilate into a syncretism with a religion like Hinduism. Salvation is freely available by grace upon Christ's finished work on the cross.

God's Word is clear regarding reincarnation, which is fundamental to Hinduism.

The Bible teaches that once a man is born on earth he has only one life and then he will die once and then face judgment.

Hebrews 9:27 teaches,

> And it is appointed unto men once to die, and after that the judgment....

There are no second chances; no reincarnation into another body to have another chance. We know this because Christ has risen from the dead! That is not a theological theory or philosophical ideal; it is a historical fact.

Acts 1:3 says,

> ...He shewed himself alive after his passion by many infallible proofs....

This same Lord Jesus Christ promises that those who believe in Him and die, as He lives, they shall live also: John 11:25-26. To die as a Christian is to be absent from the body and to be present with the Lord: 2 Corinthians 5:6.

Christ is so clear and precise regarding what death without Him will be like: hell. In Luke 16 Jesus taught that it is in this lifetime alone that man's eternal destiny will be determined. The determining factor will be whether or not that person has repented of sin and believed in the gospel of the Lord Jesus Christ. That is why Paul emphasises in 2 Corinthians 6:2:

> ...now is the day of salvation....

Tragically Hindus all over the world are trying to earn their salvation by various manmade ways. Hindus have no reality of forgiveness of sins in their life; they are striving towards a goal rather than realising what has already been accomplished.

The one major difference between Bible Christianity and any other religion or cult in the world is that Christianity is the only faith that begins at the end, where Christ cried from the cross,

> It is finished: John 19:30.

Christians begin where Christ finished and what a message this is to share with a lost world: Christ, the sinless Son of God took the suffering of the world upon Himself. He was wounded for our transgressions and He was bruised for our iniquities. Through faith we can be delivered eventually from all those sufferings. The true enlightenment that God, the living God, gives is through His Son Jesus Christ, the One who said in John 8:12,

> I am the light of the world, he that followeth shall not walk in darkness but shall have the light of life.

Paul was a religious Jew who struggled with sin and self, but he came to the realisation that Christ died for him and was his substitute, and therefore his sin died with Jesus on the cross.

Paul declared in Galatians 2:20,

> I am crucified with Christ: nevertheless I live; yet not I, but Christ liveth in me: and the life which I now live in the flesh I live by the faith of the Son of God, who loved me, and gave himself for me.

Mahatma Gandhi once said,

> I shall say to the Hindus that your lives will be incomplete unless you reverently study the teachings of Jesus.

All men's lives are incomplete until they put their faith in the Lord Jesus Christ who is the only Saviour. That requires more than just a polite acknowledgement of the worth of Christ's teachings. It necessitates a personal repentant act of faith in the Lord Jesus Christ and what He has accomplished through His sacrifice at the cross and His resurrection.

Footnotes

1   Bruce J. Nicholls, Hinduism, in The World's Religions p.136.
2   Os Guinness, The Dust of Death, p.195
3   Cited in Enroth, The Lure of the Cults, p.42.

Chapter 14
Oneness Pentecostalism

'Oneness Pentecostalism' is an umbrella term designating those who believe in the 'Oneness' doctrine rather than belief in the Trinity.

The 'Jesus-Only Churches', 'The Apostolic Pentecostals', 'The Jesus' Name Movement', 'The Assemblies of the Lord Jesus Christ' and 'The Bible Way Churches of our Lord Jesus Christ' are but some of the hundreds of different independent Oneness Pentecostal denominations worldwide: the largest two being the United Pentecostal Church International and the United Apostolic Church.

Whatever the name is of a particular Oneness Pentecostal denomination, they all are easily identifiable by their doctrine.

It is important at the beginning of this chapter, as with all the other chapters, to remind readers that this particular critique has not set out to offend anyone unduly. However, it is necessary when engaging in a biblical examination of other beliefs to set aside emotional and relational ties in order to ensure an impartial and unprejudiced assessment of what the truth really is.

Whilst Christian fellowship is of great importance, the New Testament teaches that all Christian unity must be on the grounds of fundamental biblical truth. Our primary duty, therefore, is always to discern the truth.

In reaction to the announcement of this study in the local press, the following question was asked, 'How can Oneness Pentecostalism be included among all the other religious groups critiqued in this series?'

Such a question portrays the common, yet erroneous, perception that Oneness Pentecostalism is an orthodox Christian group, like any other. The strict monotheism of the Oneness Pentecostals and their strenuous defence of the deity of Christ; that He is God manifest in flesh, have contributed to this perception in the minds of many.

As a result of this misconception some evangelicals have embraced this group. There is no doubt in my mind that true believers are amongst the numbers of the Oneness Pentecostal Churches because of the belief that their Oneness Church is an orthodox, biblically fundamental and evangelical Church.

To explore whether the Oneness Pentecostal Movement is indeed orthodox, biblically fundamental and evangelical, a brief history of its origins is necessary.

Origins and History

Historically the Oneness Movement differs significantly from classic Pentecostalism. The modern Pentecostal Movement had its beginnings in 1901 at a chapel prayer meeting in Topeka, Kansas, which was being led by Charles Parham. Later, in 1906, it was claimed that during a revival meeting in an African-American Baptist Church on Azusa Street in Los Angeles, California the Pentecostal experience burst onto the scene; manifesting itself in speaking in tongues and the baptism of the Spirit. This was hailed as the birth of the Pentecostal Movement. Pentecostal preachers and doctrines spread very rapidly from that moment.

In 1913 a popular Pentecostal teacher called R.E. McAlister of Toronto, Ontario, began teaching that the doctrine of the Trinity was erroneous. R.E. McAlister taught that Jesus was the only God and that the three manifestations, Father, Son and Holy Spirit were simply manifestations of the Lord Jesus.

In addition R.E. McAlister claimed that God, using Acts 2:38, had given to him a revelation that baptism should be correctly administered in the name of Jesus alone.

Acts 2:38 states,

> Then Peter said unto them, Repent, and be baptized every one of you in the name of Jesus Christ for the remission of sins, and ye shall receive the gift of the Holy Ghost.

This **new revelation,** in effect a **theological** characteristic of a cult, claimed that the baptismal formula of the Trinity given by the Lord in Matthew 28:19 was obsolete.

Eventually other preachers joined R.E. McAlister and by 1916 Oneness views were being propounded by some of the ministers in the Assemblies of God Movement: one of the largest Pentecostal denominations in the USA. However, the Assemblies of God Movement strongly rejected the Oneness doctrine and its Denominational Council in 1916 adopted a very definite Trinitarian stance in its statement of faith.

More than 160 of those Oneness ministers in the Assemblies of God were expelled and subsequently they formed alliances in order to propagate this Oneness doctrine. One of these alliances was the 'Pentecostal Assemblies of the World'.

Thus in a strict sense, the Oneness Movement cannot be considered mainstream Pentecostal even though they are pentecostal in their understanding of the ministry of the Holy Spirit.

What Is The Oneness Doctrine And Is It Biblical?

Does this doctrine conflict with the Oneness Movement's claim to be mainstream evangelical?

The Oneness doctrine is simply the belief that there are no distinctions in the Godhead. Though the Bible speaks of the Father, Son and Holy Spirit, according to the Oneness Movement these are only designations for representations of the Lord Jesus Christ. Oneness proponents maintain, Jesus is the Father, Jesus is the Son, Jesus is the Holy Spirit and Jesus is all three. This view teaches that in eternity past Christ was a uni-personal God; there was no Father or Spirit, only the Lord Jesus Christ. The Oneness Movement teaches that, in time, Christ begot a human Son, the human Jesus who was born in Bethlehem.

Oneness proponents teach that the divine nature of the earthly Christ became known as God the Father and in addition the human nature of Jesus, His flesh, is designated as the Son of God.

If Christ's divine nature is God the Father and His bodily human nature is God the Son then who or what is the Holy Spirit?

It is the belief of the Oneness Movement, that the Spirit, is simply Jesus, in a spiritual form, dwelling in the midst of His people. Oneness teachers explain it thus: in the same sense that Jesus is Prophet, Priest, and King so the Lord Jesus Christ is Father, Son and Holy Spirit. The Oneness Movement view these designations as different offices of the one person, Jesus: Jesus is the Father, Jesus is the Son and Jesus is the Holy Spirit.

This, in effect, is a denial of the New Testament doctrine of the eternal Sonship of the Lord Jesus Christ. Oneness teachers tell us that the concept of Sonship only relates to the human nature of Christ. They maintain that the term 'son' is a human term and is a figure of time, which also conveys a sense of inferiority. Sonship, to the Oneness Movement, was part of Christ's humiliation.

Oneness teaching is in fact an ancient heresy known in the early Church as Sabellianism. It was known also as Modalism and was taught by some in the late first and early second century.

Before assessing this Oneness teaching in detail let it be noted that the fundamental error of the Oneness Movement is how they seek to understand the Bible.

The Oneness Movement has attempted to explain the inexplicable: God Himself. God cannot be explained to the satisfaction of human reason and intellect. If we do not start on this premise when studying the biblical doctrine of the Godhead inevitably, we will fall into serious error.

Trinitarians do not claim to have a complete or perfect understanding of the Godhead for such knowledge is unachievable. The first man to understand God has made himself God! Here, I believe, lies one of the fatal downfalls of the Oneness Movement. In order to achieve a clearer and simpler understanding of the Godhead, they have adopted an imbalanced view. It may be a simpler understanding of the Godhead, but in effect it is an overly *simplistic* view because it does not deal with all the facts and indeed it contradicts many clear Scriptures.

If only one aspect of the Godhead is emphasised, then only a partial understanding of the Godhead will be achieved. To omit and contradict clear Scriptural facts regarding the Godhead in order to create an argument, is, at the very least, misleading and more seriously, spiritually dangerous.

The Oneness Movement claims that Constantine introduced the Trinity in the year 325AD at the Council of Nicea. That is not the case.

There is plenty of evidence, as we shall see from the New Testament, that long before 325AD the early Church had a simple belief in one God existing in three persons. It is also evident from the writing of the early Christian apologists and Church fathers that they believed in one God in three persons and that they opposed heretical misrepresentations of God's nature.

It was only when false teachings regarding the Godhead arose that it was necessary to formulate a crystallised and explicit doctrine on the nature of God. The Council of Nicea was the culmination of the Church's process over a period of three hundred years of grappling with the issues of the Godhead in order to achieve a systematised truth to counter heresy.

Misrepresentations of Trinitarianism

Oneness teachers misrepresent what Trinitarians believe.

In Oneness Movement literature and preaching their version of Trinitarianism is established and is then systematically demolished. This type of theological spin is a characteristic of many misguided religious groups.

Let us look at of some of these misrepresentations of the Trinitarian position.

The Oneness Movement claim that the Trinity is,

> The Rome three-god theory.

It is true that Roman Catholics believe in the Trinity but a study of Church history will show that it was not the Roman Catholic Church which introduced the doctrine of the Trinity to Christianity. The Trinity can be traced back to the Apostles' Doctrine, which is the teaching of the New Testament.

Oneness proponents make the claim that Trinitarians believe in the 'three-god theory'. However, Trinitarianism is not a belief in three gods; such a belief in three separate gods is in fact called tritheism. Trinitarians are monotheists: believing in one true and living God, as taught in Deuteronomy 6:4. This one God according to Trinitarianism, has been revealed in the Holy Scriptures in the unity of that Godhead as three distinct Persons, yet one in divine substance and being.

This indeed is a mystery: it is baffling, no one can understand it. Man is not asked to understand the Godhead. He is, however, asked to accept and believe, unreservedly, what clearly has been declared in God's revelation of Himself.

Another false argument Oneness proponents use is that the word 'Trinity' is not found in the Bible, therefore it must not be truth. It is correct to say that the word 'Trinity' is not in the Bible, but the teaching of the Triune Godhead is found in its pages. Incidentally, Oneness Pentecostals use the words 'millennium', 'theocracy' and 'incarnation' extensively, yet none of these are found in the Bible, but they must concede that, just like the Trinity, the truths are present in the Scriptures.

It is therefore spurious for Oneness proponents to claim that the Trinity should be rejected because the word is not found in the Bible.

In an attempt not to misrepresent the Oneness Movement position on the Godhead, Gordon Magee's publication *Is Jesus in the Godhead, or Is the Godhead in Jesus?* has been used in this chapter as a standard representation of the Oneness position.

Gordon Magee on p.16 wrongly implies that Trinitarians believe that there are two Spirits in the Godhead:

> Do Trinitarians imagine that there are two Spirits in the Godhead, namely, the Father, the so-called 'First Person' Who is termed a Spirit (John 4:24) and the Holy Spirit, the so-called 'Third Person'? There are not two Spirits in the Godhead because 'There is one Spirit' (Ephesians 4:4).

Here we see an example of where the Oneness Movement have misunderstood the original language of the New Testament and how it has been translated into English. The Authorised Version of John 4:24 should be translated 'God is spirit', and not 'is a spirit.'

John is not claiming that God as a personal being is a spirit, but rather, John is referring to God's nature: He is not material, or physical like us.

Colossians 1:15 tells us that God is invisible, as does 1 Timothy 1:17.

John 1:18 tell us that no man has ever seen God. This is reinforced in 1 John 4:12.

First Timothy 6:16 teaches that no man will ever see God.

It is an invention of Oneness Pentecostals to say that Trinitarians believe they shall see two spirits in heaven. Trinitarians' belief that 'God is spirit' does not mean that there are two personal spirits in heaven, but rather that God in His nature and essence is not material but spirit!

From the beginning of the Bible we see that the Scriptural record does not present the uni-personal god that Oneness Pentecostalism presents.

Genesis 1:26 reads,

> And God said, Let **us** make man in **our** image, after **our** likeness: and let them have dominion over the fish of the sea, and over the fowl of the air, and over the cattle, and over all the earth, and over every creeping thing that creepeth upon the earth.

Oneness proponents claim that God uses the plural pronoun because He is speaking collectively of Himself and the angels. This is impossible as it was not the angels and God that made creation. Further, the angels *and* God did not make man in the image of the divine *and* the angelic. In fact in Genesis 1:27 we see,

> So God created man in **his own** image, in the **image of God** created he him; male and female created he them.

It is very clear that God made man in His own image, and that the plural pronouns 'us' and 'our' signify, from the very beginning of creation, the plurality in the personality of the Godhead.

Genesis 1:26 is not an isolated proof text.

In Genesis 11 we read the account of the building of the Tower of Babel. Genesis 11:7 God says,

> Go to, let **us** go down, and there confound their language, that they may not understand one another's speech.

Again, Oneness Pentecostals claim that here God is speaking to the angels, yet contextually, throughout this whole story of the Tower of Babel, there is not a single mention of the angels. However it is recorded in Genesis 11:8 and 9 that,

> The LORD scattered them abroad....

Immediately it is clear that the plural pronoun was used of the Godhead.

Trinitarian Literary Structure In The Bible

As far back as Genesis 1 we see the Triune Godhead reflected even in the literary structure of the creation narrative.

Genesis 1:1 tells us that God was in the beginning. Genesis 1:2 tells us that God's Spirit hovered above the waters. Then in Genesis 1:3 we have the first reference to the Word of God, Christ, as God, speaks and creation is brought into being. This same literary expression of the Trinity is reflected in the opening chapter of John's Gospel. Christ is set forth as being One with God and dwelling with God as His Word who was the agent of creation.

We also see the Triune Godhead reflected in other Old Testament literature. The Aaronic blessing is an example of this.

Numbers 6:24-26 reads,

> The LORD bless thee, and keep thee:
> The LORD make his face shine upon thee, and be gracious unto thee:
> The LORD lift up his countenance upon thee, and give thee peace.

These three verses reflect clearly a triune blessing.

This triune pattern, in reference to God, is observed also in Isaiah 6:3. There it is recorded that the seraphim cried one to another in worship of God,

> Holy, holy, holy, is the LORD of hosts: the whole earth is full of his glory.

This definite triune pattern is repeated also in the New Testament when we read exactly the same words in Revelation 4:8.

Favourite Oneness Proof Texts

One favourite Scripture used by Oneness proponents is Isaiah 9:6. Speaking prophetically of the Lord Jesus, Isaiah says,

> For unto us a child is born, unto us a son is given: and the government shall be upon his shoulder: and his name shall be called Wonderful, Counsellor, The mighty God, the everlasting Father, the Prince of Peace.

The Oneness Movement interprets Isaiah 9:6 as Christ being prophetically designated as God the Father. This is incorrect. A good marginal reference Bible will show that 'everlasting Father' can be translated 'Father of eternity.' The meaning of the Hebrew word literally translates 'one over eternity', or 'the eternal one'.

Isaiah clearly wishes to communicate the concept of God's eternality. This verse has nothing whatsoever to do with the Son's relationship to the Father and vice versa. Here, Oneness teachers have repeated the mistake they made in their interpretation of John 4:24: confusing Gods nature and the persons of the Godhead.

Like John, Isaiah is conveying something of the nature of God: Christ as God being eternal. Isaiah is not addressing how the Father relates to the Son. In Isaiah 9:6 Isaiah certainly does not teach that Jesus is God the Father as the Oneness Movement claims.

A similar mistake is made in the Oneness Movement's explanation of John 10:30, when Jesus says,

> I and the Father are one.

Oneness proponents claim here that the Lord Jesus is calling Himself the Father. Note, however, that the Lord Jesus does not say '**I am** the Father' but rather, choosing His words carefully He says, 'I and the Father are one': one in nature and in substance. Effectively, Christ is saying, 'we are God.'

In fact, Christ uses the neuter of the Gk word 'one', to convey that both He and His Father are one substance. Therefore, the meaning of John 10:30 is, 'I and the Father are one in substance.' Christ would have used the masculine for 'one' rather than the neuter if He meant that He was the Father.

Grammatically, Christ shows with certainty that He is referring to the nature of God. Note also that whilst Christ says He is one with the Father, He is determined to distinguish Himself from the Father - 'I and **the Father** are one.'

Of course the Old Testament is only a partial revelation, and the persons of the Godhead are distinguished more clearly in the New Testament. In fact, in the New Testament Jesus, over 200 times, speaks of the Father as another person distinct from Himself. Over 50 times the Father and the Son are distinguished from each other in the same verse.

The distinct persons of the Godhead are evidenced in Matthew 3:16-17,

> And Jesus, when he was baptized, went up straightway out of the water: and, lo, the heavens were opened unto him, and he saw the Spirit of God descending like a dove, and lighting upon him: And lo a voice from heaven, saying, This is my beloved Son, in whom I am well pleased.

Here we see the three persons of the Godhead distinguished from each other: co-existing at the same moment.

Some Oneness teachers have interpreted this revelation to be that the Spirit did not come upon the Lord Jesus Christ but rather it was only a symbol of the Spirit which descended. If so, whose voice spoke from heaven? – Was it, as the teaching of the Oneness Pentecostal Movement would imply, only the divine nature of Christ?

Mercifully, Scripture answers these doubts: the Son is in the water being baptised, the Father is speaking from heaven, and the Holy Spirit was descending as a dove upon the Lord Jesus. All the Gospel writers concur that the Spirit actually descended on the Lord Jesus Christ. Indeed, it is recorded that Jesus saw the Holy Spirit descending as a dove.

Other Contradictions

The Oneness doctrine contradicts Scripture in many other places, not least, in regard to the Sonship of the Lord Jesus Christ. Oneness proponents teach that the Sonship of Christ is only the human part of Jesus: the flesh.

Gordon Magee writes under the subtitle 'The Son Is The Flesh', in *Is Jesus in the Godhead or is the Godhead in Jesus?* p.13,

> What part of Him was the Son? The angel told Mary, 'Mary that holy thing which shall be born of thee is the Son.' Paul told the Galatians,

'God sent forth a Son made of a woman.' *The Son is the flesh or humanity*.

The book of Hebrews abounds with evidence against this teaching.

Hebrews 1:1-2 states,

> God, who at sundry times and in divers manners spake in time past unto the fathers by the prophets, Hath in these last days spoken unto us by his Son, whom he hath appointed heir of all things, by whom also he made the worlds.

When did the Son make the worlds if it was not before He was born in Bethlehem? Clearly, Christ was the Son before He was born into humanity. God made the worlds through the Son. Did He do this before or after Bethlehem?

The Oneness Movement's answer to this question is that God made creation through the One who would become the Son. However, Hebrews 1:8 shows clearly that these words were spoken directly to the Son, for,

> …unto the Son God saith, Thy throne, O God, is for ever and ever: a sceptre of righteousness is the sceptre of thy kingdom.

Additional evidence to prove that Christ was the pre-existent Son can be found in Hebrews 5:7-8, where we read that Christ,

> … in the days of his flesh, when he had offered up prayers and supplications with strong crying and tears unto him that was able to save him from death, and was heard in that he feared; Though he were a Son, yet learned he obedience by the things which he suffered.

'Though he was Son' in Greek grammar is in the concessive clause, showing that the literal meaning is, 'in spite of him being Son he learned obedience.' In spite of Him being the Son of God, divine, He learned obedience. If Sonship speaks only of Christ's 'humanity', what does this verse mean? It cannot simply mean 'because He was the Son he learned obedience.' The Greek concessive clause means that it must carry the sense that even though He was the Son of God, He learned obedience. This verse, therefore, actually proves that Sonship signifies deity, rather than humanity.

Further, in Hebrews 7:3 the Old Testament figure of Melchisedec is presented as a type[1] of Christ. Melchisdec is a type simply because his priesthood appears to never cease.

Hebrews 7:3,

> Without father, without mother, without descent, having neither beginning of days, nor end of life; but made like unto the Son of God; abideth a priest continually.

How was Melchisedec made like unto the Son of God? Melchisedec did not have beginning of days nor end of days, just as the Son of God is without beginning or ending.

The Oneness Movement, however, teaches that Christ had a beginning as a Son in Bethlehem. Oneness Pentecostalism even go as far as to teach, using 1 Corinthians 15:27-28, that His Sonship will have an end when He offers up to God the Kingdom. This is despite the same verse telling us that He, the Son, will be again subjected to the Father.

In Hebrews 7:28 we observe also that the Son's priesthood is an unchangeable one,

> For the law maketh men high priests which have infirmity; but the word of the oath, which was since the law, maketh the Son, who is consecrated for evermore.

Another cult-like and mistaken argumentation of the Oneness Movement on this same issue can be found in *Is Jesus in the Godhead or is the Godhead in Jesus?* p.17 where Gordon Magee claims that Trinitarians teach that Christ had two fathers.

He writes,

> A classical example of the confusion of thought implicit in Trinitarian belief is seen when, under questioning, they are obliged to confess that Christ must have had *two Fathers*, namely, the First Person of the Trinity, to Whom He prayed (they say), and the Holy Spirit, Who performed the miracle act of paternity in the virgin womb.

Here, Oneness proponents obviously confuse the divine Sonship of Christ with His human Sonship. The divine Sonship and human Sonship of Christ is not one and the same thing. The divine Sonship of Christ speaks of how Christ is begotten of God eternally, but the human Sonship of Christ speaks of Him being begotten in the womb of Mary by the Holy Spirit in time. Oneness teachers confuse these distinct truths.

Additionally Oneness teachers contradict the Scriptures regarding Christ's work on the cross. In *Is Jesus in the Godhead or is the Godhead in Jesus?* p.28 Gordon Magee's under the subtitle, 'My God, my God, why hast Thou forsaken me?' says,

> Would to God Trinitarians would carefully consider the logical conclusions of their objections before making them. Think of it, if Jesus was *actually* forsaken by God then He is *not* God. The Trinitarian explanation of this verse, namely, that here we see one Divine Person forsaking another, compels us to ask where then is their professed belief in the unity of the Godhead.

Gordon Magee goes on to say that if Jesus was actually forsaken of God then He is not God, but God did not forsake Him - Jesus only 'felt' forsaken! John 16:32 is quoted,

> Behold, the hour cometh, yea, is now come, that ye shall be scattered, every man to his own, and shall leave me alone: and yet I am not alone, because the Father is with me.

Oneness proponents forget to admit that these words were said and fulfilled before Christ's substitutionary work on the cross.

Still Gordon Magee (p.29) speaking of Christ, claims that,

> Jesus felt God-forsaken. He had to, because He was the sinner's substitute. . . .

Gordon Magee is stating that Christ had to feel forsaken to be Saviour and therefore when the Lord said, 'My God, my God, why hast Thou forsaken me?'; Matthew 27:46. He was expressing how He felt: He was not literally forsaken.

Matthew 27:46 reveals that Christ did not say, 'I feel forsaken.'

If Christ only felt forsaken, as Gordon Magee claims, then it follows that Christ entertained wrong ideas on the cross because He thought He was forsaken! Oneness proponents are implying that in the midst of man's redemption Christ had mistaken feelings about what was taking place: Christ felt forsaken, yet He was not forsaken! The implications of this are staggering. If Christ was not forsaken but only felt He was: you can only feel saved! You cannot actually be saved!

Isaiah 53:6, 10 of course, tell us that the LORD laid on Christ the iniquity of us all and was pleased to bruise Him. In the light of Isaiah 53 the Oneness Movement must answer the question: was the divine part of Jesus laying punishment on the human part? If this is so, then it follows, that the part of Christ that actually bore our sins was not God!

The mystery of the cross is: God cannot die yet the man who died was God.

As Martin Luther said,

> God forsaking God, who can understand it?

Yes, this is a mystery but we must never deny what the Scriptures clearly teach in an attempt to explain its mysteries!

The Oneness Movement also misrepresents Christ's prayers. There is confusion as to whom was Christ praying?

Gordon Magee has no definitive answers.

In *Is Jesus in the Godhead or is the Godhead in Jesus?* p.11 Gordon Magee recites an apparent conversation with a Trinitarian: -

> Trinitarian: Then did not He pray to Himself?
>
> Magee: No! He did not pray to Himself!
>
> Trinitarian: What did He do?
>
> Magee: I replied, In His human nature He prayed to His Divine nature.
>
> Trinitarian: Well, he said, that is praying to Himself!
>
> Magee: You can have it that way, if Jesus were an ordinary person I would agree with you that it is praying to Himself. But, Jesus was not ordinary - Jesus was extraordinary - Jesus was God and man! If Jesus Christ had a dual nature why then should we think it incredible that he should perform a dual role?

Clearly, Gordon Magee contradicts himself. He *is* teaching that Christ is praying to Himself by claiming that His human nature prayed to His divine nature.

If Christ was praying to Himself, why does He, in His prayer in John 17 call Himself 'I' - yet when He addresses His Father He says 'My Father.' Christ also addresses the Father as 'Thou'. He implies in His address to the Father that He and the Father are two distinct personalities.

Christ is not praying to Himself or a divine part of Himself, He is praying to His Father.

Christ's commission teaches us that there are distinct persons in the Godhead.

In John 16:28 He said,

> I came forth from the Father, and am come into the world: again, I
> leave the world, and go to the Father.

Two personalities are implied in saying: 'I am going to the Father.'

If the divine part of Christ is the Father, why is it that Christ never uses the word 'I' when He refers to the Father? Why does Jesus always use the word 'You'? Why does Jesus never speak *as* the Father, and say 'I sent the Son'?

The answer is because Christ did not send the Son, He is the Son sent by the Father.

In Gethsemane this truth of the personality of the Father and of the Son is observed again. Christ prays to the Father, and says,

> Not my will, but Thine be done.

Plainly we see the existence of two wills. Consequently, there must be two personalities. To leave someone, to talk to another, to have a different will from another; all these necessitate two distinct personalities.

Problem Bible Texts For Oneness Proponents

John 17, referring to the love that exists between the Father and the Son, poses problematic for Oneness proponents. How can two natures love one another? Natures cannot love one another, natures cannot speak to one another, only persons can love one another, only people can speak to one another and only people can leave one another and go towards one another.

Another troublesome text for Onessness proponents is when Jesus said in John 6:38,

> I came down from heaven, not to do mine own will, but the will of
> him that sent me.

Here, when Christ is speaking of God, He distinguishes Himself from the Father.

In John 8:17-18 we read an indisputable text showing again how the Lord Jesus distinguishes between the Father and the Son.

> It is also written in your law, that the testimony of two men is true. I am one that bear witness of myself, and the Father that sent me beareth witness of me.

Christ is referring to Himself and the Father as two witnesses, two people whose witness is true.

John 1:1-2 shows that Christ was God by nature, yet He was also distinct from God in the sense that the Word was with God and the Word was God. John reiterates the same fact in 1 John 1:2,

> For the life was manifested, and we have seen it, and bear witness, and shew unto you that eternal life, which was with the Father, and was manifested unto us.

How do the Oneness Pentecostals interpret these verses? Regarding John 1:1, Gordon Magee says in *Is Jesus in the Godhead or is the Godhead in Jesus?* p.27,

> I can well remember a dear brother quoting this verse to me to prove that Jesus, the Word, was a distinct Divine Person from the Father. I asked him, 'Who is your God?' He answered, 'The Trinity.'

Gordon Magee continues,

> I said, 'Let us read the verse in the light of your answer - in the beginning was the Word, and the Word was with the Trinity and the Word was the Trinity.'

Here, again we see the mistaken argumentation of the Oneness teachers. Gordon Magee has failed to recognise that the Trinity is not God. The Trinity is an understanding of the Godhead. What this verse speaks of in reference to the Word being God, is the nature of God and the substance of God. It is not the personalities of God. In this misleading argument Gordon Magee goes on to say,

> The meaning of the verse became clear to him, and it is this - the Word was God. Any idea that the Word was a distinct personality from God is destroyed by John when he emphatically declares, 'and the Word was God.' I know of no stronger Oneness verse in the whole Bible. How can we make a difference of person between God and His Word?

This reasoning is suspect.

One could equally say that the statement 'And the Word was God' was destroyed by John's statement 'the Word was with God.' However, rather than destroying it, John affirms what Oneness teachers deny: that Jesus is God and yet is His own person.

Philippians 2:6 teaches clearly that Christ was in the form of God before coming to earth,

> Who, being in the form of God, thought it not robbery to be equal with God.

Christ claimed to be God and for that the Pharisees were going to stone Him. Christ may have claimed that the Father was revealed in Him: in the essence of His divinity, but He never claimed to be the Father. Holy Scripture always distinguishes the Son from the Father.

Oneness teachers have no satisfactory explanation for John 14:23:

> Jesus answered and said unto him, If a man love me, he will keep my words: and my Father will love him, and we will come unto him and make our abode with him.

In denying the Trinitarian understanding of the Godhead, Oneness teachers contradict the teaching of the Bible in regard to the Holy Spirit.

In John 14:16, Jesus said,

> I will pray the Father, and he shall give you another Comforter, that he
> may abide with you for ever.

Jesus is not the Spirit; the Spirit is sent by Jesus and sent by the Father; see John 15:26; 16:7.

The doctrine of the Trinity is a profound mystery, but note if it was a human invention, man who invented it would be able to explain it. Man cannot explain it.

Salvation And Baptism

Oneness Pentecostalism teaches that baptism in the name of Jesus, according to Acts 2:38, is intrinsic to salvation. Oneness Pentecostalism proponents do not use the Triune formula commanded by the Lord Jesus in Matthew 28:19, which reads,

> Go ye therefore, and teach all nations, baptizing them in the name of
> the Father, and of the Son, and of the Holy Ghost.

The Oneness Movement's aversion to the Trinitarian baptismal formula may be attributable to their aversion to the doctrine of the Trinity.

Oneness proponents cite the various references to baptism in the name of Jesus, as found in the book of Acts, to be proof texts for their practice. Oneness adherents, however, fail to recognise that the Acts of the Apostles is essentially a historical book. It is not the Church's epistle of instruction regarding doctrine and practice.

When baptism 'in the name of Jesus' is mentioned, it means 'in the authority', or 'by the authority of'. It certainly has nothing to do with the baptismal formula itself. The phrase refers to the authority of the One who is giving the command to baptise.

The Didache, which is understood by historians as an extra-biblical record of the teaching of the Apostles, was written in the late first and early second century. It makes clear that in the early Church baptism was practised in the Triune name of the Godhead. Justin Martyr in AD 153 declares the same.

Despite this the Oneness Pentecostals will re-baptise persons who were previously baptised in the name of the Father, and of the Son, and of the Holy Spirit.

Whilst the importance of baptism as a confession of faith is stressed in the New Testament, we must maintain that salvation is by grace through faith alone and not of works.[2]

Other issues regarding Oneness Pentecostalism, which need the attention of Christian believers are:

Soul Sleep, Annihilationism

Oneness Pentecostalism misuses and misquotes certain obscure passages, mainly from the book of Ecclesiastes, to teach that the soul sleeps until the resurrection. Some Oneness Pentecostals seem to believe that the impenitent: those who die without Christ, will be annihilated. This is: the doctrine of conditional immortality.

Paul did not teach soul sleep, rather he says in 2 Corinthians 5:8,

> We are confident, I say, and willing rather to be absent from the body, and to be present with the Lord.

The dying thief was told by the Lord Jesus in Luke 23:43,

> Today shalt thou be with me in Paradise.

In Luke 16 Jesus taught about the Rich Man in hell and the beggar Lazarus in Paradise: disproving any doctrine of soul sleep and annihilationism.

This chapter has discussed in some detail Oneness Pentecostalism's misrepresentation of the Godhead. There are other pertinent issues that need to be addressed regarding Oneness teaching but neither time nor space permits me to do so here.

British Israelism[3]

Although British Israelism does not, in itself, involve crucial doctrinal error related to salvation, it uses methods of interpretation that can lead into more serious error.[4] It should be made clear that there is not a trace of the British Israelism doctrine taught in the Bible.[5] Oswald Saunders gives this very instructive comment in his book *Heresies Ancient and Modern,*

> The theory of British Israelism is not supported by any scientist, historian or linguist of repute.

Old Testament Food Laws[6]

First Timothy 4:3 teaches that false teachers would speak,

> Forbidding to marry, and commanding to abstain from meats, which God hath created to be received with thanksgiving of them which believe and know the truth.

Paul also teaches in 1 Corinthians 8:8,

> But meat commendeth us not to God: for neither, if we eat, are we the better; neither, if we eat not, are we the worse.

It may be helpful to remember Walter Martin's observation that a cult is essentially,

> A group of people gathered around someone's misinterpretation of the Bible.

If anyone denies fundamental Scriptural truth to fit a man-made doctrinal scheme, they are false prophets. Be warned: however attractive their services are, however crowded their Churches may be, or however successful their preaching appears - Isaiah 8:20 says,

> To the law and to the testimony: if they speak not according to this word, it is because there is no light in them.

May the biblical truth of the Godhead, and the glorious gospel of grace so shine that

> Ye shall know the truth, and the truth shall make you free: John 8:32.

Footnotes

1   A foreshadowing in the Old Testament of a person or event of the Christian dispensation.

2   For more information on the error of Baptismal Regeneration see Chapter 6 The Church of Christ.

3   British Israelism or Anglo-Israelism 'teaches that ten tribes lost their national identity after they were captured by the Assyrians in the eighth century B.C. but maintains that these tribes went westward through Northern Europe and became the ancestors of the Saxons, who later invaded England. Thus the theory is that the Anglo-Saxons are the lost ten tribes. This means that white, English-speaking people are really the chosen people of God. In particular, it is maintained by the exponents of British Israelism that Ephraim is Great Britain and that Manasseh is the United States. Although Great Britain and the United States are not specifically mentioned in the Scriptures, those who hold to the theory of British Israelism see many prophecies directly related to these two countries.' Harold J. Berry Examining the Cults (Back to the Bible, 1979), p.25-26.

4   Harold J. Berry Examining the Cults (Back to the Bible, 1979), p.34.

5   For a succinct Biblical critique of British Israelism see Walter Martin The Kingdom of the Cults pp.306-316.

6   See Leviticus 11 and Deuteronomy 14:3ff.

Chapter 15
Freemasonry

The Freemasons have been persecuted for their beliefs. That is shameful, as is the persecution of anyone for his or her faith.

It is not the aim of this chapter nor indeed of this book, to ostracise or intimidate because of conscientious convictions.

This chapter sets out to compare the claims of Freemasonry with the Word of God: the Bible and to see if they are compatible.

Freemasonry has been defined as,

> A centuries old fraternal and secret society deeply entrenched in symbolism, secret oaths and secret rituals; its key themes being the universal fatherhood of God, and the brotherhood of man.

Historically, Freemasonry has an illustrious fraternity. Three British kings in the last century were Freemasons, including George VI the father of our present Queen Elizabeth II. In fact, presently, the Queen Elizabeth's cousin, the Duke of Kent, is the Worshipful Grand Master of Freemasonry in the United Kingdom.

Added to these famous names are other Freemasons of historical notoriety, including: Amadeus Mozart, Voltaire, Hayden, Sir Arthur Conan Doyle, Oscar Wilde and Sir Winston Churchill. No less than fourteen United States Presidents, including the great George Washington, were all Freemasons. A further eighteen Vice Presidents were also Freemasons. Among other well known Freemasons in the USA were: Benjamin Franklin, General MacArthur, J. Edgar Hoover, Mark Twain, Henry Ford, Harry Houdini, Cecil B. DeMille, John Wayne, Clark Gable, Roy Rogers and Norman Vincent Peele.

People join Freemasonry for a variety of reasons. Some like the idea of belonging to a secret society and of the privilege of learning some of the society's secret mysteries. Others are simply fascinated with the symbolism and overtones of mysticism in Freemasonry. There are those who simply join to increase business contacts: without feeling any deep affinity with the spiritual elements of Freemasonry. A large body of members join out of an appreciation for the Freemasonry emphasis on the brotherhood and humanitarian charity.

Characteristically, Freemasons are a very generous group of people and their commendable contributions to charity, including the care of orphans and widows of their fellow Freemasons, is widely acknowledged.

Many Freemasons resent the accusation of it being anything else, especially when evangelical Christians accuse them of being another religion or another faith. In some major Protestant denominations Freemasons are to be found amongst the clergy and church office bearers. More recently the Roman Catholic Church has also become welcoming to Freemasonry in its ranks. The fact that Freemasonry is found amongst high ranking figures in Christendom is often used as an apology for Freemasonry.

Today one of the great debates raging around the subject of Freemasonry is whether the principles of Freemasonry are compatible with historic biblical Christianity. Examining Freemasonry against the claims of Christianity and of what is revealed within the Holy Scriptures will shed some light on this.

What Is Freemasonry?

Different Freemasons, especially those in differing Degrees, will offer different answers and give different understandings of what Freemasonry is. Freemasons, who get past the first three Degrees, may admit that the symbolisms, and the philosophies behind the symbolism, take on a greater significance as progress is made through the orders. In fact, some Freemasons believe that you cannot really understand Freemasonry outside of the higher orders.

An analogy could be used that the first three Degrees are like the cover of the book of Freemasonry, and in order to understand the mysteries, the depths of the philosophies and the theology behind it all, it is necessary to open up the book and go deeper by moving on into the fourth Degree right up to the 33rd.

This is the progression of, as Freemasons call it, the light of Freemasonry.

According to Freemasons, prior to being a Freemason they were in darkness but as they progress through the Degrees they move towards the light until, they realise everything there is to know at the 33rd Degree.

The first three Degrees are: Entered Apprentice, Fellow Craft and Master Mason. A Freemason must then choose whether to take either the route of the York Rite or the Scottish Rite. The top Scottish Rite is the 33rd Degree Grand Sovereign Inspector General, and essentially the equivalent of that in the York Rite is the Order of the Knights of Templar. The significance is, as you climb up these various Degrees, more hidden Masonic mysteries are revealed.

Only men can be Freemasons, and they must be at least 21 years of age or 18 if the father is a Freemason. However, there are other related organisations available for all the family. There is the Order of the Eastern Star that includes both men and women; there is De Molay for young men, and Rainbow Girls and Job's Daughters for young girls. Consequently Freemasonry not only has influenced nations, monarchies, governments, and Churches but also the family unit.

The Origins Of Freemasonry

Masonic origins are not completely clear, and different explanations come from different sources. Essentially however, the origins of Freemasonry are shrouded in deep mystery and legend.

The Freemasons themselves claim that Freemasonry dates back to the time of King Solomon, who utilised the skills of stonemasons in building his temple in Jerusalem. The legend of Freemasonry is as follows: the original Grand Master Mason was a man called Hiram Abif, whom it is claimed had exclusive knowledge of the true name of God. Tragically some of his Mason colleagues ganged up on him and killed him and so the name of God was lost. Freemasonry claims to be the search for the lost name of God.

Freemasonry may have begun as the Freemasons claim, as a group of Gothic mediaeval English stonemasons who built Church buildings and cathedrals in their day. In order to safeguard the trade secrets of their craft they allegedly met together in Lodges and devised secret ways of communicating their skills which were then passed down from generation to generation.

Ultimately, however we find present day Masonic origins in a group of men who were appalled by the corruption in the government and Church of the 1500s. These men were essentially humanists who had read Plato's Republic and who believed that the only answer to the decline and degeneration of society was to create a New World Order that would completely change the political and religious scene. These philosophical humanists became known as 'Speculative Masons' as they no longer used the physical tools of their trade. They used the stonemason tools as images to symbolically portray moral and theological ideas.

Freemasonry, today, is much more than just a simple guild of stone tradesmen. Whatever it was at the beginning, Freemasonry has evolved into a philosophical and spiritual belief system. Some Freemasons may object by saying: 'That is not what Freemasonry is to me, I do not see it as religious.' If that is indeed the case, how can the following questions be answered? Why do Freemasons sometimes sing songs at their gatherings? Why is it that they pray? Why do they swear oaths on the sacred Law, the Old Testament? Why do Freemasons have temples with altars?

Though Freemasonry is a secret society there is a great deal of their own literature extant that proves that they are a faith community with definite theological doctrines. Several acknowledged leaders among Freemasons, whose writings are recognised as representative of Masonic beliefs attest to this. Using some of these writings, and not any caricature, this chapter will set out to show that Freemasonry is indeed an anti-Christian religion. Follow through every Masonic statement, every verse of Scripture, and let the weight of the evidence bring you to a conclusion.

What Are The Foundations Of Freemasonry?

Christianity, along with Judaism and Islam, are monotheistic religions, having belief in one God. Christianity claims to worship the one true and living Jehovah, revealed in three persons: Father, Son and Holy Spirit. Hinduism is a polytheistic religion. Paganism claims to be the oldest religion of all which traditionally was the worship of the moon god and the sun god, who were given various names in diverse cultures. Originally moon god and sun god worship emerged from Ancient Babylon, and later it manifested extensively in the Egyptian belief system.

Paganism is evidenced in the beliefs of the original 'Speculative Freemasons' who were essentially 'Rosicrucians'. A 'Rosicrucian' believes that true religion is effectively a mixture of pagan philosophy, mysticism, and the mythologies of Judaism, Christianity, Hinduism and Buddhism. This is syncretism: merging many beliefs together. Rosicrucian worship is 'pantheistic': the pagan worship of nature. This is reflected in Freemasonry in the ritual blood oaths that are sworn in initiation, which are pagan in nature. An example of this can be seen when Freemasons swear upon their life not to reveal the secrets of the society.

There are many more pagan traits involved in Freemasonry. Indeed some ex-33 Degree Masons have documented that at certain levels Freemasons actually worship various pagan deities. This is largely concealed so that these Freemasons are not aware of such worship.

David Didow a former 32nd Degree Mason, testifies that that is the case:

> In the Blue Degrees an initiate is initiated into the Egyptian trinity of the ancient mysteries of Egypt. This Egyptian Trinity is hidden from the initiate, he does not know at all what he is being initiated into, it is not even mentioned. It is based on Egyptian paganism and the worship of nature, that's really what it is: it is based on the worship of the male regenerative power, the female regenerative power ... ok ... and the product.[1]

This 32nd Degree ex-mason claims that it is based on paganism. Freemasonry is based, he says, on ancient Egyptian worship.

Freemasons, it would appear, are involved in pagan idolatrous worship, much of which is based upon the Kabbala, which is the ancient Jewish book of the occult. *Freemasonry of the Ancient Egyptians* by Manly P. Hall, a well-known and respected Freemason, refers to the Egyptians practising Freemasonry. The origins of Freemasons appear to stretch back a lot further than 1717!

Paganism can be witnessed graphically in the famous Masonic symbol: the square and compasses with the letter 'G' in the centre. Many Freemasons are misled into thinking that the letter 'G' signifies 'God' the great architect of the universe, or the geometry used by the original stonemasons. The letter 'G' represents, according to David Didow and other ex-32nd Degree Freemasons, the 'generating principle of life.' In parallel with its pagan roots, Freemasonry worships the regenerative powers. The previous quote from the 32nd Degree Mason confirms that. The real reason why women cannot become fully fledged Freemasons is because they do not possess the male regenerating and fertilising power.

Many Freemasons do not realise that both the square and compasses are symbolic of the male upon the female in the act of copulation. That is why Freemasons wear an apron around their loins; over the sexual reproductive organs, to honour the source of regenerative power. Another well-known Masonic symbol is the obelisk, which is simply a phallic symbol. Many Freemasons do not believe that this is actually the symbolism represented in these images.

Albert Mackey, a past Grand Master and a respected Masonic authority, says in his book *The Manual of the Lodge*, p.56,

> The phallus was an imitation of the male regenerative organ. It was represented usually by a column, which was surrounded by a circle at the base. The point with a circle was intended by the ancients as a type of prolific powers of nature which they worshipped under the united forms of the active or the male principle, and the passive or the female principle.

Here, Albert Mackey quite clearly states the pagan origins of Masonic worship of the regenerative power.

Albert Pike, Grand Commander of the Scottish Rite in the 1800s, in his book *Morals and Dogma,* pp.13-14, concurs with this interpretation when he writes,

> The sun and moon represent the two grand principles of all generations; the active and passive, the male and female. Both shed their light upon their offspring, the Blazing Star or Horus. . . .

These high ranking and authoritative Freemasons confirm, therefore, that the Freemasons derive its symbolism from the ancient paganism of Egypt and Babylon.

White Witchcraft too, appears to play a part in Freemasonry. In our world today White Witchcraft portrays itself fashionably as the Pagan religion. White Witchcraft has repackaged itself as a holistic, nature religion that has found common acceptance even on daytime TV. It claims to utilise the spiritual forces in nature all around us. It is also pantheism in that White Witchcraft is also the worship of the sun god and the moon god in various forms. The uncanny similarities between the initiation rites of the Freemasons and that of White Witchcraft are staggering. Similarities in ritual, phraseology and symbolism betray a common origin. This may seem far-fetched to some, but read about those who have experienced both.

Steve Warr was a practising member of a coven of witches, and shares his personal experience,

> I was involved in the occult for about 12 years . . . that is, I was constantly on a day-to-day basis reading, searching, as well as practising arts such as divination, getting in contact with the dead through mediums, tarot cards, crystal balls. Everything that we would consider occult, I was involved in. It was heavily ritualistic, with the wearing of robes, the drawing of magic circles, the invoking of gods to aid the practitioner, as well as . . . just anything you would do, even if it was not in a formal ritual, always had something to do with ritual - even if it was casting a spell, you would always light the candles, bring out the elements, set up your altar.[2]

Below is the transcript of an interview with Steve Warr that compares the experiences of initiation of a Blue Lodge Mason with an ex-occultist.

> Ex-Freemason: In the initiation in Freemasonry we had to be recommended by another Mason.

Steve Warr: Well, in order to join witchcraft you have to be first screened, you have to be recommended by somebody currently in witchcraft.

Ex-Freemason: When I was initiated I was blindfolded and bound by a rope, and on your bare chest was thrust the point of a spear.

Steve Warr: In witchcraft we were initiated through a very involved ritual, an initiation ceremony, wherein the candidate was led blindfolded, bound by a rope, to the edge of the magic circle.

Ex-Freemason: The rope is around your neck, and you're led forward. Up front, in the eastern end of the building, is a person who is the Worshipful Master. You kneel down before him as if he were a god.

Steve Warr: You were met by the high priest or high priestess at that time, usually with a sword to your chest.

Ex-Freemason: When I went to enter the Lodge, a sharp object was put to my left breast. I was warned that should I reveal any of the secrets of Freemasonry, to know what to expect.

Steve Warr: When you're presented before the high priest, a sword is held against your chest and you actually take a blood oath, promising to remain faithful to the secrets of witchcraft.

Ex-Freemason: When you're in the room this blindfold is taken away from you, and this is a time when they say that you're coming from darkness into light.

Steve Warr: During the initiation ceremony, the initiate is led by the Lieutenant of the high priest, and is challenged at the edge of the circle by someone saying: 'Who goes there?' The answer is: 'One from the world of darkness.'

Ex-Freemason: In Masonry the prayers are ended with 'So Mote it Be.'

Steve Warr: Oh and one of the other distinctives of the craft was that we would always end any spell or ritual, where we release the power, this is where the power was released, with the words 'So Mote it Be.'[3]

For those Freemasons who are still in the first three Degrees, this revelation may be startling.

Remarkably one of the differences between White Witchcraft and Freemasonry, is that White Witchcraft dismisses the idea of a personal Devil called 'Lucifer' and yet Freemasonry goes as far as actually acknowledging Lucifer and, some commentators would say, even worshipping Lucifer.

Manly Hall, who was a 33rd Degree Mason, says in is his book *The Lost Keys of Freemasonry*,

> When the Mason learns that the key to the warrior on the block is the proper application of the dynamo of living power, he has learned the mystery of his craft. The seething energies of Lucifer are in his hands, and before he may step onward and upward he must prove his ability to properly apply this energy.

If a Freemason does not venture higher than the third Degree he will never find out the significance of much of Masonic symbolism. Indeed, there is even a Christian veneer placed upon the symbolism that makes it so acceptable to many. It appears that Freemasons in the first three Degrees are deliberately deceived regarding the true significance of this symbolism. This is admitted.

Albert Pike in *Morals and Dogma*, p.819 says,

> The Blue Degrees are but the outer court or portico of the temple. Part of the symbols are displayed there to the initiate, but he is

intentionally misled by false interpretations. It is not intended that he should understand them, but it is intended that he shall imagine he understands them.

That is the reason why many Freemasons feel that they are in a Christian organisation. The foundation of Freemasonry is pagan, and ultimately the higher you go, the more you uncover the hidden mystery: it is the devotion of Lucifer himself. Pay particular attention to the references and the books in this chapter, search Masonic libraries, turn the pages, and you will find these facts are substantiated.

Where Is Christ In Freemasonry?

The Christ of the Bible is not to be found in Freemasonry. This fact should be instrumental in every Christian's understanding of the movement.

Manly Hall in *The Lost Keys of Freemasonry*, on pp.64-65 says,

> The true Mason is not creed-bound. He realises with the divine illumination of his Lodge that, as a Mason, his religion must be universal. Christ, Buddha or Mohammed, the name means little; for he recognises only the light and not the bearer. He worships at every shrine, bows before every altar whether in temple, mosque, pagoda, cathedral - and realises with his true understanding the oneness of all spiritual truths. No true Mason can be narrow, for his Lodge is the divine expression of all broadness.

The words of the Lord Jesus Christ recorded in Matthew 7:13-14 have particular relevance here.

> Enter ye in at the strait gate: for wide is the gate, and broad is the way, that leadeth to destruction, and many there be which go in thereat:

> Because strait is the gate, and narrow is the way, which leadeth unto
> life, and few there be that find it.

Yet Manly Hall says no true Freemason can be narrow, for his Lodge is the divine expression of all broadness!

It is one thing to adhere to the name of Christ, but men are commanded also to follow the teaching of Christ, and His way to be saved is a narrow way, an exclusive way.

Jesus said in John 14:6,

> I am the way...no man cometh unto the Father but by me.

The Christ of the Bible is nowhere to be found in Freemasonry.

In John 5:23 the Lord Jesus said,

> He that honoureth not the Son honoureth not the Father which hath
> sent him.

Though Freemasons claim they worship the true and living God, as the Jews and Christians do, the Bible states that if men do not worship that God, through Jesus Christ His Son, they fail to honour God by honouring His Son. Cults and false religions have the **theological** characteristic of claiming that God can be revealed in a way other than Jesus Christ. This is a **new revelation**. Freemasonry recognises 'light' in every religion and the true knowledge of the name of God is only available in Freemasonry; this is **exclusivity**.

First Timothy 2:5 says very clearly,

> For there is one God, and one mediator between God and men, the
> man Christ Jesus.

Who Is The God Of Freemasonry?

The Times newspaper on 25th October 1984, quoted a Church of England minister; the Rev Peter Moore, as saying,

> The God we worship in the Lodge is the same God that Jews and Muslims worship.

If this is the god of Freemasonry, the god of every religion; then it is not the God of the Bible. The God of the Bible is the Father of our Lord Jesus Christ, Jehovah, worshipped as the Father, Son and Holy Spirit, one substance, three persons.

The Bible in Freemasonry is only a symbol; it is not understood as an all-sufficient revelation of God to man. Although Freemason Lodges in our land use only the Bible; the Koran or the Vedas or any holy book of any other religion is legitimate to use in Masonic rites. This is witnessed when a candidate from a non-Christian religion is initiated.

Albert Pike in his *Morals and Dogma* p.11 writes,

> The Bible is an indispensable part of the furniture of a Christian Lodge only because it is the sacred book of the Christian religion. The Hebrew Pentateuch in a Hebrew Lodge, and the Koran in a Mohammedan one, belong on the Altar; and one of these, and the Square and Compass, properly understood, are the Great Lights by which a Mason must walk and work.

Contrast this with Simon Peter as he testified to Christ of His exclusivity as Saviour, in John 6:68 saying,

> Lord, to whom shall we go? Thou hast the words of eternal life.

Christ alone had the words of the eternal life. In relation to the exclusivity of the Bible, the Lord Jesus in His great prayer recorded in John 17:17, exclaimed to His Father,

> …Thy word is truth.

In the initiation into the first Degree of Freemasonry, the Freemason is introduced to the name of God, as the 'Grand Architect of the Universe'. A while later these Freemasons will learn also the divine name as the letters 'JHVH', which is a representation of 'Yahweh', the name 'Jehovah'; the Hebrew name for God.

Remember the legend behind all of Freemasonry? Freemasonry claims that Hiram Abif was murdered as he was building Solomon's Temple, and as he was the only one who knew God's name, so the divine name was lost with him. Freemasonry is trying to rediscover the lost name of God. That name of God is eventually revealed when a Freemason reaches the Royal Arch Degree. The lost name is written across the arch. It is said to be the sacred and mysterious name of the true and living God, and it is revealed by three Freemasons, to the initiate, as the threefold name: 'Jah-Bul-On'.

This name is the composition of the names of three different gods. First is the name of Yahweh, Jehovah, the God of the Old and New Testament. The second is the name of the Assyrian deity 'Baal'; the worship of whom was extensively condemned in the Old Testament. The third name is 'On', a word used in ancient Egyptian mysticism when offering prayers to the Egyptian god 'Osiris'. Therefore this composite divine name, 'Jah-Bul-On', is declared to be the missing name of God that died with Hiram Abif. This name cannot be found in any religion or spiritual system other than Freemasonry.

Our Lord Jesus Christ in Matthew 11:27 said,

> All things are delivered unto me of my Father: and no man knoweth the Son, but the Father; neither knoweth any man the Father, save the Son, and he to whomsoever the Son will reveal him.

Is it possible that all things were delivered to Christ, except the name of God which had been lost with Hiram Abif?

John 1:18 says,

> No man hath seen God at any time, the only begotten Son, which is in the bosom of the Father, he hath declared him.

The Lord Jesus Christ is the only begotten Son of God, and He has exclusively and completely declared the knowledge of God. There is a record of it in His Word, and there is no need for anyone else to reveal God. His name was not lost!

Is Salvation Found In Freemasonry?

Freemasons acknowledge Christ as a great reformer but, along with the other leaders and founders of faiths in our world. Sin is hardly mentioned in Masonic literature and when it is, sin does not carry the thought of fallen depravity in need of rescue.

Freemasons who reach the 19th Degree of Scottish Masonry are told,

> Masons who have given proof of their attachment to the statutes and rules of the Order, which in the end will make them deserving of entering the celestial Jerusalem.

Heaven, 'the celestial Jerusalem', is understood as something that can be deserved through morality.

The 28th Degree of the Scottish Rite likewise states,

> The true Mason raises himself by degrees until he reaches heaven.

According to the gospel of Freemasonry, men can be saved if, when God looks upon them, His all-seeing eye observes morality and charity. This will earn men heaven. Freemasonry has no concept of being saved by grace, which is God's unmerited favour offered to sinners; not because they earn it but because God loves them and without it they would be lost. That is Christ's gospel.

Freemasons teach the opposite to the Bible, which reads in Ephesians 2:8-9,

> For by grace are ye saved through faith; and that not of yourselves: it is the gift of God: lest any man should boast.

By His grace God has given salvation freely. All God requires of us is that we embrace His gift of salvation by faith!

Titus 3:4-5 bears out this truth,

> But after that the kindness and love of God our Saviour toward man appeared, Not by works of righteousness which we have done, but according to his mercy he saved us, by the washing of regeneration, and renewing of the Holy Spirit.

The Lord Jesus Christ died on the cross and shed His blood. He bore our shame and our punishment and the judgment that we deserved because we have fallen short of God's glory. Christ died that we might be delivered from sin and that we might go to heaven. This is achieved not by our works but by the grace of God that allowed Christ to be our sacrifice, raised Him again to be our Saviour and Lord, and offers Him to us in the gospel. What was the point of Christ dying on the cross if we could earn salvation by Freemasonry, or any other religion?

A Secret Society

A candidate being initiated into Freemasonry must make rash promises to secrets he has not yet had revealed to Him. He does not know their nature at all.

Consider A.W. Rainsbury's comment,

> The man has got to sell his conscience to the Worshipful Master before he can proceed - but what right has any man to make another the custodian of his conscience?

Few, if any Freemasons believe that the blood oath is taken seriously, or will be acted upon, and much Freemasonry is only legend and symbolism but nevertheless, for the child of God, the meaning and significance of all these ought to be a problem of the gravest nature.

D. L. Moody, that great 19th Century evangelist, made this pronouncement against Freemasonry -

> I do not see how any Christian, most of all a Christian minister, can go into these secret lodges with unbelievers. They are unequally yoked with unbelievers.

To be a member of any secret society ought to be a problem to a Christian.

The Lord Jesus Christ said in Matthew 10:26-27,

> Fear them not therefore: for there is nothing covered, that shall not be revealed; and hid, that shall not be known. What I tell you in darkness, that speak ye in light: and what ye hear in the ear, that preach ye upon the housetops.

It then follows that if you possess God's truth this revelation is not to be kept secret. It is to be declared to all men. The gospel was revealed so that it could be preached to the ends of the earth.

In John 18:20 the Saviour says of Himself,

> I spake openly to the world; I ever taught in the synagogue, and in the temple, whither the Jews always resort; and in secret have I said nothing.

That is the example of our Lord.

The Christian, in every area of his life, is duty bound to obey the Holy Spirit. The inspired instruction of the Apostle Paul in 2 Corinthians 6:14-18 is,

> Be ye not unequally yoked together with unbelievers: for what fellowship hath righteousness with unrighteousness? and what communion hath light with darkness? And what concord hath Christ with Belial (Baal)[4]? or what part hath he that believeth with an infidel? And what agreement hath the temple of God with idols? for ye are the temple of the living God; as God hath said, I will dwell in them, and walk in them; and I will be their God, and they shall be my people. Wherefore come out from among them, and be ye separate, saith the Lord, and touch not the unclean thing; and I will receive you, And will be a Father unto you, and ye shall be my sons and daughters, saith the Lord Almighty.

In the initiation ceremony a Freemason will roll up his left trouser leg to his knee and then remove his jacket and tie and open his shirt. The candidate then replaces his right shoe with a slipper and in emptying his pockets symbolises his poverty. All this is to symbolise that the candidate coming in, is in a state of poverty. To symbolise the candidates previous darkness he is blindfolded and acknowledges that while he is in that darkness he needs to be moved towards the light, which is found alone in the Degrees of Freemasonry. That indeed, is contrary to the Bible.

Jesus said in John 8:12,

> I am the light of the world: he that followeth me shall not walk in darkness, but shall have the light of life.

Christ is that light that lights every man who comes into the world. The Lord Jesus Christ is not to be set alongside Buddha, or Mohammed, or any other leader as a legitimate alternative.

First John 1:5-9 tells us

> This then is the message which we have heard of him, and declare
> unto you, that God is light, and in him is no darkness at all. If we say
> that we have fellowship with him, and walk in darkness, we lie, and
> do not the truth: But if we walk in the light, as he is in the light, we
> have fellowship one with another, and the blood of Jesus Christ God's
> Son cleanseth us from all sin. If we say that we have no sin, we
> deceive ourselves, and the truth is not in us. If we confess our sins, he
> is faithful and just to forgive us our sins, and to cleanse us from all
> unrighteousness.

Acts 4:12 makes clear,

> Neither is there salvation in any other: for there is none other name
> under heaven given among men, whereby we must be saved.

Are you 'on the square'? Do you know the foundation of what you are standing on?
Where is the Christ of the Bible in Freemasonry? Where is the God of the Bible in
Freemasonry? Where is the salvation by grace that is revealed in Christ and His Word
in Freemasonry?

First Corinthians 3:11 says,

> Other foundation can no man lay than that which is laid, which is
> Jesus Christ.

What are you resting on?

The only secure resting place as the hymn says is,

> On Christ the solid Rock I stand, all other ground is sinking
> sand!

Footnotes

1 From the video documentary Freemasonry: From Darkness to Light?, Jeremiah Films, 1987.
2 Ibid.
3 Ibid.
4 Added by author for purposes of clarity.

Conclusion

As you have read this book perhaps you have come to doubt the veracity of your personal faith. Perhaps you have been confronted with the truth of Jesus Christ and what He has accomplished for you at the cross.

If you now doubt your position before God, consider these questions, the answers of which should make clearer to you your present spiritual condition.

1. Are you sure that your sins are forgiven?

2. Do you know God in a personal rather than a religious way?

3. Have you peace within your heart?

4. Have you a life that is truly satisfying?

5. Are you sure if you died today that you would go to Heaven?

6. Are you sure that you are not going to Hell?

If you are not able to answer positively these questions with sincerity and conviction then I urge you to study further God's Word, the Bible, and to come to realize the following.

You are a sinner. The Bible says in Romans 3:23

> For all have sinned and come short of the glory of God.

This means that because no one can reach the perfect standard of God's goodness, no one can come to God on their own. Romans 5:12 states,

> Wherefore as by one man sin entered into the world, and death by sin; and so death passed upon all men, for all have sinned.

Death is the greatest evidence of sin in the world and in our own life. By our wrong actions, words and thoughts it is clear that we are sinners by nature and by habitual practice.

As a sinner you will be punished for your sin. We are debtors to God because of our sin,

> The wages of sin is death; Romans 6:23.

The punishment for our sin is eternal damnation in a place the Bible calls Hell. Hell is a real and terrible place. It is a place where there is constant torment and a *'weeping and wailing and gnashing of teeth.'* It is eternal. It will never end. The only qualification a person needs to get there is to be a sinner and since we know that, *'All have sinned'* therefore all of us are heading to that final destination. We cannot change these circumstances by trying to live a better life or to be more religious. The only way that this penalty for sin can be avoided is if God intervenes.

The Lord Jesus Christ has paid your penalty. At Calvary God did intervene on behalf of sinners. Jesus, God's Son, died for our sin. As Romans 5:8 reminds us,

> But God commendeth his love toward us, in that while we were yet sinners, Christ died for us.

Christ was not a sinner and could not sin, for He is God manifest in flesh. Being perfect He is the only one who could reach God's standard. He was also fully man; therefore He could pay the debt we owed to God on behalf of humanity. Jesus Christ, the God-Man, took our punishment upon Himself on the cross so that we could be set free from the penalty of sin and be sure of a place in heaven. Amazingly, God the Father laid all our sins on Jesus at the cross: Isaiah 53:6. The key to understanding the cross is the realization that the crucifixion was not a simple execution or miscarriage of justice, but God's plan to bring humanity back into a right relationship with Himself. God, whom we had offended, was the only one who could help and save us and He did. We cannot work for salvation; nor can we earn it or learn it. The work for our salvation was accomplished on the cross. Our proof is Jesus' cry, *'It is finished,'* and his resurrection by God three days later!

You must repent of sin and by faith accept what Jesus Christ did for you. Acts 3:19 commands,

> Repent ye therefore, and be converted, that your sins may be blotted out.

To repent from your sin means simply to change your mind about sin and Jesus Christ. God gives the power to leave sin to those who are willing to turn to God, by faith, for salvation. It takes God Himself to do a work of salvation in your life. This means having faith in Jesus Christ. It is not sufficient to have a head knowledge, you must believe that Jesus died for you to save you from your sins; you must claim Jesus as your personal Saviour. This means taking Jesus at His word, understanding that because of His great work of salvation on the cross, you can accept his gift of salvation and be saved.

Standing before God there are only two types of people in the world: those saved through the blood of the cross and those lost because they have rejected God's way of the cross. John 3:36 states,

> He that believeth on the Son hath everlasting life: and he that believeth not the Son shall not see life; but the wrath of God abideth on him.

Jesus, Himself, said,

> Verily, verily, I say unto you, He that heareth my word, and believeth on him that sent me, hath everlasting life, and shall not come into condemnation; but is passed from death unto life; John 5:24.

If, through the reading of, and reflecting on the words in this book you have been brought by God, to realise the truth and you want to put your trust in the Lord Jesus Christ for your salvation, why not use this prayer below as a starting point to pray to God? Ask Him to save you. There are no magic words. Reciting the words of this prayer will not do anything for you. You must believe in your heart the sentiments expressed and mean them personally as you pray them to God. This prayer cannot save you, but faith in Christ will.

Lord Jesus Christ, I know I am a sinner, and I deserve to pay the penalty of my sin on my own. However, I do believe that You died for me to pay the debt of my sin. I now repent of my sin and trust You now as my Saviour from sin. Amen.

If you have prayed these words, meant them personally and believed them in your heart, we would love to be of further support for you.

If you are undecided and still seeking God, we wish to make ourselves available to help you in whatever way we can.

Please take a moment to contact us at **www.preachtheword.com**. We can send you some literature to help you find the Saviour and if you have trusted Christ we can give you some pointers on how to grow in your Christian life as you seek to follow the Lord Jesus Christ. We would like to pray for you and to rejoice with you in your new-found life in Christ. May you experience God's blessing and know His presence in the days that lie ahead.